PHONICS
for Reading

Teacher Guide Second Level

Cover Design: Matt Pollock and Susan Hawk

Interior Design: Pat Lucas

Illustrators: Laurel Aiello, Lane Gregory, Leslie Alfred McGrath, Laura Nikiel, Janice Skivington, Susan Spellman, Carolyn Williams, and Wilson Williams

Editorial Project Manager: Pamela Seastrand

Anita Archer
James Flood
Diane Lapp
Linda Lungren

CA101®
Online e-training

Use this product right away, the right way!
Online e-training at **CAtraining.com**

TABLE OF CONTENTS

ISBN 978-0-7609-6900-7

©2011, 2009, 2002, 1993—Curriculum Associates, LLC
North Billerica, MA 01862

The *Phonics for Reading* Series

The *Phonics for Reading* series is a systematic, research-based, instructional program that provides explicit instruction in phonics as well as phonemic awareness, fluency, and comprehension. The series is carefully sequenced to guide and build students' learning. Each level in the series features consistent teaching routines, repeated practice, and immediate corrective feedback. The teacher may use one, two, or all three levels to help improve students' reading skills.

Florida Center for Reading Research Says . . .

Strengths

Materials are teacher friendly and easy to navigate.

The instruction is **explicit and systematic.**

The program consists of features that may be helpful for struggling readers, such as **consistent teaching routines, repeated practice, and cumulative review.**

The materials include a detailed scope and sequence and clear objectives.

The decoding strategies are taught to automaticity.

Students learn to pronounce the individual sounds in a blend.

Students are given **immediate corrective feedback.**

Weaknesses

None were noted.

Download the full review at
*fcrr.org/FCRRReports/PDF/
PhonicsReading.pdf*

First Level
focuses on:

- short vowels
- double consonants
- consonant blends
- consonant digraphs

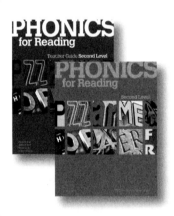

Second Level
progresses with:

- long vowels
- vowel combinations
- CVCe words
- word endings
- *r*-controlled vowel sounds

Third Level
expands concepts with:

- letter/vowel combinations
- prefixes and suffixes
- minor sounds of *c* and *g*
- minor sounds of vowel combinations

Built for a Wide Range of Students and Classroom Settings

Phonics for Reading is a supplementary phonics program designed to teach decoding skills that are generally introduced in grades one through three.

This flexible program may be used in
- regular classrooms
- special-education classrooms
- tutorial programs
- home-schooling programs
- summer-school sessions

Use with students . . .

in **3rd through 6th grade** who have not yet mastered the decoding skills taught in the primary grades.

in **the upper grades** who have significant decoding challenges.

in **adult-education classes** who are new to learning to read English.

in **1st and 2nd grade** who would benefit from systematic decoding instruction.

Created with Older Students in Mind

While *Phonics for Reading* addresses the same primary-level reading skills found in traditional phonics programs, the design of this program offers a unique appeal to older students.

- The typeface used in the material is small, thus avoiding the stigma of large type.

- Illustrations include older children and adults.

- In addition to reading one-syllable words, students also read multisyllable words, which enhances their feeling of decoding competency.

- Independent practice activities require reading words in context rather than simply adding letters to words or matching pictures to words.

Phonics for Reading, Second Level

Getting Started

Phonics for Reading, Second Level, teaches students how to read one-syllable and multisyllable words by using knowledge of letter-sound relationships as well as structural units such as root words and word endings.

The program assumes that students beginning ***Phonics for Reading, Second Level,*** can decode words that contain short vowels, single and double consonants, consonant blends (e.g., *tr, bl, sm),* and consonant digraphs (e.g., *sh, th, wh).* These skills are introduced in ***Phonics for Reading, First Level.***

It is recommended that the skills be taught in the order in which they appear in the program.

1 Place Students in the Right Level

A Placement Test is provided at the back of this teacher guide. The test can be used to place students in the First Level, Second Level, or Third Level of the ***Phonics for Reading*** series.

The test consists of numerous subtests. The teacher may begin administration with the first subtest or use a higher subtest if appropriate. If the student receives at least 80 percent accuracy, the teacher will administer the next subtest. This procedure will continue until the student scores less than 80 percent accuracy on a subtest. That subtest will determine placement in the series. (For complete procedures for administering the Placement Test, see page 181.)

2 Group Students for Instruction

Phonics for Reading, Second Level, is designed for small-group instruction of up to 10 students working at the same skill level.

Although group instruction is generally more efficient than tutorial instruction, this program may also be used on a one-to-one basis. Individual instruction can be provided by a paraprofessional, a tutor, or a volunteer, following training on program implementation.

3 Teach the Lessons Using Scripted Text

Phonics for Reading, Second Level, includes 32 teacher-directed lessons. Scripted text walks the teacher through what to do and say during each part of the scaffolded lessons. Each lesson follows the same procedures for introducing the skills students will learn.

1. A focus word (or words) is presented to students, and then the sound for a letter or letter combination within the word is introduced. Students practice the focus sound along with other previously learned sounds.

2. The letter or letter combination is incorporated into one-syllable and multisyllable words. Students employ a systematic strategy for decoding the words.

3. Root words and word endings are introduced to students. Students also practice reading words whose roots are altered when word endings are added.

4. Words containing recently taught letter-sound associations and word endings appear in decodable text (sentences and stories). Students practice reading the words within meaningful contexts.

5. Students complete independent practice activities that require decoding of one-syllable and multisyllable words with known sounds.

4 Monitor Students' Progress

There are several opportunities for monitoring students' progress during instruction with *Phonics for Reading, Second Level.*

1. Immediately following the completion of the independent practice activities, students may complete the **Work Check** activity as a group. In this activity, students self-correct their work. (For complete procedures, see page 11.)

2. The teacher may use the **Checking Up** activity as a formative-assessment measure. The teacher listens to students read a part from a reading passage in the student book and counts the number of word-reading errors. If 90 percent of the students make two errors or fewer, the group may move on to the next lesson. If this criterion is not met, the lesson should be repeated.

3. Given that fluency is a more powerful indicator of student decoding progress than accuracy alone, the teacher can use the **one-minute fluency checks** to gauge student growth. This data can be displayed on individual fluency graphs for visual examination of progress. (These fluency procedures are outlined on page 15.)

4. The **Placement Test** may also be used as a post test. When the student completes a level or a portion of a level, the appropriate subtest may be administered again to gauge the student's progress. The test may also be administered at the end of the school year to measure student growth.

1 Objectives

Goals for introducing or practicing specific sounds and word endings are identified at the beginning of each lesson.

2 New Sound

Focus sounds are presented in Lessons 1, 4, 7, 10, 13, 17, 18, 21, 24, 27, and 30.

Procedure

Students repeat the key words and focus sounds after the teacher pronounces them.

3 Sound Drill

A letter-sound correspondence activity is included in every lesson. This activity is oral, teacher directed, and appears only in the teacher guide.

Procedure

Students say the sounds from words in the lesson with the teacher.

Teaching Tip

Care should be taken not to distort the sounds, which would make subsequent decoding of words difficult.

Continuous sounds should be held for one second. These sounds are indicated as /sss/, /mmm/.

If the sound is a stop sound, such as /k/ or /ch/, the sound should be said quickly with no vowel sound added.

Teacher Guide Lessons

A teacher-directed approach is recommended during instruction with *Phonics for Reading, Second Level.* Because students must learn letter-sound relationships, decoding rules, and various strategies for pronouncing words, they benefit from systematic, teacher-directed lessons. The structure of each lesson is consistent throughout the program, so students are able to focus on the content rather than on the teaching procedures being used.

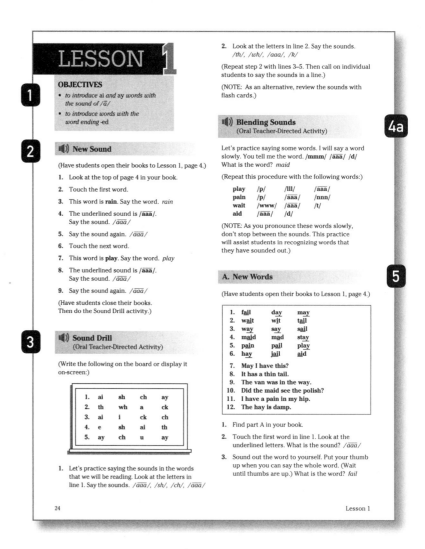

4a Blending Sounds

A phonemic awareness activity is included in Lessons 1–6. It is oral, teacher directed, and appears only in the teacher guide.

Procedure

After the teacher pronounces the separate sounds (without stopping) within a word, students say the whole word.

4b Segmenting Words into Sounds

In Lessons 7–12, this phonemic awareness activity replaces Blending Sounds. The ability to segment words is a necessary preskill for spelling phonetically regular words.

Procedure

Students repeat a word after the teacher pronounces it. Then students say the separate sounds in the word as they hold up a finger for each sound.

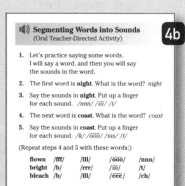

This four-page section contains facsimiles from a teacher guide lesson. Numbered boxes call out and describe each feature. Each lesson is carefully outlined and includes a specific teacher script. The teacher can use the exact wording in the script or similar wording when presenting the lessons. Being provided with such a structure allows the teacher to focus attention on the students' responses and provide immediate corrective feedback.

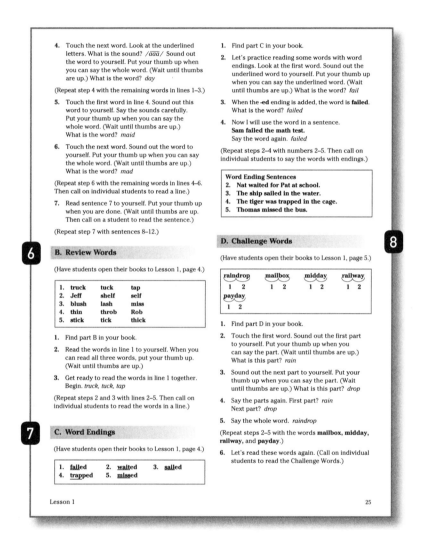

4. Touch the next word. Look at the underlined letters. What is the sound? /āāā/ Sound out the word to yourself. Put your thumb up when you can say the whole word. (Wait until thumbs are up.) What is the word? *day*

(Repeat step 4 with the remaining words in lines 1–3.)

5. Touch the first word in line 4. Sound out this word to yourself. Say the sounds carefully. Put your thumb up when you can say the whole word. (Wait until thumbs are up.) What is the word? *maid*

6. Touch the next word. Sound out the word to yourself. Put your thumb up when you can say the whole word. (Wait until thumbs are up.) What is the word? *mad*

(Repeat step 6 with the remaining words in lines 4–6. Then call on individual students to read a line.)

7. Read sentence 7 to yourself. Put your thumb up when you are done. (Wait until thumbs are up. Then call on a student to read the sentence.)

(Repeat step 7 with sentences 8–12.)

B. Review Words

(Have students open their books to Lesson 1, page 4.)

1.	truck	tuck	tap
2.	Jeff	shelf	self
3.	blush	lash	miss
4.	thin	throb	Rob
5.	stick	tick	thick

1. Find part B in your book.
2. Read the words in line 1 to yourself. When you can read all three words, put your thumb up. (Wait until thumbs are up.)
3. Get ready to read the words in line 1 together. Begin. *truck, tuck, tap*

(Repeat steps 2 and 3 with lines 2–5. Then call on individual students to read the words in a line.)

C. Word Endings

(Have students open their books to Lesson 1, page 4.)

| 1. failed | 2. waited | 3. sailed |
| 4. trapped | 5. missed | |

1. Find part C in your book.
2. Let's practice reading some words with word endings. Look at the first word. Sound out the underlined word to yourself. Put your thumb up when you can say the underlined word. (Wait until thumbs are up.) What is the word? *fail*
3. When the **-ed** ending is added, the word is **failed**. What is the word? *failed*
4. Now I will use the word in a sentence. **Sam failed the math test.** Say the word again. *failed*

(Repeat steps 2–4 with numbers 2–5. Then call on individual students to say the words with endings.)

Word Ending Sentences
2. Nat waited for Pat at school.
3. The ship sailed in the water.
4. The tiger was trapped in the cage.
5. Thomas missed the bus.

D. Challenge Words

(Have students open their books to Lesson 1, page 5.)

raindrop	mailbox	midday	railway
1 2	1 2	1 2	1 2
payday			
1 2			

1. Find part D in your book.
2. Touch the first word. Sound out the first part to yourself. Put your thumb up when you can say the part. (Wait until thumbs are up.) What is this part? *rain*
3. Sound out the next part to yourself. Put your thumb up when you can say the part. (Wait until thumbs are up.) What is this part? *drop*
4. Say the parts again. First part? *rain* Next part? *drop*
5. Say the whole word. *raindrop*

(Repeat steps 2–5 with the words **mailbox, midday, railway,** and **payday.**)

6. Let's read these words again. (Call on individual students to read the Challenge Words.)

Lesson 1   25

Immediate Corrective Feedback

If a student mispronounces a sound or a word, the error should be corrected immediately. The teacher should model the correct pronunciation and have the student repeat the sound or word. To ensure learning, the teacher should provide additional practice by having the student reread the line or sentence. If possible, at the end of the activity, the teacher should recheck the student on the sound or word.

5 New Words

A list of 18 words is presented in each lesson.

Procedure

Students say the sound for the underlined letters, sound out and say the words, and read the words in sentences.

6 Review Words

Each lesson includes a list of 15 words containing word types taught in previous lessons.

Procedure

Students read a line of words to themselves and then read the words aloud.

7 Word Endings

Each lesson introduces 5 to 10 words that contain word endings, including *-ed, -ing,* and *-er.*

Some words contain altered roots, in which the final consonant of the root is doubled or the finale *e* is dropped before the ending is added.

Procedure

Students sound out and say the underlined root word. Then they say the whole word after the teacher pronounces it. The teacher reads the word in a sentence, and students say the word again.

8 Challenge Words

At least 5 multisyllable words are presented in each lesson. Reading multisyllable words is included to enhance students' transfer of decoding skills to longer words and to increase student motivation.

Procedure

Students sound out each word part, say each word part, and then pronounce the whole word.

9 Sight Words

At least 10 high-frequency words are presented in each lesson.

Procedure

Students repeat the words after the teacher pronounces them. Students then reread the words.

Teaching Tip

Since students must memorize these words, it is important that students be certain of all words before moving on to the next activity. Students should reread the words until they are read accurately and fluently.

10 Sentences and Stories

Decodable text, in the form of a narrative or expository passage, is included in each lesson.

Procedure

After the parts of the story have been read silently and orally, students demonstrate their knowledge of what they have read by matching each part to the appropriate picture.

11 Spelling

A spelling activity is included in each lesson.

Procedure

The teacher dictates to students two short words, two longer words, and a sentence.

Students slow down the pronunciation of each word, say the sounds or parts of the word, and write down the corresponding letters or parts.

Students then self-correct their spelling against a visual model that the teacher displays.

---

9 **E. Sight Words**

(Have students open their books to Lesson 1, page 5.)

were	you	of	said	have
after	from	my	to	they

1. Find part E in your book.
2. There are some words that may be difficult to sound out. We just have to remember these words.
3. Touch the first word. This word is **were**. What is the word? *were* Spell and read. *w-e-r-e. were*
4. Touch the next word. This word is **you**. What is the word? *you* Spell and read. *y-o-u. you*

(Repeat step 4 with the remaining words.)

5. Let's read these words again. (Call on individual students to read the Sight Words.)

10 **F. Sentences and Stories**

(Have students open their books to Lesson 1, page 5.)

1. Find part F in your book.
2. Touch the title of the story. Let's read the title together. *The Day of Rain*
3. Read Part 1 to yourself. Read it very carefully. Put your thumb up when you are done. (Wait until thumbs are up.)
4. Let's read Part 1 together. When you are not reading aloud, follow along in your book. (Call on a student to read one or two sentences. Continue until Part 1 has been read.)
5. Look at the three pictures. Put a number 1 under the picture that goes with Part 1.

(Repeat steps 3–5 with Parts 2 and 3.)

Answers

G. Spelling **11**

(Have students open their books to Lesson 1, page 6.)

1. Find part G in your book.
2. Your first spelling word is **stay**. What is the word? *stay*
3. Say the sounds to yourself as you write the word. (Monitor.)
4. (Write the word on the board or display it on-screen.) Check your word. If you made a mistake, cross out the word and rewrite it. (Monitor.)

(Repeat steps 2–4 with the word **wait**.)

5. Your next spelling word is **raindrop**. Say the first part of the word. *rain* Write this part.
6. Say the second part of the word. *drop* Write this part.
7. (Write the word on the board or display it on-screen.) Check your word. If you made a mistake, cross out the word and rewrite it. (Monitor.)

(Repeat steps 5–7 with the word **payday**.)

8. Listen. **The dog has a black tail.** Say the sentence. *The dog has a black tail.* Write the sentence. (Monitor.)
9. (Write the sentence on the board or display it on-screen.) Check each word. If you made a mistake, cross out the word and rewrite it. (Monitor.)

Answers
1. stay
2. wait
3. raindrop
4. payday
5. The dog has a black tail.

Lesson 1

Time to Complete Each Lesson

Depending on the length of the instructional period, the teacher may choose to complete an entire lesson in one day or divide the lesson into two sessions.

A lesson will take 45–60 minutes to complete, depending on the number of students in the group, the pace of the instruction, and the proficiency of the students.

Lesson Part	Time
Teacher-directed activities	30–45 minutes
Independent practice activities	15 minutes

H. Practice Activity 1

(Have students open their books to Lesson 1, page 6.)

1. Find part H in your book.

2. Follow along as I read the directions. **Draw a line under the phrase that best completes each sentence.**

3. Do number 1. Put your thumb up when you are finished. (Monitor and check.)

4. You will finish part H later.

 I. Practice Activity 2

(Have students open their books to Lesson 1, page 7.)

1. Find part I in your book.

2. Follow along as I read the directions. **Draw a line under the sentence that goes with each picture.**

3. Do number 1. Put your thumb up when you are finished. (Monitor and check.)

4. Now go back and finish parts H and I.

 Work Check for Parts H and I
(Oral Teacher-Directed Activity)

1. Find part H in your book.

2. Let's check your work. If you made a mistake, circle the number. You will fix all mistakes at the end of the lesson. (Call on individual students to read their answers.)

3. Count how many correct answers you have, and write that number in the box at the bottom of the page. (Monitor students.)

(Repeat steps 1–3 with part I.)

4. Now go back and correct any mistakes. (Monitor students.)

Answers for Part H
1. a. <u>a mop in the pail</u>
2. a. <u>have a sail</u>
3. a. <u>wait in the truck</u>
4. b. <u>fail a test</u>
5. b. <u>pay the bill</u>
6. b. <u>sit in the hay</u>
7. a. <u>rain on this day</u>

Answers for Part I
1. <u>The dog has a black tail.</u>
2. <u>The cats play in the box.</u>
3. <u>The rain will fill the pail.</u>
4. <u>Rob put the nail in the box.</u>
5. <u>Chuck will wait until the bus stops.</u>
6. <u>Will Beth fail the test?</u>
7. <u>The maid will dust the lamp.</u>
8. <u>The man will pay with cash.</u>

 Checking Up
(Oral Teacher-Directed Activity)

Practice reading Part 1 of the story on page 13. I am going to listen to each of you read. Your goal is to make fewer than two errors. Keep practicing Part 1 until you can read it without any errors.

(Ask each student to read Part 1. Record the number of errors in his or her book.

NOTE: If 90 percent of the students make two errors or fewer, you may move on to Lesson 4. If not, repeat Lesson 3.)

Lesson 1

Two practice activities are presented in each lesson for students to complete independently.

Procedure

The teacher introduces each activity and monitors the first item. This procedure will ensure that students understand the directions and will be able to do the work without assistance.

13 **Work Check**

This oral teacher-directed activity, in which students self-correct their practice activities, provides an informal measure of students' progress.

Procedure

Individual students are called on to read aloud their answer to each item.

Students circle the numeral for each incorrect item and then write the total number of correct items in the box below each activity.

Students then go back and correct their errors.

Teaching Tip

The Work Check activity should be done as a group immediately following the practice activities. If time is limited, however, the correct answers may be read to students. Or students may correct their own work, using a copy of the Answer Key on pages 152–167.

14 **Checking Up**

This activity is a formal measure of students' skills and appears at the end of Lessons 3, 6, 9, 12, 16, 20, 23, 26, 29, and 32. This activity is oral and teacher directed.

Procedure

The teacher listens to students read a story part and counts the number of errors. If 90 percent of the students make two errors or fewer, the group may move on to the next lesson. Otherwise, the lesson should be repeated.

Teaching Tip

The best time to listen to individual students read is during their independent work session. No words should be corrected during the Checking Up activity. After the story has been read, errors may then be corrected.

1 New Sound

A focus sound (or sounds) is introduced.

2 New Words

One-syllable words are introduced, and the words are read in sentences.

3 Review Words

One-syllable words that contain word types taught in previous lessons are presented to maintain and reinforce students' decoding skills.

4 Word Endings

Root words with the word endings *-ed*, *-ing*, and *-er* are introduced and practiced. Some root words contain altered spellings when the endings are added.

5 Challenge Words

Multisyllable words that include known letter-sound correspondences and configuration patterns are introduced.

Each word is divided into pronounceable units referred to as word parts.

6 Sight Words

High-frequency words are introduced and practiced. These include irregular words that are not spelled as they sound as well as words that can be decoded but contain elements that have not yet been introduced to students.

7 Sentences and Stories

A three-part story with several paragraphs is presented for students to decode and comprehend.

Student Book Lessons

Phonics for Reading, Second Level, includes 11 types of activities. This two-page section contains facsimiles from a student book lesson. Numbered boxes call out and describe each type of activity.

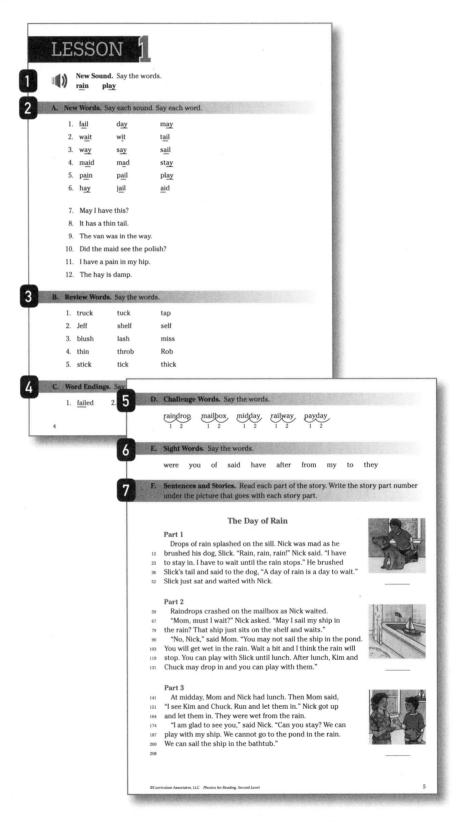

Sample Pages from Lesson 1

8   **G. Spelling.** Write the words and sentence that your teacher says.

1. _____   3. _____

2. _____   4. _____

5. _____

_____

9   **H. Practice Activity 1.** Fill in each blank with the best word.

1.	The ships were in the _____.	bat	bay	bait
2.	It may _____ at midday.	trail	grain	rain
3.	Gail put the dish on the _____.	tray	trip	play
4.	Fish will grab the _____.	bay	bait	train
5.	Jan will fill the pail with _____.	grain	plain	bay
6.	Jill put the _____ in the mailbox.	raid	pain	mail
7.	The children will _____ with us.	way	stay	may
8.	Chuck will pay Jill to _____.	paint	plain	grain
9.	Beth has a black _____.	bay	rain	braid
10.	Dad will fix the _____.	drain	wait	may

14

10   ☐ Correct

---

9   **I. Practice Activity 2.** Draw a line under the sentence that goes with each picture.

1. The men will stay in the cabin.
   The men will stay on the ship.

2. Paint is on the tray.
   Paint is in the can.

3. Bess will play in the bay.
   Bess will play in the rain.

4. Ray has bait in a pail.
   Ray has grain in a pail.

5. The hat has red dots.
   The hat is plain.

6. The dog will raid the box.
   The dog will run up the trail.

7. Nick and Gail play with clay.
   Nick and Gail pay with clay.

8. The mail is on the train.
   The mail is in the mailbox.

10 ☐ Correct   **11** ☐ Checking Up   15

Sample Pages from Lesson 3

---

8 **Spelling**

Two short words, two long words, and a sentence are dictated to students by the teacher.

Students then compare their spelling to a model and rewrite incorrect words.

9 **Practice Activities**

Two practice activities are presented for students to complete independently.

The types of activities vary from lesson to lesson to keep students engaged, but each type remains consistent in its format.

The activities require students to complete sentences, match sentences to pictures, answer questions, reorder words into meaningful sentences, and recall details from story passages.

10 **Self-Correct Boxes**

Students self-correct their practice activities and record the total number of correct answers in the boxes.

Receiving feedback on their own answers is more helpful than examining another student's work.

11 **Checking Up Box**

Students read a part from the story passage as the teacher counts and records the number of word-reading errors.

Teacher Guide Resources

Included at the back of this teacher guide are several reproducible resources the teacher may find useful while instructing students with *Phonics for Reading, Second Level*.

Individual Education Plan (IEP)

A long-term goal and short-term objectives can be set for individual students.

(pages 174–177)

Placement Test

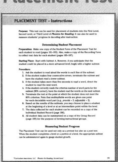

Placement Test instructions explain how to use the Student Forms that students read, as well as the Recording Form, Individual Student Record, and Group Record that the teacher uses.

(pages 181–189)

Letters of Progress

Three letters of progress may be sent home to family members (after the completion of Lessons 1–12, 13–20, and 21–32) to inform them about their child's performance.

(pages 178–180)

Reading Fluency Graph

This graph may be used by the teacher and students to record and plot the progress of how many words each student reads correctly per minute.

(page 190)

Games for Additional Word Practice

These games are fun and require no preparation. Students may use the words from the activities or the Word Lists in their books.

Cross-Out

To begin this activity, students circle three words on their individual word list. Then the teacher reads words from the list in random order. As each word is read, the student locates and crosses out the word. The winner is the student whose circled words are crossed out first.

I'm Thinking of a Word

For this activity, the teacher makes a statement that relates to a word's meaning. For example, "I'm thinking of a word that is a tool you might use to create a picture." (paintbrush) Students locate the word and say it aloud. Students may also work with a partner to identify words.

Team Timings

Students should form teams of four to do timed readings of a word list. When the teacher says, "Begin," the team members take turns reading a word from the list. Teams should continue reading until the teacher says, "Stop." The winner is the team that reads the most words correctly.

Timed Word List Reading

After students read a list of words under teacher guidance, they may work in pairs to engage in timed readings that last 10 seconds. When the teacher says, "Begin," Partner 1 reads the list, while Partner 2 puts up a finger for each word read correctly. When 10 seconds are up, the teacher says, "Stop," and Partner 2 shows with fingers the total number of words read correctly. Then the partners switch roles.

Fluency in *Phonics for Reading*

Studies have indicated that it is important for students to be able to read material fluently as well as accurately in order for them to move their cognitive resources from decoding to comprehension.

Assessing Fluency

At any point in the program, the teacher can assess students' fluency (the number of correct words read in one minute) by using the passages in the student book. The cumulative number of words is listed to the left of each line in the story (see reading passage below).

1. Before assessing a student, make a copy of the reading passage for recording students' errors.

2. Ask the student to read for one minute and underline any errors the student makes.

3. When it is time for the student to stop (after one minute), circle the last word that the student read.

4. Count up from the number at the beginning of the line in which the circled word appears.

5. Subtract any word errors from the total number of words to figure out the number of words read correctly in one minute.

6. At this level, the student should read 100 correct words in one minute.

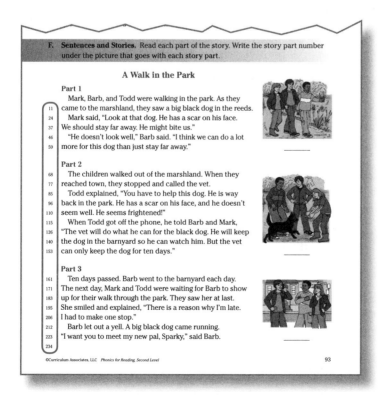

F. Sentences and Stories. Read each part of the story. Write the story part number under the picture that goes with each story part.

A Walk in the Park

Part 1
Mark, Barb, and Todd were walking in the park. As they
11   came to the marshland, they saw a big black dog in the reeds.
24   Mark said, "Look at that dog. He has a scar on his face.
37   We should stay far away. He might bite us."
46   "He doesn't look well," Barb said. "I think we can do a lot
59   more for this dog than just stay far away."

Part 2
68   The children walked out of the marshland. When they
77   reached town, they stopped and called the vet.
85   Todd explained, "You have to help this dog. He is way
96   back in the park. He has a scar on his face, and he doesn't
110 seem well. He seems frightened!"
115 When Todd got off the phone, he told Barb and Mark,
126 "The vet will do what he can for the black dog. He will keep
140 the dog in the barnyard so he can watch him. But the vet
153 can only keep the dog for ten days."

Part 3
161 Ten days passed. Barb went to the barnyard each day.
171 The next day, Mark and Todd were waiting for Barb to show
183 up for their walk through the park. They saw her at last.
195 She smiled and explained, "There is a reason why I'm late.
206 I had to make one stop."
212 Barb let out a yell. A big black dog came running.
223 "I want you to meet my new pal, Sparky," said Barb.
234

©Curriculum Associates, LLC *Phonics for Reading, Second Level*   93

Repeated Readings

Engaging students in repeated readings is one of the best ways to build fluency. Students should read the same passage a number of times, attempting each time to read more words correctly per minute.

The teacher can time individual students each day and, for each student, maintain a graph of the number of words read correctly in one minute. The blank Reading Fluency Graph on page 190 may be used for this purpose.

Partner Timed Readings

Students can also work with a partner for timed readings.

1. The teacher gives students time to practice reading a passage for a minute and teaches them how to determine the number of correct words per minute.

2. Student partners exchange books.

3. Partner 1 reads for one minute, while Partner 2 underlines any errors. (Students should be discouraged from debating about errors, since this will significantly reduce the number of words read.)

4. At the end of the minute, Partner 2 circles the last word read and then determines the number of words read accurately.

5. These steps are repeated for Partner 2.

6. Each student graphs the number of correct words per minute for each timed reading on a copy of the Reading Fluency Graph.

Research Report

Phonics for Reading is a research-based program that reflects the findings of the major national documents on reading, including *Becoming a Nation of Readers* (Anderson et al., 1985), *Preventing Reading Difficulties in Young Children* (Snow et al., 1998), and the *National Reading Panel Report* (2000), which summarized research on numerous topics, including phonemic awareness, phonics, fluency, and comprehension. In addition to these reports, the design of *Phonics for Reading* was informed by the research on beginning reading (Honig, Diamond, and Gutlohn, 2008), the research on reading interventions for older, struggling readers (Archer, Gleason, and Vachon, 2003), the research on explicit instruction (Archer and Hughes, 2011), and the research on literacy and cultural diversity (Morrow, Rueda, and Lapp, 2009).

Phonemic Awareness

Phonemic awareness refers to the understanding that words can be segmented into constituent sounds or phonemes. Students must understand that the words they say can be segmented into sounds so that they can map letters (graphemes) onto those sounds (phonemes) and use those letter-sound associations to decode unknown words (Chard and Dickson, 1999; Erhi and Roberts, 2006). A lack of this understanding is the most common cause of children's early difficulties in acquiring accurate and fluent word recognition skills (Torgesen, 2002; Torgesen, 2004). Students with strong phonological skills will likely become good readers, and students with weak phonological skills will likely become weak readers (Blachman, 2000). In fact, phonemic awareness has proven to be the best early predictor of reading difficulties (Adams, 1990) and is more highly related to learning to read than are tests of general intelligence, reading readiness, and listening comprehension (Stanovich, 1994).

Research clearly indicates that phonemic awareness can be developed through instruction, and that doing so accelerates students' reading and writing achievement (Ball and Blachman, 1991; Lane and Pullen, 2004). When phonemic awareness is taught, it enhances the reading acquisition of young students as they move into first and second grade (Foorman et al., 1997) as well as the reading gains of older, struggling readers. Torgesen and Mathes (1998) concluded that phonemic awareness training would accelerate the reading growth of all children, but is particularly vital for at least 20 percent of children to acquire useful reading skills.

Because of its importance to beginning reading acquisition, phonemic awareness activities are included in *Phonics for Reading.* Consistent with the recommendations of the National Reading Panel (2000), the authors incorporated a limited number of phonemic awareness tasks into the program. As a result, students become familiar with the tasks, allowing them to direct their cognitive energy to the content rather than the tasks. These tasks focus on blending and segmenting, which are the phonemic awareness skills that have the greatest benefit to reading and spelling acquisition (Snider, 1995). In the blending activities, students hear the sounds in a word and say the whole word. In the segmenting activities, students put up a finger as they say each sound within a word. Torgesen et al. (1994) concluded that phonemic awareness training for at-risk children must be more explicit and intense than that for other students. For this reason, the program provides explicit modeling of these blending and segmenting tasks and daily practice with increasingly difficult words.

Phonics

Phonics is the study and use of letter-sound associations to pronounce (decode) unknown words and to spell (encode) words. In the past, students were taught that there were three equal cueing systems that could be used to determine the pronunciation of an unknown word: the phonological cueing system (letter-sound associations), the semantic cueing system (context and pictures), and the syntactical cueing system (word order). However, research has shown that good readers rely on letters in a word rather than context or pictures to pronounce familiar and unfamiliar words (Ehri, 1994). Research has also determined that competent readers do not sample text as they read, but rather process the letters of each word, although this is done rapidly and unconsciously (Adams et al., 1998; Share and Stanovich, 1995; Rayner and Pollatsek,1989). For these reasons, *Phonics for Reading* teaches students to use letter-sound associations as their primary decoding tool and to utilize the semantic and syntactical cues to confirm the accuracy of their initial pronunciation of a word.

As with phonemic awareness, students—especially those struggling to acquire reading skills—benefit from very explicit instruction, in this case focused on letter-sound associations and their application to the decoding and encoding of words. In fact, one of the most well-established conclusions in all of behavioral science is that direct instruction on letter-sound associations and word decoding facilitates early reading acquisition (Stanovich,1994). To optimize student gains in decoding and encoding, *Phonics for Reading* uses the following instructional steps: a) introduce a letter-sound association, b) guide students in reading one-syllable words with the letter-sound association, c) provide reading practice with multisyllabic words containing the letter-sound association, d) have students read decodable passages containing words with the target letter-sound association, and e) dictate spelling words containing the target letter sound. The research basis for each of these steps is articulated below.

Letter-Sound Associations Many studies have confirmed that students are more successful readers if they have been taught letter-sound associations (Juel, 1991). In teaching letter-sound associations, *Phonics for Reading* is consistent with the recommendations of the National Reading Panel (2000). First, only the highest frequency letter-sound associations are introduced. Next, an explicit instructional approach is utilized in which the sounds for the letters are modeled and practiced with other graphemes during initial practice sessions, followed by distributive and cumulative practice in subsequent lessons (Archer and Hughes, 2011; Carnine et al, 2006).

Decodable Words As soon as the letter-sound associations have been introduced, they are immediately placed in words that reflect common English configurations (e.g., CVC, CVCC, CCVC, CVCe, CVVC). Students are explicitly taught the following decoding strategy: a) say the sounds for each grapheme, b) blend the sounds together, c) pronounce the entire word, and d) ask yourself if it is the "real word." Students repeatedly sound out words in which the focus grapheme is mixed with words containing previously taught graphemes deliberately chosen to promote careful scrutiny of the letters (e.g., *lake, tale, mane, man, tape, tap, fate*) to diminish "guessing" as a strategy. As Beck (2006) concluded, the ability to blend individual sounds into a recognizable word is an important component of reading.

Systematic phonics instruction has many benefits including: a) preventing reading difficulties among at-risk students (Ambruster, Lehr, and Osborn, 2001), b) helping children overcome reading difficulties, and increasing the ability to comprehend text for beginning readers and older students with reading challenges (National Reading Panel, 2000).

Multisyllabic Words   The ability to read one-syllable words does not necessarily lead to proficiency with multisyllabic words (Just and Carpenter, 1987). Decoding instruction must go beyond one-syllable words to multisyllabic words to truly prepare students for intermediate and secondary reading and also to ensure that students are not intimidated when confronted by long words. From fifth grade on, students encounter about 10,000 unknown words each year (Nagy and Anderson, 1984), the majority of which are multisyllabic words (Cunningham, 1998) that often convey the meaning of the passage. For example, when reading an article about the water cycle, students will need to decode words such as *evaporation, precipitation,* and *transpiration.* Students must be taught systematic procedures for decoding longer words, such as these.

Research indicates that when good readers encounter unfamiliar multisyllabic words, they chunk the words into manageable, decodable units (Adams, 1990; Mewhort and Campbell, 1981). To facilitate the development of this process, each level of this program presents multisyllabic words segmented into decodable chunks, or parts (Archer, Gleason, and Vachon, 2003). Loops under the words indicate the parts, which students are asked to read one by one and then to blend into a word. As suggested by research in this area, students are also taught to use affixes and vowels to pronounce longer words (Chall and Popp, 1996; Shefelbine, 1990; Shefelbine and Calhoun, 1991).

High-Frequency Words   In order to be a fluent reader, students must quickly and automatically recognize the most common words appearing in text (Blevins, 1998). Only 100 words account for approximately 50 percent of the English words in print (Fry et al., 1985). Thirteen words (*a, and, for, he, is, in, it, of, that, the, to, was, you*) account for 25 percent of the words in print (Johns, 1980). Many of the most frequent words are irregular, having unique letter-sound associations. For example, the high-frequency words *you, was, of, said, do, some,* and *what* are not pronounced as expected, given the letters in the words.

In ***Phonics for Reading***, high-frequency words are systematically introduced, practiced, and reviewed. A spell-out method is used for directly teaching high-frequency words. Students hear the word, say the word, spell the word letter by letter, and finally repeat the word (Honig et al., 2008). As suggested by Louisa Moats (2005), high-frequency, irregular words are grouped by pattern when possible (e.g., *would, could; come, some; all, call, tall*) to facilitate acquisition.

Reading Decodable Text   After students have been introduced to short, decodable words, multisyllabic, decodable words, and high-frequency words, they read decodable passages containing these words. Decodable text is useful in beginning reading for developing automaticity and fluency (Chard and Osborn, 1999) and for providing students with a strong start in reading (Blevins, 2006). Anderson et al. (1985) and Juel (1994) recommended that 90 percent of the words in a story should be decodable.

"The important point is that a high proportion of the words in the earliest selections students read should conform to the phonics they have already been taught. Otherwise, they will not have enough opportunity to practice, extend, and refine their knowledge of letter-sound relations." (*Becoming a Nation of Readers,* 1985).

Spelling   Spelling dictation was included in each ***Phonics for Reading*** lesson for a number of reasons. First, learning to read and spell rely on much of the same underlying knowledge, such as letter-sound associations, affixes, and word patterns (Joshi, Treiman, Carreker, and Moats, 2008/2009). Because of the reciprocal relationship between decoding and encoding, spelling instruction can help children better understand key knowledge, resulting in better reading (Ehri, 2000). Likewise, reading instruction focused on the patterns of words can strengthen spelling. Systematic spelling instruction is also critical to improving students' writing skills. Writers who must think too hard about how to spell words use crucial cognitive resources that could be used for higher level aspects of composition, such as organization, transcription, and revision (Singer & Bashir, 2004). Because of the importance of spelling, in each ***Phonics for Reading*** lesson, students are asked to spell words that contain letter-sound associations and affixes that they have been taught and have used in decoding words.

Fluency

Fluency has been defined as being able to read words accurately and fluently with expression or prosody (Hudson, Lane, and Pullen, 2005). Meyer and Felton (1999) concluded that fluency is "the ability to read connected text rapidly, smoothly, effortlessly, and automatically with little conscious attention to the mechanics of reading such as decoding" (p. 284). When students are able to read fluently, decoding requires less attention and cognitive effort. Instead, attention and cognition can be directed to comprehension (La Berge and Samuels, 1974; Stanovich, 1986). Not surprising, oral reading rate is strongly correlated with reading comprehension (Torgesen and Hudson, 2006). As Hasbrouck (2006) concluded, if students read slowly, they struggle to remember what was read, much less to extract meaning.

Another result of laborious decoding and low fluency is little reading practice (Moats, 2001). Because reading is arduous for struggling readers, they read less over time and fail to gain fluency, while their peers read more and more over time and become increasingly fluent; thus, the gap between the best readers and the weakest readers widens as they get older. The term "Matthew Effect" illustrates this rich-get-richer and poor-get-poorer phenomenon (Stanovich, 1986). Fluent, voracious readers are likely to gain, among other things, increased vocabulary, background knowledge, ideas that can be incorporated into written products, visual memory of words for spelling, and schema for understanding certain genre. It has even been suggested that voracious reading can alter measured intelligence (Cunningham & Stanovich, 1998).

Fluency in reading, like automaticity of any skill, is primarily gained though practice. In ***Phonics for Reading***, students are given abundant practice in reading lists of words and decodable passages. The decodable passages are read more than once. The students read the passages silently first and then orally. Oral reading has particular benefits at the beginning reading stages (National Reading Panel, 2000) for a number of reasons. First, the student can listen to his/her own reading and determine if the words are pronounced accurately. Second, the teacher can also listen to the student and gain information on the accuracy of the student's reading.

In ***Phonics for Reading, Second Level*** and ***Third Level,*** focused, intentional fluency practice is also provided by using a research-based procedure referred to as repeated readings. After completing a comprehensive review of fluency intervention studies conducted in the past 25 years, Chard, et al. (2002) concluded that repeated reading interventions with struggling readers were associated with improvement in reading rate, accuracy, and comprehension. In ***Phonics for Reading***, students read a short passage a number of times. After practice, they read the passage for a minute, count the number of words read, and graph the number. Timing student's reading is effective in increasing accuracy and fluency (Hasbrouck and Tindal, 1992).

Comprehension

The desired outcome of all reading instruction is that students can read passages, constructing meaning as they proceed and extracting the gist of the passage. Each of the reading components previously discussed contributes to increased reading comprehension. If students can decode words accurately, comprehension will be facilitated. Similarly, if students can fluently read a passage, comprehension is enhanced. Nevertheless, as in all areas of reading, students benefit from systematic instruction and intentional practice.

Phonics for Reading addresses comprehension in a number of ways. First, in response to a portion of a reading passage, the students are asked to select an illustration that depicts what has been read. They are also asked to respond to oral comprehension questions, a time-honored and research-validated procedure to increase reading comprehension (National Reading Panel, 2000; McKeown, Beck, and Blake, 2009). As Ambruster, Lehr, and Osborn (2001) suggested, responding to oral comprehension questions encourages students to form better answers and to learn more. In addition, students are taught to answer written questions on passage content in response to the most common questioning words: *who, what, when, where, how,* and *why.* This instruction, like all of the instruction in *Phonics for Reading*, involves modeling the skill followed by guided practice, support which is gradually reduced. This type of scaffolding, found in all strands of the program, is designed to increase the success experienced by students who have encountered consistent failure in the past.

References

Adams, M. J. 1990. *Beginning to Read: Thinking and Learning About Print.* Cambridge, MA: MIT Press.

Adams, M. J., R. Treiman, and M. Pressley. 1998. Reading, writing, and literacy. In *Handbook of Child Psychology* 4, edited by I. E. Sigel and K. A. Renninger, 275–355. New York: Wiley.

Ambruster, B., F. Lehr, and J. Osborn. 2001. *Put reading first: The research building blocks for teaching children to read.* Jessup, MD: National Institute for Literacy.

Anderson, R. C., E. H. Heibert, J. A. Scott, and I. A. G. Wilkinson. 1985. *Becoming a Nation of Readers: The Report of the Commission on Reading.* Washington, D.C.: National Institute of Education.

Archer, A. L., M. M. Gleason, and V. L. Vachon. 2003. Decoding and fluency: Foundation skills for struggling older readers. *Learning Disability Quarterly* 26, pp. 89–101.

Archer, A., and C. Hughes. 2011. *Explicit Instruction: Effective and Efficient Teaching.* New York: Guilford.

Ball, E. W., and B. A. Blachman. 1991. Does phoneme awareness training in kindergarten make a difference in early word recognition and developmental spelling? *Reading Research Quarterly* 26 (1): 33–44.

Beck, I. L., 2006. *Making sense of phonics: The hows and whys.* New York: Guilford.

Blachman, B. A. 2000. Phonological awareness. In M. L. Kamil, P. B. Rosenthal, P. D. Pearson, and R. Barr (eds), *Handbook of reading research,* Vol. 3 (pp. 483–502). Mahwah, NJ: Erlbaum.

Blevins, W. 1998. *Phonics from A to Z: A Practical Guide.* New York: Scholastic.

Carnine, D. W., J. Silbert, E. J. Kame'enui, S. Tarver, and K. Jungjohann. 2006. *Teaching struggling and at-risk readers.* Upper Saddle River, NJ: Pearson.

Chall, J. S. 1996. *Learning to Read: The Great Debate.* New York: McGraw-Hill.

Chall, J. S., and H. M. Popp. 1996. *Teaching and Assessing Phonics: A Guide for Teachers.* Cambridge, MA: Educator's Publishing Service.

Chard, D. J., and J. Osborn. 1999. Phonics and word-recognition instruction in early reading programs: Guidelines for accessibility. *Learning Disabilities Research and Practice* 14(2): 107–117.

Chard, D. J., and S. V. Dickson. 1999. Phonological awareness: Instructional and assessment guidelines. *Intervention in School and Clinic* 34: 261–270.

Chard, D. J., S. Vaughn, and B. J. Tyler. 2002. A synthesis of research on effective interventions for building reading fluency with elementary students with learning disabilities. *Journal of Learning Disabilities* 35, 386–406.

Cunningham, P. M., & Stanovich. 1998. The multisyllabic-word dilemma: Helping students build meaning, spell, and read "big" words. *Reading and Writing Quarterly: Overcoming Learning Difficulties* 14: 189–218

Ehri, L. 2000. Learning to read and learning to spell: Two sides of a coin. *Topics in Language Disorders,* 20(3), 19–49.

Ehri, L. 1994. Development of the ability to read words. In *Theoretical Models and Processes of Reading,* edited by R. Ruddell, M. Ruddell, and H. Singer. Newark, DE: International Reading Association.

Ehri, L. C., & T. Roberts. 2006. The roots of learning to read and write: Acquisition of letters and phonemic awareness. In *Handbook of early literacy research,* Vol. 2, eds. D. K. Dickinson & S. B. Neuman, 113–31. New York: Guilford.

Foorman, B. R., D. J. Francis, S. E. Shaywitz, B. A. Shaywitz, and J. M. Fletcher. 1997. The case for early reading intervention. In *Foundations of Reading Acquisition and Dyslexia: Implications for Early Intervention,* edited by B. A. Blachman, 243–264. Mahwah, NJ: Erlbaum.

Fry, E., D. Fountoukidis, and J. Polk. 1985. *The New Reading Teacher's Book of Lists.* Upper Saddle River, NJ: Prentice-Hall.

Hasbrouck, J. 2006, Summer. Drop everything and read—but how? *The American Educator,* 30(2), 22–31.

Hasbrouck, J. E., and G. Tindal. 1992. Curriculum-based oral reading fluency norms for students in grades 2 through 5. *Teaching Exceptional Children* 24(3): 41–44.

Honig, B., L. Diamond, and L. Gutlohn. 2008. *Teaching Reading Sourcebook for Kindergarten Through Eighth Grade.* Second Edition. Novato, CA: Arena Press.

Hudson, R. F., Lane, H. B., & Pullen, P. C. (2005). Reading fluency assessment and instruction: What, why, and how? *The Reading Teacher, 58,* 702–714.

Joshi, M., Treiman, R., Carreker, S., & Moats, L. C. (2008/2009) How words cast their spell: Spelling is an integral part of learning the language, not a matter of memorization. *American Educator, 32*(4), 6–16, 42–43.

Johns, J. L. 1980. First-graders' concepts about print. *Reading Research Quarterly* 15.

Juel, C. 1994. *Learning to Read in One Elementary School.* New York: Springer-Verlag.

Juel, C. 1991. Beginning reading. In *Handbook of Reading Research* 2, edited by R. Barr, M. L. Kamil, P. B. Mosenthal, and P. D. Pearson. Mahwah, NJ: Erlbaum.

Just, M. A., and P. A. Carpenter. 1987. *The Psychology of Reading and Language Comprehension.* Boston: Allyn and Bacon.

LaBerge, D., and S. J. Samuels. 1974. Toward a theory of automatic information processing in reading. *Cognitive Psychology* 6: 292–323.

Lane, H. B, and P. C. Pullen. 2004. *A sound beginning: Phonological awareness assessment and instruction.* Boston: Allyn & Bacon.

McKeown, M.G., Beck, I. L., and Blake, R. K. 2009, July/August/September. Rethinking reading comprehension instruction: A comparison of instruction for strategies and content approaches. *Reading Research Quarterly, 44*(3), 218–253.

Mewhort, D. J. K., and A. J. Campbell. 1981. Toward a model of skilled reading: An analysis of performance in tachistoscoptic tasks. In *Reading Research: Advances in Theory and Practice* 3, edited by G. E. MacKinnon and T. G. Walker, 39–118. New York: Academic Press.

Meyer, M. S. and R. H. Felton. 1999. Repeated reading to enhance fluency: Old approaches and new directions. *Annals of Dyslexia,* 49, 283–306.

Moats, L. C. 2005. When older students can't read. *Educational Leadership,* 58, 36–40.

Morrow, L. M., Rueda, R., & Lapp, D. (2009) *Handbook of research on literacy and diversity.* New York: Guilford.

Nagy, W., and R. C. Anderson. 1984. How many words are there in printed school English? *Reading Research Quarterly* 19: 304–330.

National Reading Panel. 2000. *Teaching Children to Read: An Evidence-based Assessment of the Scientific Research Literature on Reading and Its Implications for Reading Instruction.* Bethesda, MD: National Institute of Child Health and Human Development.

Rayner, K., and A. Pollatsek. 1989. *The Psychology of Reading.* Englewood Cliffs, NJ: Prentice Hall.

Share, D., and K. E. Stanovich. 1995. Cognitive processes in early reading development: Accommodating individual differences into a mode of acquisition. *Issues in Education: Contributions for Educational Psychology* 1: 1–57.

Shefelbine, J. 1990. A syllable-unit approach to teaching decoding of polysyllabic words to fourth- and sixth-grade disabled readers. In *Literacy Theory and Research: Analysis from Multiple Paradigms,* edited by J. Zutell and S. McCormick, 223–230. Chicago: National Reading Conference.

Shefelbine, J., and J. Calhoun. 1991. Variability in approaches to identifying polysyllabic words: A descriptive study of sixth graders with highly, moderately, and poorly developed syllabication strategies. In *Learner Factors/Teacher Factors: Issues in Literacy Research and Instruction,* edited by J. Zutell and S. McCormick, 169–177. Chicago: National Reading Conference.

Singer, B. and A. Bashir. 2004. Developmental variations in writing. In Stone, C. A., Silliman, E. R., Ehren, B. J., and Apel, K. (Eds.), *Handbook of Language and Literacy: Development and Disorders,* pp. 559–582. New York: Guilford.

Snider, V. E. 1995. A primer on phonemic awareness: What it is, why it's important, and how to teach it. *School Psychology Review* 24: 443–455.

Snow, C. E., M. S. Burns, and P. Griffin. 1998. *Preventing Reading Difficulties in Young Children.* Washington, D.C.: National Academy Press.

Stanovich, K. E. 1986. Matthew effects in reading: Some consequences of individual differences in the acquisition of literacy. *Reading Research Quarterly* 21: 360–407.

Stanovich, K. E. 1994. Romance and reality. *The Reading Teacher* 47(4): 280–291.

Torgesen, J. K. 2002. The prevention of reading difficulties. *Journal of School Psychology,* 40, 7–26.

Torgesen, J. K. 2004. Preventing early reading failure. *American Educator,* Fall.

Torgesen, J. K., R. K. Wagner, and C. A. Rashotte. 1994. Longitudinal studies of phonological processing and reading. *Journal of Learning Disabilities* 27: 276–286.

Torgesen, J. K. and R. Hudson. 2006. Reading fluency: Critical issues for struggling readers. In S. J. Samuels and A. Farstrup (Eds.), *Reading Fluency: The forgotten dimension of reading success.* Newark, DE: International Reading Association Monograph of the British Journal of Educational Psychology.

Torgesen, J. K, and P. Mathes. 1998. What every teacher should know about phonological awareness. *CORE Reading Research Anthology.* Novato, CA: Arena Press.

LESSON 1

OBJECTIVES

- *to introduce* ai *and* ay *words with the sound of* /ā/
- *to introduce words with the word ending* -ed

🔊 New Sound

(Have students open their books to Lesson 1, page 4.)

1. Look at the top of page 4 in your book.

2. Touch the first word.

3. This word is **rain**. Say the word. *rain*

4. The underlined sound is /**aaa**/. Say the sound. /āaā/

5. Say the sound again. /āaā/

6. Touch the next word.

7. This word is **play**. Say the word. *play*

8. The underlined sound is /**aaa**/. Say the sound. /āaā/

9. Say the sound again. /āaā/

(Have students close their books. Then do the Sound Drill activity.)

🔊 Sound Drill
(Oral Teacher-Directed Activity)

(Write the following on the board or display it on-screen:)

1.	ai	sh	ch	ay
2.	th	wh	a	ck
3.	ai	i	ck	ch
4.	e	sh	ai	th
5.	ay	ch	u	ay

1. Let's practice saying the sounds in the words that we will be reading. Look at the letters in line 1. Say the sounds. /āaā/, /sh/, /ch/, /āaā/

2. Look at the letters in line 2. Say the sounds. /th/, /wh/, /aaa/, /k/

(Repeat step 2 with lines 3–5. Then call on individual students to say the sounds in a line.)

(NOTE: As an alternative, review the sounds with flash cards.)

🔊 Blending Sounds
(Oral Teacher-Directed Activity)

Let's practice saying some words. I will say a word slowly. You tell me the word. /**mmm**/ /**aaa**/ /**d**/ What is the word? *maid*

(Repeat this procedure with the following words:)

play	/p/	/lll/	/āaā/
pain	/p/	/āaā/	/nnn/
wait	/www/	/āaā/	/t/
aid	/āaā/	/d/	

(NOTE: As you pronounce these words slowly, don't stop between the sounds. This practice will assist students in recognizing words that they have sounded out.)

A. New Words

(Have students open their books to Lesson 1, page 4.)

1.	f<u>ai</u>l	d<u>ay</u>	m<u>ay</u>
2.	w<u>ai</u>t	w<u>i</u>t	t<u>ai</u>l
3.	w<u>ay</u>	s<u>ay</u>	s<u>ai</u>l
4.	m<u>ai</u>d	m<u>a</u>d	st<u>ay</u>
5.	p<u>ai</u>n	p<u>ai</u>l	pl<u>ay</u>
6.	h<u>ay</u>	j<u>ai</u>l	<u>ai</u>d

7. **May I have this?**
8. **It has a thin tail.**
9. **The van was in the way.**
10. **Did the maid see the polish?**
11. **I have a pain in my hip.**
12. **The hay is damp.**

1. Find part A in your book.

2. Touch the first word in line 1. Look at the underlined letters. What is the sound? /āaā/

3. Sound out the word to yourself. Put your thumb up when you can say the whole word. (Wait until thumbs are up.) What is the word? *fail*

4. Touch the next word. Look at the underlined letters. What is the sound? /$\overline{aaa}$/ Sound out the word to yourself. Put your thumb up when you can say the whole word. (Wait until thumbs are up.) What is the word? *day*

(Repeat step 4 with the remaining words in lines 1–3.)

5. Touch the first word in line 4. Sound out this word to yourself. Say the sounds carefully. Put your thumb up when you can say the whole word. (Wait until thumbs are up.) What is the word? *maid*

6. Touch the next word. Sound out the word to yourself. Put your thumb up when you can say the whole word. (Wait until thumbs are up.) What is the word? *mad*

(Repeat step 6 with the remaining words in lines 4–6. Then call on individual students to read a line.)

7. Read sentence 7 to yourself. Put your thumb up when you are done. (Wait until thumbs are up. Then call on a student to read the sentence.)

(Repeat step 7 with sentences 8–12.)

B. Review Words

(Have students open their books to Lesson 1, page 4.)

1.	truck	tuck	tap
2.	Jeff	shelf	self
3.	blush	lash	miss
4.	thin	throb	Rob
5.	stick	tick	thick

1. Find part B in your book.

2. Read the words in line 1 to yourself. When you can read all three words, put your thumb up. (Wait until thumbs are up.)

3. Get ready to read the words in line 1 together. Begin. *truck, tuck, tap*

(Repeat steps 2 and 3 with lines 2–5. Then call on individual students to read the words in a line.)

C. Word Endings

(Have students open their books to Lesson 1, page 4.)

1.	failed	2.	waited	3.	sailed
4.	trapped	5.	missed		

1. Find part C in your book.

2. Let's practice reading some words with word endings. Look at the first word. Sound out the underlined word to yourself. Put your thumb up when you can say the underlined word. (Wait until thumbs are up.) What is the word? *fail*

3. When the **-ed** ending is added, the word is **failed**. What is the word? *failed*

4. Now I will use the word in a sentence. **Sam failed the math test.** Say the word again. *failed*

(Repeat steps 2–4 with numbers 2–5. Then call on individual students to say the words with endings.)

> **Word Ending Sentences**
> 2. **Nat waited for Pat at school.**
> 3. **The ship sailed in the water.**
> 4. **The tiger was trapped in the cage.**
> 5. **Thomas missed the bus.**

D. Challenge Words

(Have students open their books to Lesson 1, page 5.)

raindrop	mailbox	midday	railway
1 2	1 2	1 2	1 2
payday			
1 2			

1. Find part D in your book.

2. Touch the first word. Sound out the first part to yourself. Put your thumb up when you can say the part. (Wait until thumbs are up.) What is this part? *rain*

3. Sound out the next part to yourself. Put your thumb up when you can say the part. (Wait until thumbs are up.) What is this part? *drop*

4. Say the parts again. First part? *rain* Next part? *drop*

5. Say the whole word. *raindrop*

(Repeat steps 2–5 with the words **mailbox, midday, railway,** and **payday**.)

6. Let's read these words again. (Call on individual students to read the Challenge Words.)

E. Sight Words

(Have students open their books to Lesson 1, page 5.)

were	you	of	said	have
after	from	my	to	they

1. Find part E in your book.

2. There are some words that may be difficult to sound out. We just have to remember these words.

3. Touch the first word. This word is **were**.
   What is the word? *were*
   Spell and read. *w-e-r-e. were*

4. Touch the next word. This word is **you**.
   What is the word? *you*
   Spell and read. *y-o-u. you*

(Repeat step 4 with the remaining words.)

5. Let's read these words again. (Call on individual students to read the Sight Words.)

F. Sentences and Stories

(Have students open their books to Lesson 1, page 5.)

1. Find part F in your book.

2. Touch the title of the story. Let's read the title together. *The Day of Rain*

3. Read Part 1 to yourself. Read it very carefully. Put your thumb up when you are done. (Wait until thumbs are up.)

4. Let's read Part 1 together. When you are not reading aloud, follow along in your book. (Call on a student to read one or two sentences. Continue until Part 1 has been read.)

5. Look at the three pictures. Put a number 1 under the picture that goes with Part 1.

(Repeat steps 3–5 with Parts 2 and 3.)

Answers

1   3   2

G. Spelling

(Have students open their books to Lesson 1, page 6.)

1. Find part G in your book.

2. Your first spelling word is **stay**.
   What is the word? *stay*

3. Say the sounds to yourself as you write the word. (Monitor.)

4. (Write the word on the board or display it on-screen.) Check your word. If you made a mistake, cross out the word and rewrite it. (Monitor.)

(Repeat steps 2–4 with the word **wait**.)

5. Your next spelling word is **raindrop**.
   Say the first part of the word. *rain*
   Write this part.

6. Say the second part of the word. *drop*
   Write this part.

7. (Write the word on the board or display it on-screen.) Check your word. If you made a mistake, cross out the word and rewrite it. (Monitor.)

(Repeat steps 5–7 with the word **payday**.)

8. Listen. **The dog has a black tail.** Say the sentence. *The dog has a black tail.* Write the sentence. (Monitor.)

9. (Write the sentence on the board or display it on-screen.) Check each word. If you made a mistake, cross out the word and rewrite it. (Monitor.)

Answers
1. stay   3. raindrop
2. wait   4. payday
5. **The dog has a black tail.**

H. Practice Activity 1

(Have students open their books to Lesson 1, page 6.)

1. Find part H in your book.

2. Follow along as I read the directions. **Draw a line under the phrase that best completes each sentence.**

3. Do number 1. Put your thumb up when you are finished. (Monitor and check.)

4. You will finish part H later.

I. Practice Activity 2

(Have students open their books to Lesson 1, page 7.)

1. Find part I in your book.

2. Follow along as I read the directions. **Draw a line under the sentence that goes with each picture.**

3. Do number 1. Put your thumb up when you are finished. (Monitor and check.)

4. Now go back and finish parts H and I.

🔊 Work Check for Parts H and I
(Oral Teacher-Directed Activity)

1. Find part H in your book.

2. Let's check your work. If you made a mistake, circle the number. You will fix all mistakes at the end of the lesson. (Call on individual students to read their answers.)

3. Count how many correct answers you have, and write that number in the box at the bottom of the page. (Monitor students.)

(Repeat steps 1–3 with part I.)

4. Now go back and correct any mistakes. (Monitor students.)

Answers for Part H
1. a. <u>a mop in the pail</u>
2. a. <u>have a sail</u>
3. a. <u>wait in the truck</u>
4. b. <u>fail a test</u>
5. b. <u>pay the bill</u>
6. b. <u>sit in the hay</u>
7. a. <u>rain on this day</u>

Answers for Part I
1. <u>The dog has a black tail</u>.
2. <u>The cats play in the box</u>.
3. <u>The rain will fill the pail</u>.
4. <u>Rob put the nail in the box</u>.
5. <u>Chuck will wait until the bus stops</u>.
6. <u>Will Beth fail the test?</u>
7. <u>The maid will dust the lamp</u>.
8. <u>The man will pay with cash</u>.

LESSON 2

OBJECTIVES

- *to practice words with* ai *and* ay
- *to practice words with the word ending* -ed

Sound Drill
(Oral Teacher-Directed Activity)

(Write the following on the board or display it on-screen:)

1.	ay	ch	ai	th
2.	ai	sh	u	ch
3.	wh	e	ay	sh
4.	th	o	ai	i
5.	ay	cli	ck	wh

1. Let's practice saying the sounds in the words that we will be reading. Look at the letters in line 1. Say the sounds. /$\overline{aaa}$/, /ch/, /$\overline{aaa}$/, /th/

2. Look at the letters in line 2. Say the sounds. /$\overline{aaa}$/, /sh/, /uuu/, /ch/

(Repeat step 2 with lines 3–5. Then call on individual students to say the sounds in a line.)

(NOTE: As an alternative, review the sounds with flash cards.)

Blending Sounds
(Oral Teacher-Directed Activity)

Let's practice saying some words. I will say a word slowly. You tell me the word. /t/ /rrr/ /$\overline{aaa}$/ /lll/ What is the word? *trail*

(Repeat this procedure with the following words:)

clay	/k/	/lll/	/$\overline{aaa}$/	
faint	/fff/	/$\overline{aaa}$/	/nnn/	/t/
gain	/g/	/$\overline{aaa}$/	/nnn/	
braid	/b/	/rrr/	/$\overline{aaa}$/	/d/

(NOTE: As you pronounce these words slowly, don't stop between the sounds. This practice will assist students in recognizing words that they have sounded out.)

A. New Words

(Have students open their books to Lesson 2, page 8.)

1.	ray	mail	gain
2.	Jay	paint	pant
3.	trail	rail	train
4.	brain	play	lay
5.	tray	braid	gray
6.	clay	faint	fin

7. **Will you get the mail?**
8. **Mix the paint well.**
9. **I missed the train.**
10. **Did you see the play?**
11. **The gray hat fit me.**
12. **Here is a lump of clay.**

1. Find part A in your book.

2. Touch the first word in line 1. Look at the underlined letters. What is the sound? /$\overline{aaa}$/

3. Sound out the word to yourself. Put your thumb up when you can say the whole word. (Wait until thumbs are up.) What is the word? *ray*

4. Touch the next word. Look at the underlined letters. What is the sound? /$\overline{aaa}$/ Sound out the word to yourself. Put your thumb up when you can say the whole word. (Wait until thumbs are up.) What is the word? *mail*

(Repeat step 4 with the remaining words in lines 1–3.)

5. Touch the first word in line 4. Sound out this word to yourself. Say the sounds carefully. Put your thumb up when you can say the whole word. (Wait until thumbs are up.) What is the word? *brain*

6. Touch the next word. Sound out the word to yourself. Put your thumb up when you can say the whole word. (Wait until thumbs are up.) What is the word? *play*

(Repeat step 6 with the remaining words in lines 4–6. Then call on individual students to read a line.)

7. Read sentence 7 to yourself. Put your thumb up when you are done. (Wait until thumbs are up. Then call on a student to read the sentence.)

(Repeat step 7 with sentences 8–12.)

B. Review Words

(Have students open their books to Lesson 2, page 8.)

1. bunch	lunch	luck
2. hiss	check	chick
3. snack	nap	kiss
4. hit	splash	lash
5. rich	which	stick

1. Find part B in your book.

2. Read the words in line 1 to yourself. When you can read all three words, put your thumb up. (Wait until thumbs are up.)

3. Get ready to read the words in line 1 together. Begin. *bunch, lunch, luck*

(Repeat steps 2 and 3 with lines 2–5. Then call on individual students to read the words in a line.)

C. Word Endings

(Have students open their books to Lesson 2, page 8.)

1. <u>mail</u>ed	2. <u>paint</u>ed	3. <u>play</u>ed
4. <u>stop</u>ped	5. <u>check</u>ed	

1. Find part C in your book.

2. Let's practice reading some words with word endings. Look at the first word. Sound out the underlined word to yourself. Put your thumb up when you can say the underlined word. (Wait until thumbs are up.) What is the word? *mail*

3. When the **-ed** ending is added, the word is **mailed**. What is the word? *mailed*

4. Now I will use the word in a sentence. **Kim mailed the letter.** Say the word again. *mailed*

Repeat steps 2–4 with numbers 2–5. Then call on individual students to say the words with endings.)

Word Ending Sentences
2. **Last week, Hal painted the house.**
3. **Nick played in the soccer game yesterday.**
4. **At noon, the children stopped playing.**
5. **Ms. Archer checked the student's work.**

D. Challenge Words

(Have students open their books to Lesson 2, page 9.)

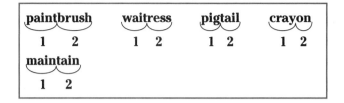

1. Find part D in your book.

2. Touch the first word. Sound out the first part to yourself. Put your thumb up when you can say the part. (Wait until thumbs are up.) What is this part? *paint*

3. Sound out the next part to yourself. Put your thumb up when you can say the part. (Wait until thumbs are up.) What is this part? *brush*

4. Say the parts again. First part? *paint* Next part? *brush*

5. Say the whole word. *paintbrush*

(Repeat steps 2–5 with the words **waitress, pigtail, crayon,** and **maintain.**)

6. Let's read these words again. (Call on individual students to read the Challenge Words.)

E. Sight Words

(Have students open their books to Lesson 2, page 9.)

were	said	you	to	of
are	look	was	my	have

1. Find part E in your book.

2. There are some words that may be difficult to sound out. We just have to remember these words.

3. Touch the first word. This word is **were.** What is the word? *were* Spell and read. *w-e-r-e. were*

4. Touch the next word. This word is **said.** What is the word? *said* Spell and read. *s-a-i-d. said*

(Repeat step 4 with the remaining words.)

5. Let's read these words again. (Call on individual students to read the Sight Words.)

F. Sentences and Stories

(Have students open their books to Lesson 2, page 9.)

1. Find part F in your book.

2. Touch the title of the story. Let's read the title together. *After the Rain*

3. Read Part 1 to yourself. Read it very carefully. Put your thumb up when you are done. (Wait until thumbs are up.)

4. Let's read Part 1 together. When you are not reading aloud, follow along in your book. (Call on a student to read one or two sentences. Continue until Part 1 has been read.)

5. Look at the three pictures. Put a number 1 under the picture that goes with Part 1.

(Repeat steps 3–5 with Parts 2 and 3.)

G. Spelling

(Have students open their books to Lesson 2, page 10.)

1. Find part G in your book.

2. Your first spelling word is **play**. What is the word? *play*

3. Say the sounds to yourself as you write the word. (Monitor.)

4. (Write the word on the board or display it on-screen.) Check your word. If you made a mistake, cross out the word and rewrite it. (Monitor.)

(Repeat steps 2–4 with the word **trail**.)

5. Your next spelling word is **paintbrush**. Say the first part of the word. *paint* Write this part.

6. Say the second part of the word. *brush* Write this part.

7. (Write the word on the board or display it on-screen.) Check your word. If you made a mistake, cross out the word and rewrite it. (Monitor.)

(Repeat steps 5–7 with the word **maintain**.)

8. Listen. **The crayon is in the box.** Say the sentence. *The crayon is in the box.* Write the sentence. (Monitor.)

9. (Write the sentence on the board or display it on-screen.) Check each word. If you made a mistake, cross out the word and rewrite it. (Monitor.)

> **Answers**
> 1. play   3. paintbrush
> 2. trail   4. maintain
> 5. The crayon is in the box.

H. Practice Activity 1

(Have students open their books to Lesson 2, page 10.)

1. Find part H in your book.

2. Follow along as I read the directions. **Read each question. Circle the answer.**

3. Do number 1. Put your thumb up when you are finished. (Monitor and check.)

4. You will finish part H later.

I. Practice Activity 2

(Have students open their books to Lesson 2, page 11.)

1. Find part I in your book.

2. Follow along as I read the directions. **Draw a line under the sentence that goes with each picture.**

3. Do number 1. Put your thumb up when you are finished. (Monitor and check.)

4. Now go back and finish parts H and I.

🔊 Work Check for Parts H and I
(Oral Teacher-Directed Activity)

1. Find part H in your book.

2. Let's check your work. If you made a mistake, circle the number. You will fix all mistakes at the end of the lesson. (Call on individual students to read their answers.)

3. Count how many correct answers you have, and write that number in the box at the bottom of the page. (Monitor students.)

(Repeat steps 1–3 with part I.)

4. Now go back and correct any mistakes. (Monitor students.)

Answers for Part H		
1. no	6.	yes
2. yes	7.	yes
3. no	8.	yes
4. yes	9.	no
5. no	10.	yes

Answers for Part I
1. Rob and Chuck play with the train.
2. Pam's muffin is on the tray.
3. A train runs on a rail.
4. The paintbrush is in the pail.
5. Mom got the mail.
6. Beth has a braid.
7. The hen stands in the hay.
8. Jay painted the shed.

LESSON 3

OBJECTIVES

- *to practice words with* ai *and* ay
- *to practice words with the word ending* -ed

 Sound Drill
(Oral Teacher-Directed Activity)

(Write the following on the board or display it on-screen:)

1.	ai	ch	e	th
2.	a	u	ay	o
3.	wh	ch	o	sh
4.	ay	i	ck	u
5.	a	sh	ai	e

1. Let's practice saying the sounds in the words that we will be reading. Look at the letters in line 1. Say the sounds. /$\overline{aaa}$/, /ch/, /eee/, /th/

2. Look at the letters in line 2. Say the sounds. /aaa/, /uuu/, /$\overline{aaa}$/, /ooo/

(Repeat step 2 with lines 3–5. Then call on individual students to say the sounds in a line.)

(NOTE: As an alternative, review the sounds with flash cards.)

 Blending Sounds
(Oral Teacher-Directed Activity)

Let's practice saying some words. I will say a word slowly. You tell me the word. /mmm/ /$\overline{aaa}$/ /nnn/ What is the word? *main*

(Repeat this procedure with the following words:)

stay	/sss/	/t/	/$\overline{aaa}$/	
drain	/d/	/rrr/	/$\overline{aaa}$/	/nnn/
raise	/rrr/	/$\overline{aaa}$/	/zzz/	
plain	/p/	/lll/	/$\overline{aaa}$/	/nnn/

(NOTE: As you pronounce these words slowly, don't stop between the sounds. This practice will assist students in recognizing words that they have sounded out.)

A. New Words

(Have students open their books to Lesson 3, page 12.)

1.	b<u>ay</u>	m<u>ai</u>n	m<u>a</u>n
2.	G<u>ai</u>l	b<u>a</u>t	b<u>ai</u>t
3.	b<u>i</u>t	pr<u>ay</u>	p<u>ay</u>
4.	st<u>ay</u>	pl<u>a</u>n	pl<u>ai</u>n
5.	dr<u>ai</u>n	gr<u>ai</u>n	r<u>ai</u>d
6.	R<u>ay</u>	spr<u>ay</u>	r<u>ai</u>se

7. That man is my boss.
8. Gail is at her desk.
9. Will Fred pay for his ticket?
10. Stay where you are.
11. The water went down the drain.
12. Spray the spot of rust.

1. Find part A in your book.

2. Touch the first word in line 1. Look at the underlined letters. What is the sound? /$\overline{aaa}$/

3. Sound out the word to yourself. Put your thumb up when you can say the whole word. (Wait until thumbs are up.) What is the word? *bay*

4. Touch the next word. Look at the underlined letters. What is the sound? /$\overline{aaa}$/ Sound out the word to yourself. Put your thumb up when you can say the whole word. (Wait until thumbs are up.) What is the word? *main*

(Repeat step 4 with the remaining words in lines 1–3.)

5. Touch the first word in line 4. Sound out this word to yourself. Say the sounds carefully. Put your thumb up when you can say the whole word. (Wait until thumbs are up.) What is the word? *stay*

6. Touch the next word. Sound out the word to yourself. Put your thumb up when you can say the whole word. (Wait until thumbs are up.) What is the word? *plan*

(Repeat step 6 with the remaining words in lines 4–6. Then call on individual students to read a line.)

7. Read sentence 7 to yourself. Put your thumb up when you are done. (Wait until thumbs are up. Then call on a student to read the sentence.)

(Repeat step 7 with sentences 8–12.)

B. Review Words

(Have students open their books to Lesson 3, page 12.)

1.	less	rash	trash
2.	which	when	hen
3.	chip	check	chick
4.	branch	ranch	ran
5.	stack	stick	tip

1. Find part B in your book.

2. Read the words in line 1 to yourself. When you can read all three words, put your thumb up. (Wait until thumbs are up.)

3. Get ready to read the words in line 1 together. Begin. *less, rash, trash*

(Repeat steps 2 and 3 with lines 2–5. Then call on individual students to read the words in a line.)

C. Word Endings

(Have students open their book to Lesson 3, page 12.)

1. <u>nail</u>ed	2. <u>play</u>ed	3. <u>stay</u>ed
4. <u>plan</u>ned	5. <u>raid</u>ed	

1. Find part C in your book.

2. Let's practice reading some words with word endings. Look at the first word. Sound out the underlined word to yourself. Put your thumb up when you can say the underlined word. (Wait until thumbs are up.) What is the word? *nail*

3. When the **-ed** ending is added, the word is **nailed**. What is the word? *nailed*

4. Now I will use the word in a sentence. **Carmen nailed the shelf to the wall.** Say the word again. *nailed*

(Repeat steps 2–4 with numbers 2–5. Then call on individual students to say the words with endings.)

> **Word Ending Sentences**
> 2. **We played a fun game.**
> 3. **He stayed in bed.**
> 4. **Josh planned a meal for his friends.**
> 5. **The girls raided the refrigerator.**

D. Challenge Words

(Have students open their books to Lesson 3, page 13.)

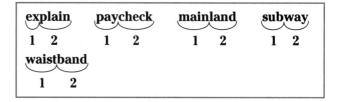

1. Find part D in your book.

2. Touch the first word. Sound out the first part to yourself. Put your thumb up when you can say the part. (Wait until thumbs are up.) What is this part? *ex*

3. Sound out the next part to yourself. Put our thumb up when you can say the part. (Wait until thumbs are up.) What is this part? *plain*

4. Say the parts again. First part? *ex* Next part? *plain*

5. Say the whole word. *explain*

(Repeat steps 2–5 with the words **paycheck, mainland, subway,** and **waistband**.)

6. Let's read these words again. (Call on individual students to read the Challenge Words.)

E. Sight Words

(Have students open their books to Lesson 3, page 13.)

they	were	said	you	after
my	have	put	saw	of

1. Find part E in your book.

2. Touch the first word. This word is **they**. What is the word? *they* Spell and read. *t-h-e-y. they*

3. Touch the next word. This word is **were**. What is the word? *were* Spell and read. *w-e-r-e. were*

(Repeat step 3 with the remaining words.)

4. Let's read these words again. (Call on individual students to read the Sight Words.)

F. Sentences and Stories

(Have students open their books to Lesson 3, page 13.)

1. Find part F in your book.

2. Touch the title of the story. Let's read the title together. *A Day at Bay Ranch*

3. Read Part 1 to yourself. Read it very carefully. Put your thumb up when you are done. (Wait until thumbs are up.)

4. Let's read Part 1 together. When you are not reading aloud, follow along in your book. (Call on a student to read one or two sentences. Continue until Part 1 has been read.)

5. Look at the three pictures. Put a number 1 under the picture that goes with Part 1.

(Repeat steps 3–5 with Parts 2 and 3.)

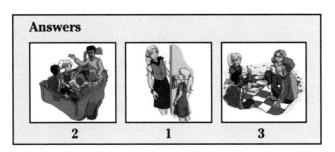

Answers

2   1   3

G. Spelling

(Have students open their books to Lesson 3, page 14.)

1. Find part G in your book.

2. Your first spelling word is **grain**. What is the word? *grain*

3. Say the sounds to yourself as you write the word. (Monitor.)

4. (Write the word on the board or display it on-screen.) Check your word. If you made a mistake, cross out the word and rewrite it. (Monitor.)

(Repeat steps 2–4 with the word **pray**.)

5. Your next spelling word is **explain**. Say the first part of the word. *ex* Write this part.

6. Say the second part of the word. *plain* Write this part.

7. (Write the word on the board or display it on-screen.) Check your word. If you made a mistake, cross out the word and rewrite it. (Monitor.)

(Repeat steps 5–7 with the word **paycheck**.)

8. Listen. **The mail is in the mailbox.** Say the sentence. *The mail is in the mailbox.* Write the sentence. (Monitor.)

9. (Write the sentence on the board or display it on-screen.) Check each word. If you made a mistake, cross out the word and rewrite it. (Monitor.)

Answers
1. grain   3. explain
2. pray   4. paycheck
5. **The mail is in the mailbox.**

H. Practice Activity 1

(Have students open their books to Lesson 3, page 14.)

1. Find part H in your book.

2. Follow along as I read the directions. **Fill in each blank with the best word.**

3. Do number 1. Put your thumb up when you are finished. (Monitor and check.)

4. You will finish part H later.

I. Practice Activity 2

(Have students open their books to Lesson 3, page 15.)

1. Find part I in your book.

2. Follow along as I read the directions. **Draw a line under the sentence that goes with each picture.**

3. Do number 1. Put your thumb up when you are finished. (Monitor and check.)

4. Now go back and finish parts H and I.

◀)) Work Check for Parts H and I
(Oral Teacher-Directed Activity)

1. Find part H in your book.

2. Let's check your work. If you made a mistake, circle the number. You will fix all mistakes at the end of the lesson. (Call on individual students to read their answers.)

3. Count how many correct answers you have, and write that number in the box at the bottom of the page. (Monitor students.)

(Repeat steps 1–3 with part I.)

4. Now go back and correct any mistakes. (Monitor students.)

Answers for Part H	
1. bay	6. mail
2. rain	7. stay
3. tray	8. paint
4. bait	9. braid
5. grain	10. drain

Answers for Part I
1. The men will stay in the cabin.
2. Paint is in the can.
3. Bess will play in the rain.
4. Ray has bait in a pail.
5. The hat has red dots.
6. The dog will run up the trail.
7. Nick and Gail play with clay.
8. The mail is in the mailbox.

◀)) Checking Up
(Oral Teacher-Directed Activity)

Practice reading Part 1 of the story on page 13. I am going to listen to each of you read. Your goal is to make fewer than two errors. Keep practicing Part 1 until you can read it without any errors.

(Ask each student to read Part 1. Record the number of errors in his or her book.

NOTE: If 90 percent of the students make two errors or fewer, you may move on to Lesson 4. If not, repeat Lesson 3.)

LESSON 4

OBJECTIVES

- *to introduce* ee *and* ea *words with the sound of* /ē/
- *to practice words with the word ending* -ed

New Sound

(Have students open their books to Lesson 4, page 16.)

1. Look at the top of page 16 in your book.

2. Touch the first word.

3. This word is **feed**. Say the word. *feed*

4. The underlined sound is /eēe/. Say the sound. /eēe/

5. Say the sound again. /eēe/

6. Touch the next word.

7. This word is **leaf**. Say the word. *leaf*

8. The underlined sound is /eēe/. Say the sound. /eēe/

9. Say the sound again. /eēe/

(Have students close their books. Then do the Sound Drill activity.)

Sound Drill
(Oral Teacher-Directed Activity)

(Write the following on the board or display it on-screen:)

1.	ee	ai	ea	ay
2.	ch	o	th	ck
3.	sh	ee	ai	wh
4.	ea	e	ay	i
5.	ai	a	ea	u

1. Let's practice saying the sounds in the words that we will be reading. Look at the letters in line 1. Say the sounds. /eēe/, /aāa/, /eēe/, /aāa/

2. Look at the letters in line 2. Say the sounds. /ch/, /ooo/, /th/, /k/

(Repeat step 2 with lines 3–5. Then call on individual students to say the sounds in a line.)

(NOTE: As an alternative, review the sounds with flash cards.)

Blending Sounds
(Oral Teacher-Directed Activity)

Let's practice saying some words. I will say a word slowly. You tell me the word. **/b/ /eēe/ /ch/** What is the word? *beach*

(Repeat this procedure with the following words:)

trail	/t/	/rrr/	/aāa/	/lll/
each	/eēe/	/ch/		
week	/www/	/eēe/	/k/	
beef	/b/	/eēe/	/fff/	

(NOTE: As you pronounce these words slowly, don't stop between the sounds. This practice will assist students in recognizing words that they have sounded out.)

A. New Words

(Have students open their books to Lesson 4, page 16.)

1.	beef	eat	sea
2.	say	week	tea
3.	meat	beach	need
4.	see	lead	feed
5.	each	deep	trail
6.	beat	bait	beets

7. The dog will eat out of the can.
8. The test is this week.
9. 1 need a new backpack.
10. Will you feed the fish?
11. Do you see the trail on the map?
12. Fill the dish with beets.

1. Find part A in your book.

2. Touch the first word in line 1. Look at the underlined letters. What is the sound? /eēe/

3. Sound out the word to yourself. Put your thumb up when you can say the whole word. (Wait until thumbs are up.) What is the word? *beef*

4. Touch the next word. Look at the underlined letters. What is the sound? /$\overline{eee}$/ Sound out the word to yourself. Put your thumb up when you can say the whole word. (Wait until thumbs are up.) What is the word? *eat*

(Repeat step 4 with the remaining words in lines 1–3.)

5. Touch the first word in line 4. Sound out this word to yourself. Say the sounds carefully. Put your thumb up when you can say the whole word. (Wait until thumbs are up.) What is the word? *see*

6. Touch the next word. Sound out the word to yourself. Put your thumb up when you can say the whole word. (Wait until thumbs are up.) What is the word? *lead*

(Repeat step 6 with the remaining words in lines 4–6. Then call on individual students to read a line.)

7. Read sentence 7 to yourself. Put your thumb up when you are done. (Wait until thumbs are up. Then call on a student to read the sentence.)

(Repeat step 7 with sentences 8–12.)

B. Review Words

(Have students open their books to Lesson 4, page 16.)

1. paint	pant	plan
2. step	stay	Spain
3. brass	brain	pain
4. tray	trip	rip
5. man	main	train

1. Find part B in your book.

2. Read the words in line 1 to yourself. When you can read all three words, put your thumb up. (Wait until thumbs are up.)

3. Get ready to read the words in line 1 together. Begin. *paint, pant, plan*

(Repeat steps 2 and 3 with lines 2–5. Then call on individual students to read the words in a line.)

C. Word Endings

(Have students open their books to Lesson 4, page 16.)

1. stayed	2. painted	3. hailed
4. needed	5. planned	

1. Find part C in your book.

2. Let's practice reading some words with word endings. Look at the first word. Sound out the underlined word to yourself. Put your thumb up when you can say the underlined word. (Wait until thumbs are up.) What is the word? *stay*

3. When the **-ed** ending is added, the word is **stayed**. What is the word? *stayed* **Jerome stayed home from school.** Say the word again. *stayed*

(Repeat steps 2 and 3 with numbers 2–5. Then call on individual students to say the words with endings.)

Word Ending Sentences
2. **Yesterday Rachel painted the living room.**
3. **During the storm, it hailed.**
4. **The cat needed aid.**
5. **Carlos planned his trip carefully.**

D. Challenge Words

(Have students open their books to Lesson 4, page 17.)

seashell	peanut	seaweed	payment
1 2	1 2	1 2	1 2
sunbeam			
1 2			

1. Find part D in your book.

2. Touch the first word. Sound out the first part to yourself. Put your thumb up when you can say the part. (Wait until thumbs are up.) What is this part? *sea*

3. Sound out the next part to yourself. Put your thumb up when you can say the part. (Wait until thumbs are up.) What is this part? *shell*

4. Say the parts again. First part? *sea* Next part? *shell*

5. Say the whole word. *seashell*

(Repeat steps 2–5 with the words **peanut, seaweed, payment,** and **sunbeam.**)

6. Let's read these words again. (Call on individual students to read the Challenge Words.)

E. Sight Words

(Have students open their books to Lesson 4, page 17.)

there	were	things	have	some
people	you	little	of	water

1. Find part E in your book.

2. Touch the first word. This word is **there**.
   What is the word? *there*
   Spell and read. *t-h-e-r-e.* there

3. Touch the next word. This word is **were**.
   What is the word? *were*
   Spell and read. *w-e-r-e.* were

(Repeat step 3 with the remaining words.)

4. Let's read these words again. (Call on individual students to read the Sight Words.)

F. Sentences and Stories

(Have students open their books to Lesson 4, page 17.)

1. Find part F in your book.

2. Touch the title of the story. Let's read the title together. *The Sea*

3. Read Part 1 to yourself. Read it very carefully. Put your thumb up when you are done. (Wait until thumbs are up.)

4. Let's read Part 1 together. When you are not reading aloud, follow along in your book. (Call on a student to read one or two sentences. Continue until Part 1 has been read.)

5. Look at the three pictures. Put a number 1 under the picture that goes with Part 1.

(Repeat steps 3–5 with Parts 2 and 3.)

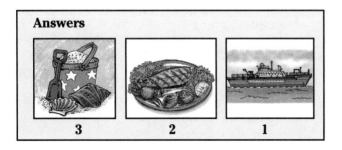

G. Spelling

(Have students open their books to Lesson 4, page 18.)

1. Find part G in your book.

2. Your first spelling word is **week**.
   What is the word? *week*

3. Say the sounds to yourself as you write the word. (Monitor.)

4. (Write the word on the board or display it on-screen.) Check your word. If you made a mistake, cross out the word and rewrite it. (Monitor.)

(Repeat steps 2–4 with the word **beach**.)

5. Your next spelling word is **peanut**.
   Say the first part of the word. *pea*
   Write this part.

6. Say the second part of the word. *nut*
   Write this part.

7. (Write the word on the board or display it on-screen.) Check your word. If you made a mistake, cross out the word and rewrite it. (Monitor.)

(Repeat steps 5–7 with the word **seashell**.)

8. Listen. **Fish swim in the deep sea.**
   Say the sentence. *Fish swim in the deep sea.*
   Write the sentence. (Monitor.)

9. (Write the sentence on the board or display it on-screen.) Check each word. If you made a mistake, cross out the word and rewrite it. (Monitor.)

> **Answers**
> 1. week 3. peanut
> 2. beach 4. seashell
> 5. **Fish swim in the deep sea.**

H. Practice Activity 1

(Have students open their books to Lesson 4, page 18.)

1. Find part H in your book.

2. Follow along as I read the directions. **Fill in each blank with the best word.**

3. Do number 1. Put your thumb up when you are finished. (Monitor and check.)

4. You will finish part H later.

I. Practice Activity 2

(Have students open their books to Lesson 4, page 19.)

1. Find part I in your book.

2. Follow along as I read the directions. **Draw a line under the sentence that goes with each picture.**

3. Do number 1. Put your thumb up when you are finished. (Monitor and check.)

4. Now go back and finish parts H and I.

◀)) Work Check for Parts H and I
(Oral Teacher-Directed Activity)

1. Find part H in your book.

2. Let's check your work. If you made a mistake, circle the number. You will fix all mistakes at the end of the lesson. (Call on individual students to read their answers.)

3. Count how many correct answers you have, and write that number in the box at the bottom of the page. (Monitor students.)

(Repeat steps 1–3 with part I.)

4. Now go back and correct any mistakes. (Monitor students.)

Answers for Part H	
1. bee	5. tea
2. see	6. sea
3. feed	7. each
4. week	8. eat

Answers for Part I
1. The van will need gas.
2. Rob leans on the mailbox.
3. The seaweed is on the beach.
4. He will feed the dog each day.
5. Fish swim in the deep sea.
6. Nan will cut each beet.
7. Beth saw a bee on the seat.
8. Rain fell on the leaf.

LESSON 5

OBJECTIVES

- *to practice words with ee and ea*
- *to practice words with the word ending -ed*

 Sound Drill
(Oral Teacher-Directed Activity)

(Write the following on the board or display it on-screen:)

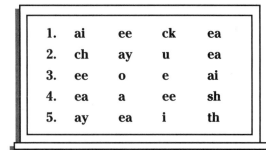

1.	ai	ee	ck	ea
2.	ch	ay	u	ea
3.	ee	o	e	ai
4.	ea	a	ee	sh
5.	ay	ea	i	th

1. Let's practice saying the sounds in the words that we will be reading. Look at the letters in line 1. Say the sounds. */āāā/, /ēēē/, /k/, /ēēē/*

2. Look at the letters in line 2. Say the sounds. */ch/, /āāā/, /uuu/, /ēēē/*

(Repeat step 2 with lines 3–5. Then call on individual students to say the sounds in a line.)

(NOTE: As an alternative, review the sounds with flash cards.)

 Blending Sounds
(Oral Teacher-Directed Activity)

Let's practice saying some words. I will say a word slowly. You tell me the word. **/t/ /ēēē/ /mmm/** What is the word? *team*

(Repeat this procedure with the following words:)

pail	/p/	/āāā/	/lll/	
clean	/k/	/lll/	/ēēē/	/nnn/
treat	/t/	/rrr/	/ēēē/	/t/
fail	/f/	/āāā/	/lll/	

(NOTE: As you pronounce these words slowly, don't stop between the sounds. This practice will assist students in recognizing words that they have sounded out.)

A. New Words

(Have students open their books to Lesson 5, page 20.)

1.	deep	keep	team
2.	fail	feel	read
3.	raid	jeep	weed
4.	peel	pail	seal
5.	clean	meet	treat
6.	trait	hail	cream
7.	Nat is on the tennis team.		
8.	Did he clean his jeep?		
9.	You must tug at the weed.		
10.	Gail put cream on the peach.		
11.	Will you meet me at six?		
12.	How did you feel?		

1. Find part A in your book.

2. Touch the first word in line 1. Look at the underlined letters. What is the sound? */ēēē/*

3. Sound out the word to yourself. Put your thumb up when you can say the whole word. (Wait until thumbs are up.) What is the word? *deep*

4. Touch the next word. Look at the underlined letters. What is the sound? */ēēē/* Sound out the word to yourself. Put your thumb up when you can say the whole word. (Wait until thumbs are up.) What is the word? *keep*

(Repeat step 4 with the remaining words in lines 1–3.)

5. Touch the first word in line 4. Sound out this word to yourself. Say the sounds carefully. Put your thumb up when you can say the whole word. (Wait until thumbs are up.) What is the word? *peel*

6. Touch the next word. Sound out the word to yourself. Put your thumb up when you can say the whole word. (Wait until thumbs are up.) What is the word? *pail*

(Repeat step 6 with the remaining words in lines 4–6. Then call on individual students to read a line.)

7. Read sentence 7 to yourself. Put your thumb up when you are done. (Wait until thumbs are up. Then call on a student to read the sentence.)

(Repeat step 7 with sentences 8–12.)

B. Review Words

(Have students open their books to Lesson 5, page 20.)

1.	main	man	than
2.	spray	Ray	pray
3.	paint	saint	sat
4.	train	trip	thin
5.	plan	play	pay

1. Find part B in your book.

2. Read the words in line 1 to yourself. When you can read all three words, put your thumb up. (Wait until thumbs are up.)

3. Get ready to read the words in line 1 together. Begin. *main, man, than*

(Repeat steps 2 and 3 with lines 2–5. Then call on individual students to read the words in a line.)

C. Word Endings

(Have students open their books to Lesson 5, page 20.)

1. <u>played</u>	2. <u>weeded</u>	3. <u>peeled</u>
4. <u>cleaned</u>	5. <u>healed</u>	

1. Find part C in your book.

2. Let's practice reading some words with word endings. Look at the first word. Sound out the underlined word to yourself. Put your thumb up when you can say the underlined word. (Wait until thumbs are up.) What is the word? *play*

3. When the **-ed** ending is added, the word is **played**. What is the word? *played*
Bess played at the beach.
Say the word again. *played*

(Repeat steps 2 and 3 with numbers 2–5. Then call on individual students to say the words with endings.)

Word Ending Sentences
2. **Jay weeded at midday.**
3. **Eddie peeled the banana.**
4. **Nick cleaned the jeep.**
5. **The cut finally healed.**

D. Challenge Words

(Have students open their books to Lesson 5, page 21.)

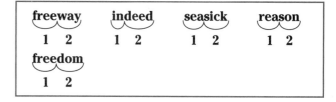

1. Find part D in your book.

2. Touch the first word. Sound out the first part to yourself. Put your thumb up when you can say the part. (Wait until thumbs are up.) What is this part? *free*

3. Sound out the next part to yourself. Put your thumb up when you can say the part. (Wait until thumbs are up.) What is this part? *way*

4. Say the parts again. First part? *free*
Next part? *way*

5. Say the whole word. *freeway*

(Repeat steps 2–5 with the words **indeed, seasick, reason,** and **freedom**.)

6. Let's read these words again. (Call on individual students to read the Challenge Words.)

E. Sight Words

(Have students open their books to Lesson 5, page 21.)

there	things	they	were	some
water	into	you	from	people

1. Find part E in your book.

2. Touch the first word. This word is **there**. What is the word? *there*
Spell and read. *t-h-e-r-e. there*

3. Touch the next word. This word is **things**. What is the word? *things*
Spell and read. *t-h-i-n-g-s. things*

(Repeat step 3 with the remaining words.)

4. Let's read these words again. (Call on individual students to read the Sight Words.)

F. Sentences and Stories

(Have students open their books to Lesson 5, page 21.)

1. Find part F in your book.

2. Touch the title of the story. Let's read the title together. *Keep the Sea Clean*

3. Read Part 1 to yourself. Read it very carefully. Put your thumb up when you are done. (Wait until thumbs are up.)

4. Let's read Part 1 together. When you are not reading aloud, follow along in your book. (Call on a student to read one or two sentences. Continue until Part 1 has been read.)

5. Look at the three pictures. Put a number 1 under the picture that goes with Part 1.

(Repeat steps 3–5 with Parts 2 and 3.)

Answers

2	1	3

G. Spelling

(Have students open their books to Lesson 5, page 22.)

1. Find part G in your book.

2. Your first spelling word is **deep**. What is the word? *deep*

3. Say the sounds to yourself as you write the word. (Monitor.)

4. (Write the word on the board or display it on-screen.) Check your word. If you made a mistake, cross out the word and rewrite it. (Monitor.)

(Repeat steps 2–4 with the word **clean**.)

5. Your next spelling word is **freedom**. Say the first part of the word. *free* Write this part.

6. Say the second part of the word. *dom* Write this part.

7. (Write the word on the board or display it on-screen.) Check your word. If you made a mistake, cross out the word and rewrite it. (Monitor.)

(Repeat steps 5–7 with the word **freeway**.)

8. Listen. **I need to clean my hands.** Say the sentence. *I need to clean my hands.* Write the sentence. (Monitor.)

9. (Write the sentence on the board or display it on-screen.) Check each word. If you made a mistake, cross out the word and rewrite it. (Monitor.)

Answers
1. deep   3. freedom
2. clean   4. freeway
5. I need to clean my hands.

H. Practice Activity 1

(Have students open their books to Lesson 5, page 22.)

1. Find part H in your book.

2. Follow along as I read the directions. **Read each group of words. Change the order of the groups to make a sentence. Write each sentence on the line.**

3. Do number 1. Put your thumb up when you are finished. (Monitor and check.)

4. You will finish part H later.

I. Practice Activity 2

(Have students open their books to Lesson 5, page 23.)

1. Find part I in your book.

2. Follow along as I read the directions. **Draw a line under the sentence that goes with each picture.**

3. Do number 1. Put your thumb up when you are finished. (Monitor and check.)

4. Now go back and finish parts H and I.

◀))) Work Check for Parts H and I
(Oral Teacher-Directed Activity)

1. Find part H in your book.

2. Let's check your work. If you made a mistake, circle the number. You will fix all mistakes at the end of the lesson. (Call on individual students to read their answers.)

3. Count how many correct answers you have, and write that number in the box at the bottom of the page. (Monitor students.)

(Repeat steps 1–3 with part I.)

4. Now go back and correct any mistakes. (Monitor students.)

Answers for Part H
1. Bess and Pat fill the pail with sand.
2. The seal will play on the rocks.
3. The swim team will get a treat.
4. Jay will clean the paintbrush.
5. Dad will hail a cab.
6. Mom will peel the skin off the peach.
7. We got free tickets to the train.

Answers for Part I
1. Ted peeled the egg.
2. Jill reads each day.
3. The seal swims in the water.
4. Nan feels sad.
5. Chuck will meet you at the bus stop.
6. She put weeds in the pail.
7. Dad keeps nails in a box.
8. 1 need to clean my hands.

LESSON 6

OBJECTIVES

- *to practice words with* ee *and* ea
- *to practice words with the word ending* -ed

🔊 Sound Drill
(Oral Teacher-Directed Activity)

(Write the following on the board or display it on-screen:)

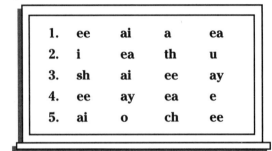

1.	ee	ai	a	ea
2.	i	ea	th	u
3.	sh	ai	ee	ay
4.	ee	ay	ea	e
5.	ai	o	ch	ee

1. Let's practice saying the sounds in the words that we will be reading. Look at the letters in line 1. Say the sounds. /ēēē/, /āāā/, /aaa/, /ēēē/

2. Look at the letters in line 2. Say the sounds. /iii/, /ēēē/, /th/, /uuu/

(Repeat step 2 with lines 3–5. Then call on individual students to say the sounds in a line.)

(NOTE: As an alternative, review the sounds with flash cards.)

🔊 Blending Sounds
(Oral Teacher-Directed Activity)

Let's practice saying some words. I will say a word slowly. You tell me the word. /sh/ /ēēē/ /p/ What is the word? *sheep*

(Repeat this procedure with the following words:)

spray	/sss/	/p/	/rrr/	/āāā/
steal	/sss/	/t/	/ēēē/	/lll/
dream	/d/	/rrr/	/ēēē/	/mmm/
teeth	/t/	/ēēē/	/th/	

(NOTE: As you pronounce these words slowly, don't stop between the sounds. This practice will assist students in recognizing words that they have sounded out.)

A. New Words

(Have students open their books to Lesson 6, page 24.)

1.	reach	three	sheep
2.	tree	tray	leak
3.	heel	hail	wheel
4.	sleep	green	grain
5.	speak	steal	teeth
6.	dream	scream	spray

7. Where can I reach you?
8. The tree fell with a thud.
9. The jeep lost a wheel.
10. Let him sleep for a bit.
11. The dentist will look at your teeth.
12. You must have had a bad dream.

1. Find part A in your book.

2. Touch the first word in line 1. Look at the underlined letters. What is the sound? /ēēē/

3. Sound out the word to yourself. Put your thumb up when you can say the whole word. (Wait until thumbs are up.) What is the word? *reach*

4. Touch the next word. Look at the underlined letters. What is the sound? /ēēē/ Sound out the word to yourself. Put your thumb up when you can say the whole word. (Wait until thumbs are up.) What is the word? *three*

(Repeat step 4 with the remaining words in lines 1–3.)

5. Touch the first word in line 4. Sound out this word to yourself. Say the sounds carefully. Put your thumb up when you can say the whole word. (Wait until thumbs are up.) What is the word? *sleep*

6. Touch the next word. Sound out the word to yourself. Put your thumb up when you can say the whole word. (Wait until thumbs are up.) What is the word? *green*

(Repeat step 6 with the remaining words in lines 4–6. Then call on individual students to read a line.)

7. Read sentence 7 to yourself. Put your thumb up when you are done. (Wait until thumbs are up. Then call on a student to read the sentence.)

(Repeat step 7 with sentences 8–12.)

B. Review Words

(Have students open their books to Lesson 6, page 24.)

1.	braid	rain	thin
2.	step	stay	ship
3.	raid	rid	mist
4.	press	raise	spend
5.	wait	wit	mitt

1. Find part B in your book.

2. Read the words in line 1 to yourself. When you can read all three words, put your thumb up. (Wait until thumbs are up.)

3. Get ready to read the words in line 1 together. Begin. *braid, rain, thin*

(Repeat steps 2 and 3 with lines 2–5. Then call on individual students to read the words in a line.)

C. Word Endings

(Have students open their books to Lesson 6, page 24.)

1. <u>scream</u>ed	2. <u>drain</u>ed	3. <u>reach</u>ed
4. <u>spray</u>ed	5. <u>stay</u>ed	

1. Find part C in your book.

2. Let's practice reading some words with word endings. Look at the first word. Sound out the underlined word to yourself. Put your thumb up when you can say the underlined word. (Wait until thumbs are up.) What is the word? *scream*

3. When the **-ed** ending is added, the word is **screamed**. What is the word? *screamed* **Denise screamed, "Help! Help!"** Say the word again. *screamed*

(Repeat steps 2 and 3 with numbers 2–5. Then call on individual students to say the words with endings.)

> **Word Ending Sentences**
> 2. **Anna drained the water out of the sink.**
> 3. **She reached with her hand.**
> 4. **Helena sprayed paint on the bench.**
> 5. **During the rain, Lim stayed in the house.**

D. Challenge Words

(Have students open their books to Lesson 6, page 25.)

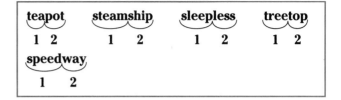

1. Find part D in your book.

2. Touch the first word. Sound the first part to yourself. Put your thumb up when you can say the part. (Wait until thumbs are up.) What is this part? *tea*

3. Sound out the next part to yourself. Put your thumb up when you can say the part. (Wait until thumbs are up.) What is this part? *pot*

4. Say the parts again. First part? *tea* Next part? *pot*

5. Say the whole word. *teapot*

(Repeat steps 2–5 with the words **steamship, sleepless, treetop,** and **speedway.**)

6. Let's read these words again. (Call on individual students to read the Challenge Words.)

E. Sight Words

(Have students open their books to Lesson 6, page 25.)

said	were	there	saw	down
have	you	was	to	little

1. Find part E in your book.

2. Touch the first word. This word is **said**. What is the word? *said* Spell and read. *s-a-i-d. said*

3. Touch the next word. This word is **were**. What is the word? *were* Spell and read. *w-e-r-e. were*

(Repeat step 3 with the remaining words.)

4. Let's read these words again. (Call on individual students to read the Sight Words.)

F. Sentences and Stories

(Have students open their books to Lesson 6, page 25.)

1. Find part F in your book.

2. Touch the title of the story. Let's read the title together. *Rush to the Beach*

3. Read Part 1 to yourself. Read it very carefully. Put your thumb up when you are done. (Wait until thumbs are up.)

4. Let's read Part 1 together. When you are not reading aloud, follow along in your book. (Call on a student to read one or two sentences. Continue until Part 1 has been read.)

5. Look at the three pictures. Put a number 1 under the picture that goes with Part 1.

(Repeat steps 3–5 with Parts 2 and 3.)

Answers

| 1 | 3 | 2 |

G. Spelling

(Have students open their books to Lesson 6, page 26.)

1. Find part G in your book.

2. Your first spelling word is **green**. What is the word? *green*

3. Say the sounds to yourself as you write the word. (Monitor.)

4. (Write the word on the board or display it on-screen.) Check your word. If you made a mistake, cross out the word and rewrite it. (Monitor.)

(Repeat steps 2–4 with the word **speak**.)

5. Your next spelling word is **teapot**. Say the first part of the word. *tea* Write this part.

6. Say the second part of the word. *pot* Write this part.

7. (Write the word on the board or display it on-screen.) Check your word. If you made a mistake, cross out the word and rewrite it. (Monitor.)

(Repeat steps 5–7 with the word **sleepless**.)

8. Listen. **The leaf fell off the tree.** Say the sentence. *The leaf fell off the tree.* Write the sentence. (Monitor.)

9. (Write the sentence on the board or display it on-screen.) Check each word. If you made a mistake, cross out the word and rewrite it. (Monitor.)

Answers
1. green   3. teapot
2. speak   4. sleepless
5. **The leaf fell off the tree.**

H. Practice Activity 1

(Have students open their books to Lesson 6, page 26.)

1. Find part H in your book.

2. Follow along as I read the directions. **Read each group of words. Change the order of the groups to make a sentence. Write each sentence on the line.**

3. Do number 1. Put your thumb up when you are finished. (Monitor and check.)

4. You will finish part H later.

I. Practice Activity 2

(Have students open their books to Lesson 6, page 27.)

1. Find part I in your book.

2. Follow along as I read the directions. **Draw a line under the sentence that goes with each picture.**

3. Do number 1. Put your thumb up when you are finished. (Monitor and check.)

4. Now go back and finish parts H and I.

Work Check for Parts H and I
(Oral Teacher-Directed Activity)

1. Find part H in your book.

2. Let's check your work. If you made a mistake, circle the number. You will fix all mistakes at the end of the lesson. (Call on individual students to read their answers.)

3. Count how many correct answers you have, and write the number in the box at the bottom of the page. (Monitor students.)

(Repeat steps 1–3 with part I.)

4. Now go back and correct any mistakes. (Monitor students.)

Answers for Part H
1. That shop will fix my mom's heel.
2. Jay speaks to the men on the beach.
3. Jan sprayed the wheels green.
4. The jeep is next to three trees.
5. Bill can reach the gray tray.
6. Sam dreams in his sleep.
7. Clean teeth feel slick.

Answers for Part I
1. Pam speaks to Tom.
2. Stan cleaned his teeth.
3. The pot was filled with steam.
4. Sheep eat green grass.
5. The teen can reach the tray.
6. He can fix the heel.
7. Snow fell on the trees.
8. Bess played at the beach.

Checking Up
(Oral Teacher-Directed Activity)

Practice reading Part 1 of the story on page 25. I am going to listen to each of you read. Your goal is to make fewer than two errors. Keep practicing Part 1 until you can read it without any errors.

(Ask each student to read Part 1. Record the number of errors in his or her book.

NOTE: If 90 percent of the students make two errors or fewer, you may move on to Lesson 7. If not, repeat Lesson 6.)

LESSON 7

OBJECTIVES

- *to introduce* oa *and* ow *words with the sound of* /ō/
- *to introduce words with both word endings* -ed *and* -ing

🔊 New Sound

(Have students open their books to Lesson 7, page 28.)

1. Look at the top of page 28 in your book.

2. Touch the first word.

3. This word is **coat**. Say the word. *coat*

4. The underlined sound is /**ooo**/. Say the sound. /ōoo/

5. Say the sound again. /ōoo/

6. Touch the next word.

7. This word is **snow**. Say the word. *snow*

8. The underlined sound is /**ooo**/. Say the sound. /ōoo/

9. Say the sound again. /ōoo/

(Have students close their books. Then do the Sound Drill activity.)

🔊 Sound Drill
(Oral Teacher-Directed Activity)

(Write the following on the board or display it on-screen:)

1.	oa	ee	ai	ow
2.	o	ay	oa	u
3.	ow	oa	ea	a
4.	ee	ow	ai	oa
5.	ay	oa	ea	ow

1. Let's practice saying the sounds in the words that we will be reading. Look at the letters in line 1. Say the sounds. /ōoo/, /ēee/, /āaa/, /ōoo/

2. Look at the letters in line 2. Say the sounds. /ooo/, /āaa/, /ōoo/, /uuu/

(Repeat step 2 with lines 3–5. Then call on individual students to say the sounds in a line.)

(NOTE: As an alternative, review the sounds with flash cards.)

🔊 Segmenting Words into Sounds
(Oral Teacher-Directed Activity)

1. Let's practice saying some words. I will say a word, and then you will say the sounds in the word.

2. The first word is **show**. What is the word? *show*

3. Say the sounds in **show**. Put up a finger for each sound. /sh/ /ōoo/

4. The next word is **bowl**. What is the word? *bowl*

5. Say the sounds in **bowl**. Put up a finger for each sound. /b/ /ōoo/ /lll/

(Repeat steps 4 and 5 with these words:)

leaf	/lll/	/ēee/	/fff/
grow	/g/	/rrr/	/ōoo/
toad	/t/	/ōoo/	/d/

A. New Words

(Have students open their books to Lesson 7, page 28.)

1.	own	fl**oa**t	t**oa**d
2.	r**oa**d	read	fl**ow**
3.	b**ai**l	b**ow**l	gr**ow**
4.	s**oa**p	leaf	l**oa**f
5.	b**ai**t	b**oa**t	sh**ow**
6.	s**oa**k	l**ow**	m**oa**n

7. Can you float on your back?
8. Where does this road go?
9. The kitten will grow fast.
10. The soap is in the bathtub.
11. Show Glen the snapshot.
12. We are low on gas.

1. Find part A in your book.

2. Touch the first word in line 1. Look at the underlined letters. What is the sound? /ōoo/

3. Sound out the word to yourself. Put your thumb up when you can say the whole word. (Wait until thumbs are up.) What is the word? *own*

4. Touch the next word. Look at the underlined letters. What is the sound? /$\overline{ooo}$/ Sound out the word to yourself. Put your thumb up when you can say the whole word. (Wait until thumbs are up.) What is the word? *float*

(Repeat step 4 with the remaining words in lines 1–3.)

5. Touch the first word in line 4. Sound out this word to yourself. Say the sounds carefully. Put your thumb up when you can say the whole word. (Wait until thumbs are up.) What is the word? *soap*

6. Touch the next word. Sound out the word to yourself. Put your thumb up when you can say the whole word. (Wait until thumbs are up.) What is the word? *leaf*

(Repeat step 6 with the remaining words in lines 4–6. Then call on individual students to read a line.)

7. Read sentence 7 to yourself. Put your thumb up when you are done. (Wait until thumbs are up. Then call on a student to read the sentence.)

(Repeat step 7 with sentences 8–12.)

B. Review Words

(Have students open their books to Lesson 7, page 28.)

1.	week	west	went
2.	meat	beat	best
3.	fed	feed	speed
4.	each	teach	tack
5.	sheep	chip	need

1. Find part B in your book.

2. Read the words in line 1 to yourself. When you can read all three words, put your thumb up. (Wait until thumbs are up.)

3. Get ready to read the words in line 1 together. Begin. *week, west, went*

(Repeat steps 2 and 3 with lines 2–5. Then call on individual students to read the words in a line.)

C. Word Endings

(Have students open their books to Lesson 7, page 28.)

1.	baited baiting	2.	needed needing	3.	snowed snowing
4.	chipped chipping	5.	showed showing		

1. Find part C in your book.

2. Let's practice reading some words with word endings. Look at the first word. Sound out the underlined word to yourself. Put your thumb up when you can say the underlined word. (Wait until thumbs are up.) What is the word? *bait*

3. When the **-ed** ending is added, the word is **baited**. What is the word? *baited* **Maria baited her hook with a worm.** Say the word again. *baited*

4. Look at the next word. With the **-ing** ending, the word is **baiting**. What is the word? *baiting* **Maria was baiting her hook with a worm.** Say the word again. *baiting*

5. Read the words again. *baited, baiting*

(Repeat steps 2–5 with numbers 2–5. Then call on individual students to say the words with endings.)

Word Ending Sentences

2. **Liz needed three pieces to finish the puzzle. John asked, "What will you be needing for your trip?"**
3. **Yesterday it snowed. It was snowing outside.**
4. **The dish was chipped. Manuel was chipping the bark off the log.**
5. **Juan showed me his new bike. Juan was showing his bike to everyone.**

D. Challenge Words

(Have students open their books to Lesson 7, page 29.)

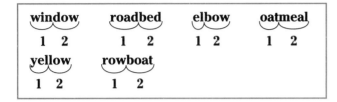

1. Find part D in your book.

2. Touch the first word. Sound out the word to yourself. Put your thumb up when you can say the word. (Wait until thumbs are up.) What is the word? *window*

3. Sound out the next word to yourself. Put your thumb up when you can say the word. (Wait until thumbs are up.) What is the word? *roadbed*

(Repeat step 3 with the words **elbow, oatmeal, yellow** and **rowboat**.)

4. Let's read these words again. (Call on individual students to read the Challenge Words.)

E. Sight Words

(Have students open their books to Lesson 7, page 29.)

all	there	water	they	work
you	said	were	from	put

1. Find part E in your book.

2. Touch the first word. This word is **all**.
What is the word? *all*
Spell and read. *a-l-l. all*

3. Touch the next word. This word is **there**.
What is the word? *there*
Spell and read. *t-h-e-r-e. there*

(Repeat step 3 with the remaining words.)

4. Let's read these words again. (Call on individual students to read the Sight Words.)

F. Sentences and Stories

(Have students open their books to Lesson 7, page 29.)

1. Find part F in your book.

2. Touch the title of the story. Let's read the title together. *A Day of Rest*

3. Read Part 1 to yourself. Read it very carefully. Put your thumb up when you are done.
(Wait until thumbs are up.)

4. Let's read Part 1 together. When you are not reading aloud, follow along in your book.
(Call on a student to read one or two sentences. Continue until Part 1 has been read.)

5. Look at the three pictures. Put a number 1 under the picture that goes with Part 1.

(Repeat steps 3–5 with Parts 2 and 3.)

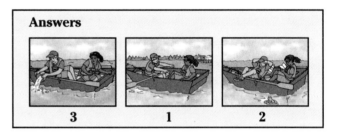

G. Spelling

(Have students open their books to Lesson 7, page 30.)

1. Find part G in your book.

2. Your first spelling word is **soap**.
What is the word? *soap*

3. Say the sounds to yourself as you write the word. (Monitor.)

4. (Write the word on the board or display it on-screen.) Check your word. If you made a mistake, cross out the word and rewrite it. (Monitor.)

(Repeat steps 2–4 with the word **grow**.)

5. Your next spelling word is **window**. Say the first part of the word. *win* Write this part.

6. Say the second part of the word. *dow* Write this part.

7. (Write the word on the board or display it on-screen.) Check your word. If you made a mistake, cross out the word and rewrite it. (Monitor.)

(Repeat steps 5–7 with the word **oatmeal**.)

8. Listen. **There is soap in the bowl.** Say the sentence. *There is soap in the bowl.* Write the sentence. (Monitor.)

9. (Write the sentence on the board or display it on-screen.) Check each word. If you made a mistake, cross out the word and rewrite it. (Monitor.)

Answers			
1.	soap	3.	window
2.	grow	4.	oatmeal
5.	There is soap in the bowl.		

H. Practice Activity 1

(Have students open their books to Lesson 7, page 30.)

1. Find part H in your book.

2. Follow along as I read the directions. **Draw a line under the sentence that goes with each picture.**

3. Do number 1. Put your thumb up when you are finished. (Monitor and check.)

4. You will finish part H later.

I. Practice Activity 2

(Have students open their books to Lesson 7, page 31.)

1. Find part I in your book.

2. Follow along as I read the directions. **Read each story. Fill in each blank with the best word.**

3. Find Story 1. Read the story to yourself. Do number 1. Put your thumb up when you are finished. (Monitor and check.)

4. Now go back and finish parts H and I.

Work Check for Parts H and I
(Oral Teacher-Directed Activity)

1. Find part H in your book.

2. Let's check your work. If you made a mistake, circle the number. You will fix all mistakes at the end of the lesson. (Call on individual students to read their answers.)

3. Count how many correct answers you have, and write that number in the box at the bottom of the page. (Monitor students.)

(Repeat steps 1–3 with part I.)

4. Now go back and correct any mistakes. (Monitor students.)

Answers for Part H
1. <u>The boat has a yellow sail.</u>
2. <u>The leaf fell off the tree.</u>
3. <u>Fran will soak her socks.</u>
4. <u>Matt and Jill will row the boat.</u>
5. <u>The van cannot go past the low tree.</u>

Answers for Part I			
Story 1		**Story 2**	
1.	coat	1.	bowl
2.	snow	2.	soap
3.	road	3.	load
4.	own	4.	soak

LESSON 8

OBJECTIVES

- *to practice words with oa and ow*
- *to practice words with both word endings -ed and -ing*

🔊 Sound Drill
(Oral Teacher-Directed Activity)

(Write the following on the board or display it on-screen:)

1.	oa	ay	ee	ow
2.	ea	o	oa	a
3.	ay	ow	ea	ai
4.	ee	oa	i	u
5.	ow	ea	ai	oa

1. Let's practice saying the sounds in the words that we will be reading. Look at the letters in line 1. Say the sounds. /$\overline{ooo}$/, /$\overline{aaa}$/, /$\overline{eee}$/, /$\overline{ooo}$/

2. Look at the letters in line 2. Say the sounds. /$\overline{eee}$/, /ooo/, /$\overline{ooo}$/, /$\overline{aaa}$/

(Repeat step 2 with lines 3–5. Then call on individual students to say the sounds in a line.)

(NOTE: As an alternative, review the sounds with flash cards.)

🔊 Segmenting Words into Sounds
(Oral Teacher-Directed Activity)

1. Let's practice saying some words. I will say a word, and then you will say the sounds in the word.

2. The first word is **loan**. What is the word? *loan*

3. Say the sounds in **loan**. Put up a finger for each sound. /lll/ /$\overline{ooo}$/ /nnn/

4. The next word is **mean**. What is the word? *mean*

5. Say the sounds in **mean**. Put up a finger for each sound. /mmm/ /$\overline{eee}$/ /nnn/

(Repeat steps 4 and 5 with these words:)

coach	/k/	/$\overline{ooo}$/	/ch/
throw	/th/	/rrr/	/$\overline{ooo}$/
glow	/g/	/lll/	/$\overline{ooo}$/

A. New Words

(Have students open their books to Lesson 8, page 32.)

1.	t<u>ow</u>	g<u>oa</u>t	l<u>oa</u>n
2.	l<u>ea</u>n	gl<u>ow</u>	r<u>ai</u>l
3.	r<u>oa</u>st	b<u>ay</u>	b<u>ow</u>
4.	bl<u>ow</u>n	m<u>ea</u>n	fl<u>oa</u>t
5.	t<u>ea</u>	t<u>oa</u>st	c<u>oa</u>ch
6.	c<u>oa</u>st	fl<u>ee</u>t	thr<u>ow</u>

7. **Did she get her loan at the bank?**
8. **Did you see the comet glow?**
9. **Mom will roast the hen.**
10. **The wind has blown the tree down.**
11. **The coach will let you have the ball.**
12. **Is the cabin on the coast?**

1. Find part A in your book.

2. Touch the first word in line 1. Look at the underlined letters. What is the sound? /$\overline{ooo}$/

3. Sound out the word to yourself. Put your thumb up when you can say the whole word. (Wait until thumbs are up.) What is the word? *tow*

4. Touch the next word. Look at the underlined letters. What is the sound? /$\overline{ooo}$/ Sound out the word to yourself. Put your thumb up when you can say the whole word. (Wait until thumbs are up.) What is the word? *goat*

(Repeat step 4 with the remaining words in lines 1–3.)

5. Touch the first word in line 4. Sound out this word to yourself. Say the sounds carefully. Put your thumb up when you can say the whole word. (Wait until thumbs are up.) What is the word? *blown*

6. Touch the next word. Sound out the word to yourself. Put your thumb up when you can say the whole word. (Wait until thumbs are up.) What is the word? *mean*

(Repeat step 6 with the remaining words in lines 4–6. Then call on individual students to read a line.)

7. Read sentence 7 to yourself. Put your thumb up when you are done. (Wait until thumbs are up. Then call on a student to read the sentence.)

(Repeat step 7 with sentences 8–12.)

B. Review Words

(Have students open their books to Lesson 8, page 32.)

1.	sweet	wed	weed
2.	stem	cream	stream
3.	sprain	rain	spent
4.	pill	peel	plant
5.	team	hill	thrill

1. Find part B in your book.

2. Read the words in line 1 to yourself. When you can read all three words, put your thumb up. (Wait until thumbs are up.)

3. Get ready to read the words in line 1 together. Begin. *sweet, wed, weed*

(Repeat steps 2 and 3 with lines 2–5. Then call on individual students to read the words in a line.)

C. Word Endings

(Have students open their books to Lesson 8, page 32.

1.	<u>loaned</u>	2.	<u>floated</u>	3.	<u>planted</u>
	<u>loaning</u>		<u>floating</u>		<u>planting</u>
4.	<u>peeled</u>	5.	<u>moaned</u>
	<u>peeling</u>		<u>moaning</u>

1. Find part C in your book.

2. Let's practice reading some words with word endings. Look at the first word. Sound out the underlined word to yourself. Put your thumb up when you can say the underlined word. (Wait until thumbs are up.) What is the word? *loan*

3. Add the **-ed** ending to **loan**. What is the word? *loaned* **Ed loaned Tom some cash.** Say the word again. *loaned*

4. Look at the next word. With the **-ing** ending, the word is **loaning**. What is the word? *loaning* **Brian was loaning Pete a dollar.** Say the word again. *loaning*

5. Read the words again. *loaned, loaning*

(Repeat steps 2–5 with numbers 2–5. Then call on individual students to say the words with endings.)

> **Word Ending Sentences**
> 2. **The boat floated on the water.**
>   **The boats were floating on the water.**
> 3. **Last week Lani planted a tree.**
>   **Lani is planting a tree.**
> 4. **Molly peeled the potatoes.**
>   **Molly is peeling the potatoes.**
> 5. **Eduardo moaned in pain.**
>   **We could hear Eduardo moaning.**

D. Challenge Words

(Have students open their books to Lesson 8, page 33.)

pillow	boatload	snowman	rainbow
1 2	1 2	1 2	1 2
fellow	roadway		
1 2	1 2		

1. Find part D in your book.

2. Touch the first word. Sound out this word to yourself. Put your thumb up when you can say the word. (Wait until thumbs are up.) What is the word? *pillow*

3. Sound out the next word to yourself. Put your thumb up when you can say the word. (Wait until thumbs are up.) What is the word? *boatload*

(Repeat step 3 with the words **snowman, rainbow, fellow,** and **roadway**.)

4. Let's read these words again. (Call on individual students to read the Challenge Words.)

E. Sight Words

(Have students open their books to Lesson 8, page 33.)

all	they	there	water	are
were	said	little	you	saw

1. Find part E in your book.

2. Touch the first word. This word is **all**.
   What is the word? *all*
   Spell and read. *a-l-l. all*

3. Touch the next word. This word is **they**.
   What is the word? *they*
   Spell and read. *t-h-e-y. they*

(Repeat step 3 with the remaining words.)

4. Let's read these words again. (Call on individual students to read the Sight Words.)

F. Sentences and Stories

(Have students open their books to Lesson 8, page 33.)

1. Find part F in your book.

2. Touch the title of the story. Let's read the title together. *The Boat Has a Leak*

3. Read Part 1 to yourself. Read it very carefully. Put your thumb up when you are done. (Wait until thumbs are up.)

4. Let's read Part 1 together. When you are not reading aloud, follow along in your book. (Call on a student to read one or two sentences. Continue until Part 1 has been read.)

5. Look at the three pictures. Put a number 1 under the picture that goes with Part 1.

(Repeat steps 3–5 with Parts 2 and 3.)

Answers

1   3   2

G. Spelling

(Have students open their books to Lesson 8, page 34.)

1. Find part G in your book.

2. Your first spelling word is **throw**.
   What is the word? *throw*

3. Say the sounds to yourself as you write the word. (Monitor.)

4. (Write the word on the board or display it on-screen.) Check your word. If you made a mistake, cross out the word and rewrite it. (Monitor.)

(Repeat steps 2–4 with the word **roast**.)

5. Your next spelling word is **pillow**.
   Say the first part of the word. *pil*
   Write this part.

6. Say the second part of the word. *low*
   Write this part.

7. (Write the word on the board or display it on-screen.) Check your word. If you made a mistake, cross out the word and rewrite it. (Monitor.)

(Repeat steps 5–7 with the word **roadway**.)

8. Listen. **Pam got a loan at the bank.**
   Say the sentence. *Pam got a loan at the bank.*
   Write the sentence. (Monitor.)

9. (Write the sentence on the board or display it on-screen.) Check each word. If you made a mistake, cross out the word and rewrite it. (Monitor.)

Answers
1. throw   3. pillow
2. roast   4. roadway
5. Pam got a loan at the bank.

H. Practice Activity 1

(Have students open their books to Lesson 8, page 34.)

1. Find part H in your book.

2. Follow along as I read the directions. **Draw a line under the sentence that goes with each picture.**

3. Do number 1. Put your thumb up when you are finished. (Monitor and check.)

4. You will finish part H later.

I. Practice Activity 2

(Have students open their books to Lesson 8, page 35.)

1. Find part I in your book.

2. Follow along as I read the directions. **Read each story. Fill in each blank with the best word.**

3. Find Story 1. Read the story to yourself. Do number 1. Put your thumb up when you are finished. (Monitor and check.)

4. Now go back and finish parts H and I.

🔊 Work Check for Parts H and I
(Oral Teacher-Directed Activity)

1. Find part H in your book.

2. Let's check your work. If you made a mistake, circle the number. You will fix all mistakes at the end of the lesson. (Call on individual students to read their answers.)

3. Count how many correct answers you have, and write that number in the box at the bottom of the page. (Monitor students.)

(Repeat steps 1–3 with part I.)

4. Now go back and correct any mistakes. (Monitor students.)

Answers for Part H
1. Jeff will toss a pass to his coach.
2. The goat eats weeds.
3. Lee saw a crack in the teapot.
4. The tugboat tows the big ship.
5. The coast has lots of rocks.

Answers for Part I

Story 1	Story 2
1. ill	1. boat
2. toast	2. tow
3. beef	3. coats
4. moaned	4. lead

LESSON 9

OBJECTIVES

- *to practice words with* oa *and* ow
- *to practice words with both word endings* -ed *and* -ing

🔊 Sound Drill
(Oral Teacher-Directed Activity)

(Write the following on the board or display it on-screen:)

1.	oa	ee	ow	a
2.	ai	i	u	ay
3.	sh	ow	oa	ck
4.	ea	e	ai	oa
5.	ow	ay	o	ch

1. Let's practice saying the sounds in the words that we will be reading. Look at the letters in line 1. Say the sounds. /$\overline{ooo}$/, /$\overline{eee}$/, /$\overline{ooo}$/, /aaa/

2. Look at the letters in line 2. Say the sounds. /$\overline{aaa}$/, /iii/, /uuu/, /$\overline{aaa}$/

(Repeat step 2 with lines 3–5. Then call on individual students to say the sounds in a line.)

(NOTE: As an alternative, review the sounds with flash cards.)

🔊 Segmenting Words into Sounds
(Oral Teacher-Directed Activity)

1. Let's practice saying some words. I will say a word, and then you will say the sounds in the word.

2. The first word is **groan**. What is the word? *groan*

3. Say the sounds in **groan**. Put up a finger for each sound. /g/ /rrr/ /$\overline{ooo}$/ /nnn/

4. The next word is **flown**. What is the word? *flown*

5. Say the sounds in **flown**. Put up a finger for each sound. /fff/ /lll/ /$\overline{ooo}$/ /nnn/

(Repeat steps 4 and 5 with these words:)

growth	/g/	/rrr/	/$\overline{ooo}$/	/th/
beast	/b/	/$\overline{eee}$/	/sss/	/t/
shown	/sh/	/$\overline{ooo}$/	/nnn/	

A. New Words

(Have students open their books to Lesson 9, page 36.)

1.	coal	slow	flown
2.	may	mow	goal
3.	throw	Gail	foam
4.	groan	shown	green
5.	growth	soak	gray
6.	cloak	boast	beast

7. The traffic is very slow here.
8. Did you get a goal?
9. 1 will throw your hat in the water.
10. Have I shown you my plan?
11. Soak the spot in water.
12. He has a mask and a cloak.

1. Find part A in your book.

2. Touch the first word in line 1. Look at the underlined letters. What is the sound? /$\overline{ooo}$/

3. Sound out the word to yourself. Put your thumb up when you can say the whole word. (Wait until thumbs are up.) What is the word? *coal*

4. Touch the next word. Look at the underlined letters. What is the sound? /$\overline{ooo}$/ Sound out the word to yourself. Put your thumb up when you can say the whole word. (Wait until thumbs are up.) What is the word? *slow*

(Repeat step 4 with the remaining words in lines 1–3.)

5. Touch the first word in line 4. Sound out this word to yourself. Say the sounds carefully. Put your thumb up when you can say the whole word. (Wait until thumbs are up.) What is the word? *groan*

6. Touch the next word. Sound out the word to yourself. Put your thumb up when you can say the whole word. (Wait until thumbs are up.) What is the word? *shown*

(Repeat step 6 with the remaining words in lines 4–6. Then call on individual students to read a line.)

7. Read sentence 7 to yourself. Put your thumb up when you are done. (Wait until thumbs are up. Then call on a student to read the sentence.)

(Repeat step 7 with sentences 8–12.)

B. Review Words

(Have students open their books to Lesson 9, page 36.)

1.	sprain	shift	lift
2.	brain	brass	chain
3.	cheek	feed	fed
4.	math	faith	flash
5.	clean	lean	cream

1. Find part B in your book.

2. Read the words in line 1 to yourself. When you can read all three words, put your thumb up. (Wait until thumbs are up.)

3. Get ready to read the words in line 1 together. Begin. *sprain, shift, lift*

(Repeat steps 2 and 3 with lines 2–5. Then call on individual students to read the words in a line.)

C. Word Endings

(Have students open their books to Lesson 9, page 36.)

1. soaked	2. mowed	3. cleaned
soaking	mowing	cleaning
4. lifted	5. foamed	
lifting	foaming	

1. Find part C in your book.

2. Let's practice reading some words with word endings. Look at the first word. Sound out the underlined word to yourself. Put your thumb up when you can say the underlined word. (Wait until thumbs are up.) What is the word? *soak*

3. Add the **-ed** ending to **soak**. What is the word? *soaked* **Linda soaked her sore foot.** Say the word again. *soaked*

4. Add the **-ing** ending to **soak**. What is the word? *soaking* **Linda was soaking her sore foot.** Say the word again. *soaking*

5. Read the words again. *soaked, soaking*

(Repeat steps 2–5 with numbers 2–5. Then call on individual students to say the words with endings.)

> **Word Ending Sentences**
> 2. **Maria mowed the lawn.**
>   **Maria is mowing the lawn.**
> 3. **Yesterday I cleaned the kitchen.**
>   **I am cleaning the kitchen.**
> 4. **James lifted the heavy box.**
>   **James is lifting the heavy box.**
> 5. **The soap foamed in the water.**
>   **The soap is foaming in the water.**

D. Challenge Words

(Have students open their books to Lesson 9, page 37.)

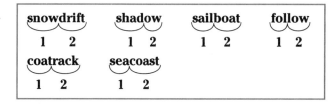

1. Find part D in your book.

2. Touch the first word. Sound out this word to yourself. Put your thumb up when you can say the word. (Wait until thumbs are up.) What is the word? *snowdrift*

3. Sound out the next word to yourself. Put your thumb up when you can say the word. (Wait until thumbs are up.) What is the word? *shadow*

(Repeat step 3 with the words **sailboat, follow, coatrack,** and **seacoast.**)

4. Let's read these words again. (Call on individual students to read the Challenge Words.)

E. Sight Words

(Have students open their books to Lesson 9, page 37.)

there	to	work	all	after
was	you	little	said	were

1. Find part E in your book.

2. Touch the first word. This word is **there**.
   What is the word? *there*
   Spell and read. *t-h-e-r-e. there*

3. Touch the next word. This word is **to**.
   What is the word? *to*
   Spell and read. *t-o. to*

(Repeat step 3 with the remaining words.)

4. Let's read these words again. (Call on individual students to read the Sight Words.)

F. Sentences and Stories

(Have students open their books to Lesson 9, page 37.)

1. Find part F in your book.

2. Touch the title of the story. Let's read the title together. *A Deal with Dad*

3. Read Part 1 to yourself. Read it very carefully. Put your thumb up when you are done. (Wait until thumbs are up.)

4. Let's read Part 1 together. When you are not reading aloud, follow along in your book. (Call on a student to read one or two sentences. Continue until Part 1 has been read.)

5. Look at the three pictures. Put a number 1 under the picture that goes with Part 1.

(Repeat steps 3–5 with Parts 2 and 3.)

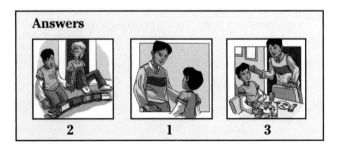

Answers

2 1 3

G. Spelling

(Have students open their books to Lesson 9, page 38.)

1. Find part G in your book.

2. Your first spelling word is **shown**.
   What is the word? *shown*

3. Say the sounds to yourself as you write the word. (Monitor.)

4. (Write the word on the board or display it on-screen.) Check your word. If you made a mistake, cross out the word and rewrite it. (Monitor.)

(Repeat steps 2–4 with the word **boast**.)

5. Your next spelling word is **seacoast**.
   Say the first part of the word. *sea*
   Write this part.

6. Say the second part of the word. *coast*
   Write this part.

7. (Write the word on the board or display it on-screen.) Check your word. If you made a mistake, cross out the word and rewrite it. (Monitor.)

(Repeat steps 5–7 with the word **sailboat**.)

8. Listen. **The sailboat is very slow.**
   Say the sentence. *The sailboat is very slow.*
   Write the sentence. (Monitor.)

9. (Write the sentence on the board or display it on-screen.) Check each word. If you made a mistake, cross out the word and rewrite it. (Monitor.)

Answers
1. shown   3. seacoast
2. boast   4. sailboat
5. **The sailboat is very slow.**

H. Practice Activity 1

(Have students open their books to Lesson 9, page 38.)

1. Find part H in your book.

2. Follow along as I read the directions. **Draw a line under the sentence that goes with each picture.**

3. Do number 1. Put your thumb up when you are finished. (Monitor and check.)

4. You will finish part H later.

I. Practice Activity 2

(Have students open their books to Lesson 9, page 39.)

1. Find part I in your book.

2. Follow along as I read the directions. **Read each story. Fill in each blank with the best word.**

3. Find Story 1. Read the story to yourself. Do number 1. Put your thumb up when you are finished. (Monitor and check.)

4. Now go back and finish parts H and I.

 ## Work Check for Parts H and I
(Oral Teacher-Directed Activity)

1. Find part H in your book.

2. Let's check your work. If you made a mistake, circle the number. You will fix all mistakes at the end of the lesson. (Call on individual students to read their answers.)

3. Count how many correct answers you have, and write that number in the box at the bottom of the page. (Monitor students.)

(Repeat steps 1–3 with part I.)

4. Now go back and correct any mistakes. (Monitor students.)

Answers for Part H
1. <u>The little tree will grow.</u>
2. <u>The gulls have flown to the rocks.</u>
3. <u>Ed soaks his feet in the tub.</u>
4. <u>Lim has shown his train set to Nat.</u>
5. <u>1 saw my shadow.</u>

Answers for Part I

Story 1	Story 2
1. fleet	1. cleaned
2. flown	2. soak
3. pack	3. green
4. fresh	4. goal

 ## Checking Up
(Oral Teacher-Directed Activity)

Practice reading Part 1 of the story on page 37. I am going to listen to each of you read. Your goal is to make fewer than two errors. Keep practicing Part 1 until you can read it without any errors.

(Ask each student to read Part 1. Record the number of errors in his or her book.

NOTE: If 90 percent of the students make two errors or fewer, you may move on to Lesson 10. If not, repeat Lesson 9.)

LESSON 10

OBJECTIVES

- *to introduce* igh *words with the sound of* /ī/
- *to practice words with both word endings* -ed *and* -ing

🔊 New Sound

(Have students open their books to Lesson 10, page 40.)

1. Look at the top of page 40 in your book.

2. Touch the word.

3. This word is **light**. Say the word. *light*

4. The underlined sound is /īī/. Say the sound. /īī/

5. Say the sound again. /īī/

(Have students close their books. Then do the Sound Drill activity.)

🔊 Sound Drill
(Oral Teacher-Directed Activity)

(Write the following on the board or display it on-screen:)

1.	igh	ee	oa	u
2.	ai	ay	e	ea
3.	ee	ow	igh	i
4.	ai	igh	oa	a
5.	ow	o	ea	ay

1. Let's practice saying the sounds in the words that we will be reading. Look at the letters in line 1. Say the sounds. /īī/, /eee/, /ooo/, /uuu/

2. Look at the letters in line 2. Say the sounds. /āāā/, /āāā/, /eee/, /eee/

(Repeat step 2 with lines 3–5. Then call on individual students to say the sounds in a line.)

(NOTE: As an alternative, review the sounds with flash cards.)

🔊 Segmenting Words into Sounds
(Oral Teacher-Directed Activity)

1. Let's practice saying some words. I will say a word, and then you will say the sounds in the word.

2. The first word is **night**. What is the word? *night*

3. Say the sounds in **night**. Put up a finger for each sound. /nnn/ /īī/ /t/

4. The next word is **coast**. What is the word? *coast*

5. Say the sounds in **coast**. Put up a finger for each sound. /k/ /ooo/ /sss/ /t/

(Repeat steps 4 and 5 with these words:)

flown	/fff/	/lll/	/ooo/	/nnn/
bright	/b/	/rrr/	/īī/	/t/
bleach	/b/	/lll/	/eee/	/ch/

A. New Words

(Have students open their books to Lesson 10, page 40.)

1.	h**igh**	n**igh**t	f**igh**t
2.	fl**ow**n	s**igh**t	s**ai**nt
3.	bl**ow**n	br**igh**t	t**ee**th
4.	ch**ea**t	c**oa**st	r**igh**t
5.	s**igh**	s**ee**	s**ay**
6.	h**ay**	bl**ea**ch	bl**ow**

7. He did not jump high.
8. Jill was a sight to see.
9. The comet was very bright.
10. My right hand is best for this.
11. 1 will sigh when I see you.
12. The wind blows at night.

1. Find part A in your book.

2. Touch the first word in line 1. Look at the underlined letters. What is the sound? /īī/

3. Sound out the word to yourself. Put your thumb up when you can say the whole word. (Wait until thumbs are up.) What is the word? *high*

4. Touch the next word. Look at the underlined letters. What is the sound? /īī/ Sound out the word to yourself. Put your thumb up when you can say the whole word. (Wait until thumbs are up.) What is the word? *night*

(Repeat step 4 with the remaining words in lines 1–3.)

5. Touch the first word in line 4. Sound out this word to yourself. Say the sounds carefully. Put your thumb up when you can say the whole word. (Wait until thumbs are up.) What is the word? *cheat*

6. Touch the next word. Sound out the word to yourself. Put your thumb up when you can say the whole word. (Wait until thumbs are up.) What is the word? *coast*

(Repeat step 6 with the remaining words in lines 4–6. Then call on individual students to read a line.)

7. Read sentence 7 to yourself. Put your thumb up when you are done. (Wait until thumbs are up. Then call on a student to read the sentence.)

(Repeat step 7 with sentences 8–12.)

B. Review Words

(Have students open their books to Lesson 10, page 40.)

1.	clamp	clasp	lamp
2.	twist	west	thick
3.	fresh	rush	plush
4.	stand	stamp	tramp
5.	bench	lunch	brunch

1. Find part B in your book.

2. Read the word in line 1 to yourself. When you can read all three words, put your thumb up. (Wait until thumbs are up.)

3. Get ready to read the words in line 1 together. Begin. *clamp, clasp, lamp*

(Repeat steps 2 and 3 with lines 2–5. Then call on individual students to read the words in a line.)

C. Word Endings

(Have students open their books to Lesson 10, page 40.)

1.	cheated cheating	2.	bleached bleaching	3.	twisted twisting
4.	rushed rushing	5.	clamped clamping		

1. Find part C in your book.

2. Let's practice reading some words with word endings. Look at the first word. Sound out the underlined word to yourself. Put your thumb up when you can say the underlined word. (Wait until thumbs are up.) What is the word? *cheat*

3. Add the **-ed** ending to **cheat**.
What is the word? *cheated*
Carmen cheated on the test.
Say the word again. *cheated*

4. Add the **-ing** ending to **cheat**.
What is the word? *cheating*
Carmen was seen cheating on the test.
Say the word again. *cheating*

5. Read the words again. *cheated, cheating*

(Repeat steps 2–5 with numbers 2–5. Then call on individual students to say the words with endings.)

Word Ending Sentences
2. Yesterday Billy bleached the white shirts. **Billy is bleaching the white shirts.**
3. Jerry twisted the handle. **Jerry was twisting the handle.**
4. On Wednesday, Marcia rushed to school on her bike. **Marcia was rushing to school.**
5. Yesterday Heidi clamped the two pieces of wood together. **Heidi was clamping the two pieces of wood together.**

D. Challenge Words

(Have students open their books to Lesson 10, page 41.)

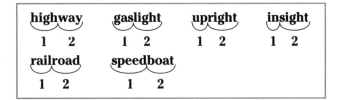

1. Find part D in your book.

2. Touch the first word. Sound out this word to yourself. Put your thumb up when you can say the word. (Wait until thumbs are up.) What is the word? *highway*

3. Sound out the next word to yourself. Put your thumb up when you can say the word. (Wait until thumbs are up.) What is the word? *gaslight*

(Repeat step 3 with the words **upright, insight, railroad,** and **speedboat**.)

4. Let's read these words again. (Call on individual students to read the Challenge Words.)

E. Sight Words

(Have students open their books to Lesson 10, page 41.)

do	after	all	saw	of
were	water	you	was	there

1. Find part E in your book.

2. Touch the first word. This word is **do**. What is the word? *do* Spell and read. *d-o. do*

3. Touch the next word. This word is **after**. What is the word? *after* Spell and read. *a-f-t-e-r. after*

(Repeat step 3 with the remaining words.)

4. Let's read these words again. (Call on individual students to read the Sight Words.)

F. Sentences and Stories

(Have students open their books to Lesson 10, page 41.)

1. Find part F in your book.

2. Touch the title of the story. Let's read the title together. *Pat to Gail*

3. Read Part 1 to yourself. Read it very carefully. Put your thumb up when you are done. (Wait until thumbs are up.)

4. Let's read Part 1 together. When you are not reading aloud, follow along in your book. (Call on a student to read one or two sentences. Continue until Part 1 has been read.)

5. Look at the three pictures. Put a number 1 under the picture that goes with Part 1.

(Repeat steps 3–5 with Parts 2 and 3.)

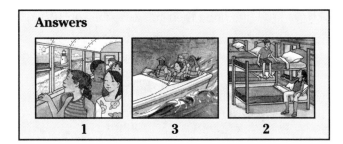

G. Spelling

(Have students open their books to Lesson 10, page 42.)

1. Find part G in your book.

2. Your first spelling word is **night**. What is the word? *night*

3. Say the sounds to yourself as you write the word. (Monitor.)

4. (Write the word on the board or display it on-screen.) Check your word. If you made a mistake, cross out the word and rewrite it. (Monitor.)

(Repeat steps 2–4 with the word **bright**.)

5. Your next spelling word is **highway**. Say the first part of the word. *high* Write this part.

6. Say the second part of the word. *way* Write this part.

7. (Write the word on the board or display it on-screen.) Check your word. If you made a mistake, cross out the word and rewrite it. (Monitor.)

(Repeat steps 5–7 with the word **insight**.)

8. Listen. **The highway went to the right.** Say the sentence. *The highway went to the right.* Write the sentence. (Monitor.)

9. (Write the sentence on the board or display it on-screen.) Check each word. If you made a mistake, cross out the word and rewrite it. (Monitor.)

Answers		
1. night	3.	highway
2. bright	4.	insight
5. The highway went to the right.		

H. Practice Activity 1

(Have students open their books to Lesson 10, page 42.)

1. Find part H in your book.

2. Follow along as I read the directions. **Draw a line under the sentence that goes with each picture.**

3. Do number 1. Put your thumb up when you are finished. (Monitor and check.)

4. You will finish part H later.

I. Practice Activity 2

(Have students open their books to Lesson 10, page 43.)

1. Find part I in your book.

2. Follow along as I read the directions. **Read each story. Fill in each blank with the best word.**

3. Find Story 1. Read the story to yourself. Do number 1. Put your thumb up when you are finished. (Monitor and check.)

4. Now go back and finish parts H and I.

🔊 Work Check for Parts H and I
(Oral Teacher-Directed Activity)

1. Find part H in your book.

2. Let's check your work. If you made a mistake, circle the number. You will fix all mistakes at the end of the lesson. (Call on individual students to read their answers.)

3. Count how many correct answers you have, and write that number in the box at the bottom of the page. (Monitor students.)

(Repeat steps 1–3 with part I.)

4. Now go back and correct any mistakes. (Monitor students.)

Answers for Part H
1. <u>The wind blows the hay.</u>
2. <u>Her coat is tight.</u>
3. <u>The dog might frighten the cat.</u>
4. <u>The truck went on the highway.</u>
5. <u>The gulls are in flight.</u>

Answers for Part I	
Story 1	Story 2
1. gray	1. paint
2. blown	2. bleach
3. high	3. bright
4. sight	4. right

LESSON 11

OBJECTIVES

- *to practice words with* igh
- *to practice words with both word endings* -ed *and* -ing

🔊 Sound Drill
(Oral Teacher-Directed Activity)

(Write the following on the board or display it on-screen:)

1.	igh	i	oa	ee
2.	ow	ea	a	ai
3.	ay	igh	e	ow
4.	u	oa	igh	ea
5.	ai	ee	ay	igh

1. Let's practice saying the sounds in the words that we will be reading. Look at the letters in line 1. Say the sounds. /īī/, /iii/, /ōō/, /ēēē/

2. Look at the letters in line 2. Say the sounds. /ōō/, /ēē/, /aaa/, /āāā/

(Repeat step 2 with lines 3–5. Then call on individual students to say the sounds in a line.)

(NOTE: As an alternative, review the sounds with flash cards.)

🔊 Segmenting Words into Sounds
(Oral Teacher-Directed Activity)

1. Let's practice saying some words. I will say a word, and then you will say the sounds in the word.

2. The first word is **light**. What is the word? *light*

3. Say the sounds in **light**. Put up one finger for each sound. /lll/ /īī/ /t/

4. The next word is **speech**. What is the word? *speech*

5. Say the sounds in **speech**. Put up one finger for each sound. /sss/ /p/ /ēē/ /ch/

(Repeat steps 4 and 5 with these words:)

sight	/sss/	/īī/	/t/
throat	/th/	/rrr/	/ōō/	/t/
bright	/b/	/rrr/	/īī/	/t/

A. New Words

(Have students open their books to Lesson 11, page 44.)

1.	l**igh**t	sl**igh**t	h**igh**
2.	tr**ai**l	r**igh**t	scr**ee**n
3.	sn**ai**l	s**igh**t	str**ee**t
4.	thr**oa**t	sh**ee**t	th**igh**
5.	fl**igh**t	tr**ay**	spr**ay**
6.	br**igh**t	sp**ee**ch	m**igh**t

7. The frog will jump high.
8. Jill went down the path on the right.
9. You are a sight!
10. There is a cut on my thigh.
11. How was her flight?
12. Ed might miss his cat.

1. Find part A in your book.

2. Touch the first word in line 1. Look at the underlined letters. What is the sound? /īī/

3. Sound out the word to yourself. Put your thumb up when you can say the whole word. (Wait until thumbs are up.) What is the word? *light*

4. Touch the next word. Look at the underlined letters. What is the sound? /īī/ Sound out the word to yourself. Put your thumb up when you can say the whole word. (Wait until thumbs are up.) What is the word? *slight*

(Repeat step 4 with the remaining words in lines 1–3.)

5. Touch the first word in line 4. Sound out this word to yourself. Put your thumb up when you can say the whole word. (Wait until thumbs are up.) What is the word? *throat*

6. Touch the next word. Sound out the word to yourself. Put your thumb up when you can say the whole word. (Wait until thumbs are up.) What is the word? *sheet*

(Repeat step 6 with the remaining words in lines 4–6. Then call on individual students to read a line.)

7. Read sentence 7 to yourself. Put your thumb up when you are done. (Wait until thumbs are up. Then call on a student to read the sentence.)

(Repeat step 7 with sentences 8–12.)

B. Review Words

(Have students open their books to Lesson 11, page 44.)

1. class	camp	cramp
2. thick	chick	crack
3. swept	wept	spend
4. plant	plan	path
5. which	when	shift

1. Find part B in your book.

2. Read the words in line 1 to yourself. When you can read all three words, put your thumb up. (Wait until thumbs are up.)

3. Get ready to read the words in line 1 together. Begin. *class, camp, cramp*

(Repeat steps 2 and 3 with lines 2–5. Then call on a student to read the words in a line.)

C. Word Endings

(Have students open their books to Lesson 11, page 44.)

1. sprayed spraying	2. trailed trailing	3. camped camping
4. planted planting	5. planned planning	

1. Find part C in your book.

2. Let's practice reading some words with word endings. Look at the first word. Sound out the underlined word to yourself. Put your thumb up when you can say the underlined word. (Wait until thumbs are up.) What is the word? *spray*

3. Add the **-ed** ending to **spray**. What is the word? *sprayed*

4. Add the **-ing** ending to **spray**. What is the word? *spraying*

5. Now I will use the words in sentences.
    Anna sprayed the garden with water.
    Anna is spraying water on the garden.
    Say the words again. *sprayed, spraying*

(Repeat steps 2–5 with numbers 2–5. Then call on individual students to say the words with endings.)

Word Ending Sentences
2. **The pup trailed the children.**   **The pup is trailing the children.**
3. **We camped in the forest.**   **We are camping in the forest.**
4. **Liz planted a peach tree.**   **Liz is planting a peach tree.**
5. **We planned our trip last summer.**   **We are planning our trip now.**

D. Challenge Words

(Have students open their books to Lesson 11, page 45.)

sightless	stoplight	nightfall	handrail
1 2	1 2	1 2	1 2
daydream	trainload		
1 2	1 2		

1. Find part D in your book.

2. Touch the first word. Sound out this word to yourself. Put your thumb up when you can say the word. (Wait until thumbs are up.) What is the word? *sightless*

3. Sound out the next word to yourself. Put your thumb up when you can say the word. (Wait until thumbs are up.) What is the word? *stoplight*

(Repeat step 3 with the words **nightfall, handrail, daydream,** and **trainload**.)

4. Let's read these words again. (Call on individual students to read the Challenge Words.)

E. Sight Words

(Have students open their books to Lesson 11, page 45.)

do	what	all	where	said
there	have	were	they	you

1. Find part E in your book.

2. Touch the first word. This word is **do**.
   What is the word? *do*
   Spell and read. *d-o. do*

3. The next word is **what**.
   What is the word? *what*
   Spell and read. *w-h-a-t. what*

(Repeat step 3 with the remaining words.)

4. Let's read these words again. (Call on individual students to read the Sight Words.)

F. Sentences and Stories

(Have students open their books to Lesson 11, page 45.)

1. Find part F in your book.

2. Touch the title of the story. Let's read the title together. *Still at Camp*

3. Read Part 1 to yourself. Read it very carefully. Put your thumb up when you are done. (Wait until thumbs are up.)

4. Let's read Part 1 together. When you are not reading aloud, follow along in your book. (Call on a student to read one or two sentences. Continue until Part 1 has been read.)

5. Look at the three pictures. Put a number 1 under the picture that goes with Part 1.

(Repeat steps 3–5 with Parts 2 and 3.)

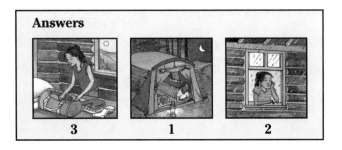

Answers

3   1   2

G. Spelling

(Have students open their books to Lesson 11, page 46.)

1. Find part G in your book.

2. Your first spelling word is **flight**.
   What is the word? *flight*

3. Say the sounds to yourself as you write the word. (Monitor.)

4. (Write the word on the board or display it on-screen.) Check your word. If you made a mistake, cross out the word and rewrite it. (Monitor.)

(Repeat steps 2–4 with the word **high**.)

5. Your next spelling word is **stoplight**.
   Say the first part of the word. *stop*
   Write this part.

6. Say the second part of the word. *light*
   Write this part.

7. (Write the word on the board or display it on-screen.) Check your word. If you made a mistake, cross out the word and rewrite it. (Monitor.)

(Repeat steps 5–7 with the word **trainload**.)

8. Listen. **Jack lifts his right hand.**
   Say the sentence. *Jack lifts his right hand.*
   Write the sentence. (Monitor.)

9. (Write the sentence on the board or display it on-screen.) Check each word. If you made a mistake, cross out the word and rewrite it. (Monitor.)

Answers
1. flight   3. stoplight
2. high   4. trainload
5. Jack lifts his right hand.

H. Practice Activity 1

(Have students open their books to Lesson 11, page 46.)

1. Find part H in your book.

2. Follow along as I read the directions. **Draw a line under the sentence that goes with each picture.**

3. Do number 1. Put your thumb up when you are finished. (Monitor and check.)

4. You will finish part H later.

I. Practice Activity 2

(Have students open their books to Lesson 11, page 47.)

1. Find part I in your book.

2. Follow along as I read the directions. **Read each story. Answer the questions.**

3. Find Story 1. Read the story to yourself. Do number 1. Put your thumb up when you are finished. (Monitor and check.)

4. Now go back and finish parts H and I.

◀)) Work Check for Parts H and I
(Oral Teacher-Directed Activity)

1. Find part H in your book.

2. Let's check your work. If you made a mistake, circle the number. You will fix all mistakes at the end of the lesson. (Call on individual students to read their answers.)

3. Count how many correct answers you have, and write that number in the box at the bottom of the page. (Monitor students.)

(Repeat steps 1–3 with part I.)

4. Now go back and correct any mistakes. (Monitor students.)

Answers for Part H
1. <u>Jack lifts his right hand</u>.
2. <u>The sheet is on the bed</u>.
3. <u>Pam put the light on at night</u>.
4. <u>The tree is in the road</u>.
5. <u>The train is fast</u>.

Answers for Part I

Story 1	Story 2
1. road	1. trail
2. light	2. show
3. sheet	3. thigh
4. night	4. right

LESSON 12

OBJECTIVES

- *to practice words with* igh
- *to practice words with both word endings* -ed *and* -ing

🔊 Sound Drill
(Oral Teacher-Directed Activity)

(Write the following on the board or display it on-screen:)

1. ea	u	igh	ow
2. o	igh	ay	a
3. ow	i	ee	ai
4. ea	ay	igh	oa
5. ee	oa	ai	e

1. Let's practice saying the sounds in the words that we will be reading. Look at the letters in line 1. Say the sounds. /$\overline{eee}$/, /uuu/, /$\overline{\imath\imath}$/, /$\overline{ooo}$/

2. Look at the letters in line 2. Say the sounds. /$\overline{ooo}$/, /$\overline{\imath\imath}$/, /$\overline{aaa}$/, /aaa/

(Repeat step 2 with lines 3–5. Then call on individual students to say the sounds in a line.)

(NOTE: As an alternative, review the sounds with flash cards.)

🔊 Segmenting Words into Sounds
(Oral Teacher-Directed Activity)

1. Let's practice saying some words. I will say a word, and then you will say the sounds in the word.

2. The first word is **faint**. What is the word? *faint*

3. Say the sounds in **faint**. Put up one finger for each sound. /fff/ /$\overline{aaa}$/ /nnn/ /t/

4. The next word is **bright**. What is the word? *bright*

5. Say the sounds in **bright**. Put up one finger for each sound. /b/ /rrr/ /$\overline{\imath\imath}$/ /t/

(Repeat steps 4 and 5 with these words:)

flight	/fff/	/lll/	/$\overline{\imath\imath}$/	/t/
steal	/sss/	/t/	/$\overline{eee}$/	/lll/
shown	/sh/	/ooo/	/nnn/	

A. New Words

(Have students open their books to Lesson 12, page 48.)

1.	l**igh**t	br**igh**t	s**igh**
2.	l**ea**st	sh**ow**	m**igh**t
3.	st**ea**l	fr**igh**t	f**ai**nt
4.	n**igh**t	br**ai**d	s**igh**t
5.	sweep	fl**igh**t	fl**oa**t
6.	sh**ow**n	r**oa**st	r**igh**t

7. This box is very light.
8. I might rub the polish off.
9. The children ran in fright.
10. You will see the spot vanish at night.
11. Nick had a ticket for the last flight.
12. Until then, you were right.

1. Find part A in your book.

2. Touch the first word in line 1. Look at the underlined letters. What is the sound? /$\overline{\imath\imath}$/

3. Sound out the word to yourself. Put your thumb up when you can say the whole word. (Wait until thumbs are up.) What is the word? *light*

4. Touch the next word. Look at the underlined letters. What is the sound? /$\overline{\imath\imath}$/ Sound out the word to yourself. Put your thumb up when you can say the whole word. (Wait until thumbs are up.) What is the word? *bright*

(Repeat step 4 with the remaining words in lines 1–3.)

5. Touch the first word in line 4. Sound out this word to yourself. Put your thumb up when you can say the whole word. (Wait until thumbs are up.) What is the word? *night*

6. Touch the next word. Sound out the word to yourself. Put your thumb up when you can say the whole word. (Wait until thumbs are up.) What is the word? *braid*

(Repeat step 6 with the remaining words in lines 4–6. Then call on a student to read a line.)

7. Read sentence 7 to yourself. Put your thumb up when you are done. (Wait until thumbs are up. Then call on a student to read the sentence.)

(Repeat step 7 with sentences 8–12.)

B. Review Words

(Have students open their books to Lesson 12, page 48.)

1.	slash	slap	crash
2.	brisk	brick	chick
3.	grant	grass	grasp
4.	check	prom	pond
5.	print	spent	swift

1. Find part B in your book.

2. Read the words in line 1 to yourself. When you can read all three words, put your thumb up. (Wait until thumbs are up.)

3. Get ready to read the words in line 1 together. Begin. *slash, slap, crash*

(Repeat steps 2 and 3 with lines 2–5. Then call on a student to read the words in a line.)

C. Word Endings

(Have students open their books to Lesson 12, page 48.)

1. <u>showed</u> <u>showing</u>	2. <u>fainted</u> <u>fainting</u>	3. <u>floated</u> <u>floating</u>
4. <u>slapped</u> <u>slapping</u>	5. <u>printed</u> <u>printing</u>	

1. Find part C in your book. Let's practice reading some words with word endings.

2. Look at number 1. Sound out the underlined word to yourself. Put your thumb up when you can say the underlined word. (Wait until thumbs are up.) What is the word? *show*

3. Add the **-ed** ending to **show**. What is the word? *showed*

4. Add the **-ing** ending to **show**. What is the word? *showing*

5. Now I will use the words in sentences.
Rosa showed us her book.
Rosa was showing us her book.
Say the words again. *showed, showing*

(Repeat steps 2–5 with numbers 2–5. Then call on individual students to say the words with endings.)

Word Ending Sentences
2. **Yesterday Todd fainted after marching in the hot sun.**
Many people were fainting in the hot sun.
3. **The boat floated in the bay.**
The boat was floating in the bay.
4. **She slapped her knee.**
She is slapping her knee.
5. **The paper was printed in the morning.**
The men were printing the paper.

D. Challenge Words

(Have students open their books to Lesson 12, page 49.)

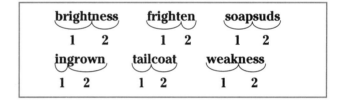

1. Find part D in your book.

2. Touch the first word. Sound out this word to yourself. Put your thumb up when you can say the word. (Wait until thumbs are up.) What is the word? *brightness*

3. Sound out the next word to yourself. Put your thumb up when you can say the word. (Wait until thumbs are up.) What is the word? *frighten*

(Repeat step 3 with the words **soapsuds, ingrown, tailcoat,** and **weakness**.)

4. Let's read these words again. (Call on individual students to read the Challenge Words.)

E. Sight Words

(Have students open their books to Lesson 12, page 49.)

do	where	all	what	people
there	saw	were	work	you

1. Find part E in your book.

2. Touch the first word. This word is **do**.
   What is the word? *do*
   Spell and read. *d-o. do*

3. The next word is **where**.
   What is the word? *where*
   Spell and read. *w-h-e-r-e. where*

(Repeat step 3 with the remaining words.)

4. Let's read these words again. (Call on individual students to read the Sight Words.)

F. Sentences and Stories

(Have students open their books to Lesson 12, page 49.)

1. Find part F in your book.

2. Touch the title of the story. Let's read the title together. *Night Sweep*

3. Read Part 1 to yourself. Read it very carefully. Put your thumb up when you are done. (Wait until thumbs are up.)

4. Let's read Part 1 together. When you are not reading aloud, follow along in your book. (Call on a student to read one or two sentences. Continue until Part 1 has been read.)

5. Look at the three pictures. Put a number 1 under the picture that goes with Part 1.

(Repeat steps 3–5 with Parts 2 and 3.)

Answers

G. Spelling

(Have students open their books to Lesson 12, page 50.)

1. Find part G in your book.

2. Your first spelling word is **right**.
   What is the word? *right*

3. Say the sounds to yourself as you write the word. (Monitor.)

4. (Write the word on the board or display it on-screen.) Check your word. If you made a mistake, cross out the word and rewrite it. (Monitor.)

(Repeat steps 2–4 with the word **sight**.)

5. Your next spelling word is **brightness**.
   Say the first part of the word. *bright*
   Write this part.

6. Say the second part of the word. *ness*
   Write this part.

7. (Write the word on the board or display it on-screen.) Check your word. If you made a mistake, cross out the word and rewrite it. (Monitor.)

(Repeat steps 5–7 with the word **frighten**.)

8. Listen. **Nell might see the sights.**
   Say the sentence. *Nell might see the sights.*
   Write the sentence. (Monitor.)

9. (Write the sentence on the board or display it on-screen.) Check each word. If you made a mistake, cross out the word and rewrite it. (Monitor.)

Answers
1. right   3. brightness
2. sight   4. frighten
5. **Nell might see the sights.**

H. Practice Activity 1

(Have students open their books to Lesson 12, page 50.)

1. Find part H in your book.

2. Follow along as I read the directions. **Draw a line under the sentence that goes with each picture.**

3. Do number 1. Put your thumb up when you are finished. (Monitor and check.)

4. You will finish part H later.

I. Practice Activity 2

(Have students open their books to Lesson 12, page 51.)

1. Find part I in your book.

2. Follow along as I read the directions. **Read each story. Answer the questions.**

3. Find Story 1. Read the story to yourself. Do number 1. Put your thumb up when you are finished. (Monitor and check.)

4. Now go back and finish parts H and I.

 ## Work Check for Parts H and I
(Oral Teacher-Directed Activity)

1. Find part H in your book.

2. Let's check your work. If you made a mistake, circle the number. You will fix all mistakes at the end of the lesson. (Call on individual students to read their answers.)

3. Count how many correct answers you have, and write that number in the box at the bottom of the page. (Monitor students.)

(Repeat steps 1–3 with part I.)

4. Now go back and correct any mistakes. (Monitor students.)

Answers for Part H
1. <u>Beth has a braid</u>.
2. <u>Don sweeps the rug</u>.
3. <u>There was bright sun at midday</u>.
4. <u>A duck floats on the pond</u>.
5. <u>The gulls are in flight</u>.

Answers for Part I

Story 1	Story 2
1. ten	1. plant shop
2. snack shop	2. three
3. ham, bun	3. three plants
4. milk	4. tree

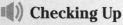 ## Checking Up
(Oral Teacher-Directed Activity)

Practice reading Part 1 of the story on page 49. I am going to listen to each of you read. Your goal is to make fewer than two errors. Keep practicing Part 1 until you can read it without any errors.

(Ask each student to read Part 1. Record the number of errors in his or her book.)

NOTE: If 90 percent of the students make two errors or fewer, you may move on to Lesson 13. If not, repeat Lesson 12.)

LESSON 13

🔊 New Sound

(Have students open their books to Lesson 13, page 52.)

1. Look at the top of page 52 in your book.

2. Touch the word.

3. This word is **rake**. Say the word. *rake*

4. Touch the letter **a**. When a word ends in **e**, we say the <u>name</u> of this letter. What is the <u>name</u> of this letter? *a*

(Have students close their books. Then do the Sound Drill activity.)

🔊 Sound Drill
(Oral Teacher-Directed Activity)

(Write the following on the board or display it on-screen:)

1.	ow	oa	ai	ee
2.	igh	ea	e	ow
3.	ai	a	ee	igh
4.	ea	ay	oa	o
5.	i	igh	ay	ee

1. Let's practice saying the sounds in the words that we will be reading. Look at the letters in line 1. Say the sounds. /ōōō/, /ōōō/, /āāā/, /ēēē/

2. Look at the letters in line 2. Say the sounds. /īīī/, /ēēē/, /eee/, /ōōō/

(Repeat step 2 with lines 3–5. Then call on individual students to say the sounds in a line.)

(NOTE: As an alternative, review the sounds with flash cards.)

A. New Words

(Have students open their books to Lesson 13, page 52.)

1.	bake	came	make
2.	made	mad	hate
3.	gave	tape	sale
4.	lake	tap	cape
5.	mane	man	wake
6.	fad	fade	late

7. The wind came from the west.
8. I hate to see you go.
9. We gave the dog a bath.
10. We will stop at the lake for a picnic.
11. Wake me up at six.
12. Will the hat fade in the sun?

1. Find part A in your book.

2. Touch the first word in line 1. This word ends in **e**. Touch the letter **a**. When a word ends in **e**, say the <u>name</u> of this letter. What is the <u>name</u> of this letter? *a*

3. This word is **bake**. What is the word? *bake*

4. Touch the next word in line 1. Does this word end in **e**? *yes*

5. Will you say the name or the sound for the letter **a**? *the name*

6. What is the name? *a*

7. Sound out the word to yourself. Put your thumb up when you can say the whole word. (Wait until thumbs are up.) What is the word? *came*

8. Touch the next word. Does this word end in **e**? *yes*

9. Will you say the name or the sound for the letter **a**? *the name*

10. What is the name? *a*

11. Sound out the word to yourself. Put your thumb up when you can say the whole word. (Wait until thumbs are up.) What is the word? *make*

12. Touch the first word in line 2. Does the word end in **e**? *yes*

13. Will you say the name or the sound for the letter **a**? *the name*

14. What is the name? *a*

15. Sound out the word to yourself. Put your thumb up when you can say the whole word. (Wait until thumbs are up.) What is the word? *made*

16. Touch the next word. Does this word end in **e**? *no*

17. Will you say the name or the sound for the letter **a**? *the sound*

18. What is the sound? */aaa/*

19. Sound out the word to yourself. Put your thumb up when you can say the whole word. (Wait until thumbs are up.) What is the word? *mad*

(Repeat steps 16–19 with the remaining words in lines 2–3. Adjust step 18 to the specific word— "What is the name?" or "What is the sound?")

20. Touch the first word in line 4. Sound out this word to yourself. Say the sounds carefully. Put your thumb up when you can say the whole word. (Wait until thumbs are up.) What is the word? *lake*

21. Touch the next word. Sound out the word to yourself. Put your thumb up when you can say the whole word. (Wait until thumbs are up.) What is the word? *tap*

(Repeat step 21 with the remaining words in lines 4–6. Then call on a student to read a line.)

22. Read sentence 7 to yourself. Put your thumb up when you are done. (Wait until thumbs are up. Then call on a student to read the sentence.)

(Repeat step 22 with sentences 8–12.)

B. Review Words

(Have students open their books to Lesson 13, page 52.)

1. sprain	pain	spin
2. tree	bright	spray
3. steam	chain	stream
4. roast	fleet	speed
5. tray	sped	street

1. Find part B in your book.

2. Read the words in line 1 to yourself. When you can read all three words, put your thumb up. (Wait until thumbs are up.)

3. Get ready to read the words in line 1 together. Begin. *sprain, pain, spin*

(Repeat steps 2 and 3 with lines 2–5. Then call on a student to read the words in a line.)

C. Word Endings—Altered Roots

1. ba<u>k</u>ing	2. ma<u>k</u>ing	3. ha<u>t</u>ing
4. ta<u>p</u>ing	5. wa<u>k</u>ing	

(Write **fading** on the board.)

1. (Point to the **d** in **fading**.) When there is one **d** in the middle of the word, you say the name for this letter. Point to the **a**. What is the name for this letter? *a*

2. This word is **fading**. What is the word? *fading*

(Have students open their books to Lesson 13, page 52.)

3. Find part C in your book.

4. Look at the first word. How many **k**'s are in the middle of this word? *one*

5. When there is one **k** in the middle of the word, you say the name for the letter **a**. What is the name? *a*

6. Sound out the word to yourself. Put your thumb up when you can say the whole word. (Wait until thumbs are up.) What is the word? *baking*

7. Look at the second word. How many **k**'s are in the middle of this word? *one*

8. When there is one **k** in the middle of the word, do you say the name for the letter **a**? *yes* What is the name? *a*

9. Sound out the word to yourself. Put your thumb up when you can say the whole word. (Wait until thumbs are up.) What is the word? *making*

10. Look at the third word. How many **t**'s are in the middle of this word? *one*

11. When there is one **t** in the middle of the word, do you say the name for the letter **a**? *yes* What is the name? *a*

12. Sound out the word to yourself. Put your thumb up when you can say the whole word. (Wait until thumbs are up.) What is the word? *hating*

13. Look at the fourth word. How many **p**'s are in the middle of this word? *one*

14. When there is one **p** in the middle of the word, do you say the name for the letter **a**? *yes* What is the name? *a*

15. Sound out the word to yourself. Put your thumb up when you can say the whole word. (Wait until thumbs are up.) What is the word? *taping*

16. Look at the fifth word. How many **k**'s are in the middle of this word? *one*

17. When there is one **k** in the middle of the word, do you say the name for the letter **a**? *yes* What is the name? *a*

18. Sound out the word to yourself. Put your thumb up when you can say the whole word. (Wait until thumbs are up.) What is the word? *waking*

19. Let's read these words again. (Call on individual students to read the words.)

D. Challenge Words

(Have students open their books to Lesson 13, page 53.)

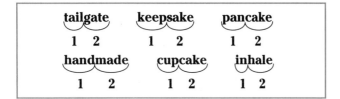

tailgate	keepsake	pancake
1 2	1 2	1 2
handmade	cupcake	inhale
1 2	1 2	1 2

1. Find part D in your book.

2. Touch the first word. Sound out this word to yourself. Put your thumb up when you can say the word. (Wait until thumbs are up.) What is the word? *tailgate*

3. Sound out the next word to yourself. Put your thumb up when you can say the word. (Wait until thumbs are up.) What is the word? *keepsake*

(Repeat step 3 with the words **pancake, handmade, cupcake,** and **inhale.**)

4. Let's read these words again. (Call on individual students to read the Challenge Words.)

E. Sight Words

(Have students open their books to Lesson 13, page 53.)

be	he	we	she	me
they	do	what	work	where
all	you	there	said	have

1. Find part E in your book.

2. Touch the first word. This word is **be**. What is the word? *be* Spell and read. *b-e. be*

3. The next word is **he**. What is the word? *he* Spell and read. *h-e. he*

(Repeat step 3 with the remaining words.)

4. Let's read these words again. (Call on individual students to read the Sight Words.)

F. Sentences and Stories

(Have students open their books to Lesson 13, page 53.)

1. Find part F in your book.

2. Touch the title of the story. Let's read the title together. *Trish Has a Plan*

3. Read Part 1 to yourself. Read it very carefully. Put your thumb up when you are done. (Wait until thumbs are up.)

4. Let's read Part 1 together. When you are not reading aloud, follow along in your book. (Call on a student to read one or two sentences. Continue until Part 1 has been read.)

5. Look at the three pictures. Put a number 1 under the picture that goes with Part 1.

(Repeat steps 3–5 with Parts 2 and 3.)

Answers

2   3   1

G. Spelling

(Have students open their books to Lesson 13, page 54.)

1. Find part G in your book.

2. Your first spelling word is **came**. Write **came**.

3. (Write the word on the board or display it on-screen.) Check and correct your word. (Monitor.)

(Repeat steps 2 and 3 with the word **lake**.)

4. Your next spelling word is **pancake**. Say the parts in **pancake**. First part. *pan* Next part. *cake* Write the word.

5. (Write the word on the board or display it on-screen.) Check and correct your word.

(Repeat steps 4 and 5 with the word **handmade**.)

6. Listen. **Nan can bake bran muffins.** Write the sentence. (Monitor.)

7. (Write the sentence on the board or display it on-screen.) Check and correct each word. (Monitor.)

```
Answers
1.  came      3.  pancake
2.  lake      4.  handmade
5.  Nan can bake bran muffins.
```

H. Practice Activity 1

Have students open their books to Lesson 13, page 54.)

1. Find part H in your book.

2. Follow along as I read the directions. **Draw a line under the sentence that goes with each picture.**

3. Do number 1. Put your thumb up when you are finished. (Monitor and check.)

4. You will finish part H later.

I. Practice Activity 2

(Have students open their books to Lesson 13, page 55.)

1. Find part I in your book.

2. Follow along as I read the directions. **Read each story. Answer the questions.**

3. Find Story 1. Read the story to yourself. Do number 1. Put your thumb up when you are finished. (Monitor and check.)

4. Now go back and finish parts H and I.

◀) Work Check for Parts H and I
(Oral Teacher-Directed Activity)

1. Find Part H in your book.

2. Let's check your work. If you made a mistake, circle the number. You will fix all mistakes at the end of the lesson. (Call on individual students to read their answers.)

3. Count how many correct answers you have, and write that number in the box at the bottom of the page. (Monitor students.)

(Repeat steps 1–3 with part I.)

4. Now go back and correct any mistakes. (Monitor students.)

```
Answers for Part H
1.  Tom wakes up at six.
2.  Nan can bake bran muffins.
3.  Fran put tape on the box.
4.  The duck floated on the lake.
5.  Chet will put cash in the safe.
```

```
Answers for Part I
Story 1      Story 2
1.  three    1.  lunch
2.  cape     2.  lake
3.  desk     3.  cake
4.  play     4.  cake pan
```

LESSON 14

OBJECTIVES

- *to practice CVCe words with* a
- *to practice words altered by the word ending* -ing

🔊 Sound Drill
(Oral Teacher-Directed Activity)

(Write the following on the board or display it on-screen:)

1.	oa	igh	a	ay
2.	igh	ai	ow	ea
3.	ee	e	igh	i
4.	ea	o	oa	ee
5.	al	ow	ay	oa

1. Let's practice saying the sounds in the words that we will be reading. Look at the letters in line 1. Say the sounds. /$\overline{oo}$/, /$\overline{\imath\imath}$/, /aaa/, /$\overline{aaa}$/

2. Look at the letters in line 2. Say the sounds. /$\overline{\imath\imath}$/, /$\overline{aaa}$/, /$\overline{oo}$/, /$\overline{eee}$/

(Repeat step 2 with lines 3–5. Then call on individual students to say the sounds in a line.)

(NOTE: As an alternative, review the sounds with flash cards.)

A. New Words

(Have students open their books to Lesson 14, page 56.)

1.	name	safe	take
2.	same	Sam	pane
3.	mate	pan	rack
4.	rake	mat	flame
5.	gate	cane	can
6.	rat	late	rate
7.	His name is Bill.		
8.	Bess and I have the same dentist.		
9.	Do you have a cabin mate?		
10.	The flame got very hot.		
11.	Glen sped past the gate.		
12.	At this rate, you will be late.		

1. Find part A in your book.

2. Touch the first word in line 1. Does the word end in **e**? *yes*

3. Will you say the name or the sound or the letter **a**? *the name*

4. What is the name? *a*

5. Sound out the word to yourself. Put your thumb up when you can say the whole word. (Wait until thumbs are up.) What is the word? *name*

6. Touch the next word in line 1. Does this word end in **e**? *yes*

7. Will you say the name or the sound for the letter **a**? *the name*

8. What is the name? *a*

9. Sound out the word to yourself. Put your thumb up when you can say the whole word. (Wait until thumbs are up.) What is the word? *safe*

10. Touch the next word. Does this word end in **e**? *yes*

11. Will you say the name or the sound for the letter **a**? *the name*

12. What is the name? *a*

13. Sound out the word to yourself. Put your thumb up when you can say the whole word. (Wait until thumbs are up.) What is the word? *take*

14. Touch the first word in line 2. Does the word end in **e**? *yes*

15. Will you say the name or the sound for the letter **a**? *the name*

16. What is the name? *a*

17. Sound out the word to yourself. Put your thumb up when you can say the whole word. (Wait until thumbs are up.) What is the word? *same*

18. Touch the next word. Does this word end in **e**? *no*

19. Will you say the name or the sound for the letter **a**? *the sound*

20. What is the sound? /aaa/

21. Sound out the word to yourself. Put your thumb up when you can say the whole word. (Wait until thumbs are up.) What is the word? *Sam*

(Repeat steps 18–21 with the remaining words in lines 2–3. Adjust step 20 to the specific word— What is the name?" or "What is the sound?")

22. Touch the first word in line 4. Sound out this word to yourself. Say the sounds carefully. Put your thumb up when you can say the whole word. (Wait until thumbs are up.) What is the word? *rake*

23. Touch the next word. Sound out the word to yourself. Put your thumb up when you can say the whole word. (Wait until thumbs are up.) What is the word? *mat*

(Repeat step 23 with the remaining words in lines 4–6. Then call on a student to read a line.)

24. Read sentence 7 to yourself. Put your thumb up when you are done. (Wait until thumbs are up. Then call on a student to read the sentence.)

(Repeat step 24 with sentences 8–12.)

B. Review Words

(Have students open their books to Lesson 14, page 56.)

1. feast	heat	fast
2. strain	cost	train
3. sweep	claim	coast
4. clam	swept	bleed
5. bled	grown	pray

1. Find part B in your book.

2. Read the words in line 1 to yourself. When you can read all three words, put your thumb up. (Wait until thumbs are up.)

3. Get ready to read the words in line 1 together. Begin. *feast, heat, fast*

(Repeat steps 2 and 3 with lines 2–5. Then call on a student to read the words in a line.)

C. Word Endings—Altered Roots

(Have students open their books to Lesson 14, page 56.)

1. taping	2. taking	3. raking
4. naming	5. waking	

1. Find part C in your book.

2. Look at the first word. How many **p's** are in the middle of this word? *one*

3. When there is one **p** in the middle of the word, you say the name for the letter **a**. What is the name? *a*

4. Sound out the word to yourself. Put your thumb up when you can say the whole word. (Wait until thumbs are up.) What is the word? *taping*

5. Look at the second word. How many **k's** are in the middle of this word? *one*

6. When there is one **k** in the middle of the word, you say the name for the letter **a**. What is the name? *a*

7. Sound out the word to yourself. Put your thumb up when you can say the whole word. (Wait until thumbs are up.) What is the word? *taking*

8. Look at the third word. How many **k's** are in the middle of this word? *one*

9. When there is one **k** in the middle of the word, do you say the name for the letter **a**? *yes* What is the name? *a*

10. Sound out the word to yourself. Put your thumb up when you can say the whole word. (Wait until thumbs are up.) What is the word? *raking*

11. Look at the fourth word. How many **m's** are in the middle of this word? *one*

12. When there is one **m** in the middle of the word, do you say the name for the letter **a**? *yes* What is the name? *a*

13. Sound out the word to yourself. Put your thumb up when you can say the whole word. (Wait until thumbs are up.) What is the word? *naming*

14. Look at the fifth word. How many **k's** are in the middle of this word? *one*

15. When there is one **k** in the middle of the word, do you say the name for the letter **a**? *yes* What is the name? *a*

16. Sound out the word to yourself. Put your thumb up when you can say the whole word. (Wait until thumbs are up.) What is the word? *waking*

17. Let's read these words again. (Call on individual students to read the words.)

D. Challenge Words

(Have students open their books to Lesson 14, page 57.)

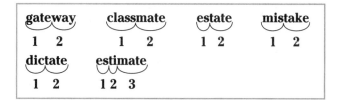

1. Find part D in your book.

2. Touch the first word. Sound out this word to yourself. Put your thumb up when you can say the word. (Wait until thumbs are up.) What is the word? *gateway*

3. Sound out the next word to yourself. Put your thumb up when you can say the word. (Wait until thumbs are up.) What is the word? *classmate*

(Repeat step 3 with the words **estate, mistake, dictate,** and **estimate.**)

4. Let's read these words again. (Call on individual students to read the Challenge Words.)

E. Sight Words

(Have students open their books to Lesson 14, page 57.)

me	she	he	be	we
were	do	what	people	where
they	there	you	all	of

1. Find part E in your book.

2. Touch the first word. This word is **me**. What is the word? *me* Spell and read. *m-e. me*

3. The next word is **she**. What is the word? *she* Spell and read. *s-h-e. she*

(Repeat step 3 with the remaining words.)

4. Let's read these words again. (Call on individual students to read the Sight Words.)

F. Sentences and Stories

(Have students open their books to Lesson 14, page 57.)

1. Find part F in your book.

2. Touch the title of the story. Let's read the title together. *Sale Day*

3. Read Part 1 to yourself. Read it very carefully. Put your thumb up when you are done. (Wait until thumbs are up.)

4. Let's read Part 1 together. When you are not reading aloud, follow along in your book. (Call on a student to read one or two sentences. Continue until Part 1 has been read.)

5. Look at the three pictures. Put a number 1 under the picture that goes with Part 1.

(Repeat steps 3–5 with Parts 2 and 3.)

G. Spelling

(Have students open their books to Lesson 14, page 58.)

1. Find part G in your book.

2. Your first spelling word is **name**. Write **name**.

3. (Write the word on the board or display it on-screen.) Check and correct your word. (Monitor.)

(Repeat steps 2 and 3 with the word **late.**)

4. Your next spelling word is **classmate**. Say the parts in **classmate**. First part. *class* Next part. *mate* Write the word.

5. (Write the word on the board or display it on-screen.) Check and correct your word.

(Repeat steps 4 and 5 with the word **mistake.**)

6. Listen. **Tom will rake the grass.**
   Write the sentence. (Monitor.)

7. (Write the sentence on the board or display it on-screen.) Check and correct each word. (Monitor.)

Answers
1. name 3. classmate
2. late 4. mistake
5. **Tom will rake the grass.**

H. Practice Activity 1

(Have students open their books to Lesson 14, page 58.)

1. Find part H in your book.

2. Follow along as I read the directions. **Draw a line under the sentence that goes with each picture.**

3. Do number 1. Put your thumb up when you are finished. (Monitor and check.)

4. You will finish part H later.

I. Practice Activity 2

(Have students open their books to Lesson 14, page 59.)

1. Find part I in your book.

2. Follow along as I read the directions. **Read each story. Answer the questions.**

3. Find Story 1. Read the story to yourself. Do number 1. Put your thumb up when you are finished. (Monitor and check.)

4. Now go back and finish parts H and I.

🔊 Work Check for Parts H and I
(Oral Teacher-Directed Activity)

1. Find part H in your book.

2. Let's check your work. If you made a mistake, circle the number. You will fix all mistakes at the end of the lesson. (Call on individual students to read their answers.)

3. Count how many correct answers you have, and write that number in the box at the bottom of the page. (Monitor students.)

(Repeat steps 1–3 with part I.)

4. Now go back and correct any mistakes. (Monitor students.)

Answers for Part H
1. <u>Tom can rake the grass.</u>
2. <u>Liz chats with her classmate.</u>
3. <u>That man has a cane.</u>
4. <u>Tom is waking up.</u>
5. <u>Beth and Kit have the same dress.</u>

Answers for Part I

Story 1	Story 2
1. six	1. ten
2. grill	2. jeep
3. beef	3. snack
4. grill	4. lake

LESSON 15

OBJECTIVES

- to practice CVCe words with a
- to practice words altered by the word ending -ing

 Sound Drill
(Oral Teacher-Directed Activity)

(Write the following on the board or display it on-screen:)

1.	ea	igh	oa	ai
2.	ay	ow	ee	e
3.	a	a	igh	i
4.	ea	oa	o	ay
5.	igh	ee	ai	ow

1. Let's practice saying the sounds in the words that we will be reading. Look at the letters in line 1. Say the sounds. /ēēē/, /īīī/, /ōōō/, /āāā/

2. Look at the letters in line 2. Say the sounds. /āāā/, /ōōō/, /ēēē/, /eee/

(Repeat step 2 with lines 3–5. Then call on individual students to say the sounds in a line.)

(NOTE: As an alternative, review the sounds with flash cards.)

A. New Words

(Have students open their books to Lesson 15, page 60.)

1.	state	ate	brave
2.	fate	at	plane
3.	brake	fat	plan
4.	glad	whale	shape
5.	clap	lame	grape
6.	snake	slap	wave

7. Which state sees the sunset last?
8. You will miss your plane.
9. The brakes on the car are new.
10. What shape dish do you want?
11. Do not sit on the grape!
12. We saw him wave from that cabin.

1. Find part A in your book.

2. Touch the first word in line 1. Does the word end in **e**? *yes*

3. Will you say the name or the sound for the letter **a**? *the name*

4. What is the name? *a*

5. Sound out the word to yourself. Put your thumb up when you can say the whole word. (Wait until thumbs are up.) What is the word? *state*

6. Touch the next word in line 1. Does this word end in **e**? *yes*

7. Will you say the name or the sound for the letter **a**? *the name*

8. What is the name? *a*

9. Sound out the word to yourself. Put your thumb up when you can say the whole word. (Wait until thumbs are up.) What is the word? *ate*

10. Touch the next word. Does this word end in **e**? *yes*

11. Will you say the name or the sound for the letter **a**? *the name*

12. What is the name? *a*

13. Sound out the word to yourself. Put your thumb up when you can say the whole word. (Wait until thumbs are up.) What is the word? *brave*

14. Touch the first word in line 2. Does the word end in **e**? *yes*

15. Will you say the name or the sound for the letter **a**? *the name*

16. What is the name? *a*

17. Sound out the word to yourself. Put your thumb up when you can say the whole word. (Wait until thumbs are up.) What is the word? *fate*

18. Touch the next word. Does this word end in **e**? *no*

19. Will you say the name or the sound for the letter **a**? *the sound*

20. What is the sound? /aaa/

21. Sound out the word to yourself. Put your thumb up when you can say the whole word. (Wait until thumbs are up.) What is the word? *at*

(Repeat steps 18–21 with the remaining words in lines 2–3. Adjust step 20 to the specific word— "What is the name?" or "What is the sound?")

22. Touch the first word in line 4. Sound out this word to yourself. Say the sounds carefully. Put your thumb up when you can say the whole word. (Wait until thumbs are up.) What is the word? *glad*

23. Touch the next word. Sound out the word to yourself. Put your thumb up when you can say the whole word. (Wait until thumbs are up.) What is the word? *whale*

(Repeat step 23 with the remaining words in lines 4–6. Then call on a student to read a line.)

24. Read sentence 7 to yourself. Put your thumb up when you are done. (Wait until thumbs are up. Then call on a student to read the sentence.)

(Repeat step 24 with sentences 8–12.)

B. Review Words

(Have students open their books to Lesson 15, page 60.)

1.	throw	snail	steal
2.	cheat	flow	flee
3.	peach	paint	pack
4.	right	soak	seek
5.	clay	wheat	speech

1. Find part B in your book.

2. Read the words in line 1 to yourself. When you can read all three words, put your thumb up. (Wait until thumbs are up.)

3. Get ready to read the words in line 1 together. Begin. *throw, snail, steal*

(Repeat steps 2 and 3 with lines 2–5. Then call on a student to read the words in a line.)

C. Word Endings—Altered Roots

1.	ta<u>p</u>ing	4.	ba<u>tt</u>ing	7.	wa<u>k</u>ing
2.	ta<u>pp</u>ing	5.	cla<u>pp</u>ing	8.	ma<u>pp</u>ing
3.	ra<u>k</u>ing	6.	ra<u>t</u>ing		

(Write **taping** and **tapping** on the board.)

1. (Point to the **p** in **taping**.) When there is one **p** in the middle of the word, you say the name for this letter. (Point to the **a**.) What is the name? *a*

2. This word is **taping**. What is the word? *taping*

3. (Point to the **p**'s in **tapping**.) When there are two **p**'s in the middle of the word, you say the sound for this letter. (Point to the **a**.) When there are two **p**'s, do you say the name or the sound? *the sound* What is the sound? */aaa/*

4. This word is **tapping**. What is the word? *tapping*

(Have students open their books to Lesson 15, page 60.)

5. Find part C in your book.

6. Look at number 1. How many **p**'s? *one*

7. Will you say the name or the sound for the letter **a**? *the name*

8. What is the name? *a*

9. Sound out the word to yourself. What is the word? *taping*

10. Look at number 2. How many **p**'s? *two*

11. Will you say the name or the sound for the letter **a**? *the sound*

12. What is the sound? */aaa/*

13. Sound out the word to yourself. What is the word? *tapping*

14. Look at number 3. How many **k**'s? *one*

15. Will you say the name or the sound for the letter **a**? *the name*

16. What is the name? *a*

17. Sound out the word. What is the word? *raking*

18. Look at number 4. How many **t**'s? *two*

19. Will you say the name or the sound for the letter **a**? *the sound*

20. What is the sound? */aaa/*

21. Sound out the word. What is the word? *batting*

22. Look at number 5. How many **p**'s? *two*

23. Will you say the name or the sound for the letter **a**? *the sound*

24. What is the sound? */aaa/*

25. Sound out the word. What is the word? *clapping*

(Repeat steps 22–25 with the remaining words. Adjust step 24 to the specific word—"What is the name?" or "What is the sound?")

26. Let's read these words again. (Call on individual students to read the words.)

D. Challenge Words

(Have students open their books to Lesson 15, page 61.)

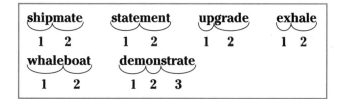

shipmate statement upgrade exhale
  1 2   1 2   1 2   1 2
whaleboat   demonstrate
  1 2   1 2 3

1. Find part D in your book.

2. Touch the first word. Sound out this word to yourself. Put your thumb up when you can say the word. (Wait until thumbs are up.) What is the word? *shipmate*

3. Sound out the next word to yourself. Put your thumb up when you can say the word. (Wait until thumbs are up.) What is the word? *statement*

(Repeat step 3 with the words **upgrade, exhale, whaleboat,** and **demonstrate**.)

4. Let's read these words again. (Call on individual students to read the Challenge Words.)

E. Sight Words

(Have students open their books to Lesson 15, page 61.)

he	me	she	we	be
where	they	do	what	water
there	down	look	all	were

1. Find part E in your book.

2. Touch the first word. This word is **he**.
   What is the word? *he*
   Spell and read. *h-e. he*

3. The next word is **me**.
   What is the word? *me*
   Spell and read. *m-e. me*

(Repeat step 3 with the remaining words.)

4. Let's read these words again. (Call on individual students to read the Sight Words.)

F. Sentences and Stories

(Have students open their books to Lesson 15, page 61.)

1. Find part F in your book.

2. Touch the title of the story. Let's read the title together. *A Whale Tale*

3. Read Part 1 to yourself. Read it very carefully. Put your thumb up when you are done. (Wait until thumbs are up.)

4. Let's read Part 1 together. When you are not reading aloud, follow along in your book. (Call on a student to read one or two sentences. Continue until Part 1 has been read.)

5. Look at the three pictures. Put a number 1 under the picture that goes with Part 1.

(Repeat steps 3–5 with Parts 2 and 3.)

Answers

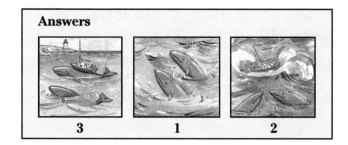

3   1   2

G. Spelling

(Have students open their books to Lesson 15, page 62.)

1. Find part G in your book.

2. Your first spelling word is **plane**. Write **plane**.

3. (Write the word on the board or display it on-screen.) Check and correct your word. (Monitor.)

(Repeat steps 2 and 3 with the word **whale**.)

4. Your next spelling word is **statement**.
   Say the parts in **statement**. First part. *state*
   Next part. *ment* Write the word.

5. (Write the word on the board or display it on-screen.) Check and correct your word.

(Repeat steps 4 and 5 with the word **demonstrate**.)

6. Listen. **You may miss your plane.**
   Write the sentence. (Monitor.)

7. (Write the sentence on the board or display it on-screen.) Check and correct each word. (Monitor.)

Answers
1. plane   3. statement
2. whale   4. demonstrate
5. **You may miss your plane.**

H. Practice Activity 1

(Have students open their books to Lesson 15, page 62.)

1. Find part H in your book.

2. Follow along as I read the directions.
   Fill in each blank with the best word.

3. Do number 1. Put your thumb up when you are finished. (Monitor and check.)

4. You will finish part H later.

I. Practice Activity 2

(Have students open their books to Lesson 15, page 63.)

1. Find part I in your book.

2. Follow along as I read the directions.
   Read each story. Answer the questions.

3. Find Story 1. Read the story to yourself. Do number 1. Put your thumb up when you are finished. (Monitor and check.)

4. Now go back and finish parts H and I.

Work Check for Parts H and I
(Oral Teacher-Directed Activity)

1. Find part H in your book.

2. Let's check your work. If you made a mistake, circle the number. You will fix all mistakes at the end of the lesson. (Call on individual students to read their answers.)

3. Count how many correct answers you have, and write that number in the box at the bottom of the page. (Monitor students.)

(Repeat steps 1–3 with part I.)

4. Now go back and correct any mistakes. (Monitor students.)

Answers for Part H
1. flame   6. ate
2. game   7. whale
3. grape   8. rake
4. plane   9. tape
5. snake   10. state

Answers for Part I

Story 1	Story 2
1. three	1. last night
2. gate	2. bake shop
3. black	3. muffins
4. snack	4. take

LESSON 16

OBJECTIVES

- *to practice CVCe words with* a
- *to practice words altered by the word ending* -ing

 Sound Drill
(Oral Teacher-Directed Activity)

(Write the following on the board or display it on-screen:)

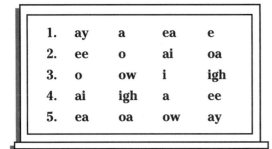

1.	ay	a	ea	e
2.	ee	o	ai	oa
3.	o	ow	i	igh
4.	ai	igh	a	ee
5.	ea	oa	ow	ay

1. Let's practice saying the sounds in the words that we will be reading. Look at the letters in line 1. Say the sounds. /āāā/, /aaa/, /ēēē/, /eee/

2. Look at the letters in line 2. Say the sounds. /ēēē/, /ooo/, /āāā/, /ōōō/

(Repeat step 2 with lines 3–5. Then call on individual students to say the sounds in a line.)

(NOTE: As an alternative, review the sounds with flash cards.)

A. New Words

(Have students open their books to Lesson 16, page 64.)

1.	case	flat	shame
2.	ham	rate	trade
3.	flake	date	lack
4.	plate	van	slave
5.	sale	plant	vane
6.	fame	skate	crate
7.	She put the fossil in a little case.		
8.	Will you trade jobs with me?		
9.	Did you see a flake of snow?		
10.	Dip the plate in water.		
11.	When do tickets go on sale?		
12.	He fell when his skate hit the rock.		

1. Find part A in your book.

2. Touch the first word in line 1. Does the word end in **e**? *yes*

3. Will you say the name or the sound for the letter **a**? *the name*

4. What is the name? *a*

5. Sound out the word to yourself. Put your thumb up when you can say the whole word. (Wait until thumbs are up.) What is the word? *case*

6. Touch the next word in line 1. Does this word end in **e**? *no*

7. Will you say the name or the sound for the letter **a**? *the sound*

8. What is the sound? */aaa/*

9. Sound out the word to yourself. Put your thumb up when you can say the whole word. (Wait until thumbs are up.) What is the word? *flat*

10. Touch the next word. Does this word end in **e**? *yes*

11. Will you say the name or the sound for the letter **a**? *the name*

12. What is the name? *a*

13. Sound out the word to yourself. Put your thumb up when you can say the whole word. (Wait until thumbs are up.) What is the word? *shame*

14. Touch the first word in line 2. Does the word end in **e**? *no*

15. Will you say the name or the sound for the letter **a**? *the sound*

16. What is the sound? */aaa/*

17. Sound out the word to yourself. Put your thumb up when you can say the whole word. (Wait until thumbs are up.) What is the word? *ham*

18. Touch the next word. Does this word end in **e**? *yes*

19. Will you say the name or the sound for the letter **a**? *the name*

20. What is the name? *a*

21. Sound out the word to yourself. Put your thumb up when you can say the whole word. (Wait until thumbs are up.) What is the word? *rate*

(Repeat steps 18–21 with the remaining words in lines 2–3. Adjust step 20 to the specific word— "What is the name?" or "What is the sound?")

22. Touch the first word in line 4. Sound out this word to yourself. Say the sounds carefully. Put your thumb up when you can say the whole word. (Wait until thumbs are up.) What is the word? *plate*

23. Touch the next word. Sound out the word to yourself. Put your thumb up when you can say the whole word. (Wait until thumbs are up.) What is the word? *van*

(Repeat step 23 with the remaining words in lines 4–6. Then call on a student to read a line.)

24. Read sentence 7 to yourself. Put your thumb up when you are done. (Wait until thumbs are up. Then call on a student to read the sentence.)

(Repeat step 24 with sentences 8–12).

B. Review Words

(Have students open their books to Lesson 16, page 64.)

1. trail	step	blown
2. steep	beat	boat
3. bowl	sail	seal
4. stay	weak	bail
5. peel	pail	sell

1. Find part B in your book.

2. Read the words in line 1 to yourself. When you can read all three words, put your thumb up. (Wait until thumbs are up.)

3. Get ready to read the words in line 1 together. Begin. *trail, step, blown*

(Repeat steps 2 and 3 with lines 2–5. Then call on a student to read the words in a line.)

C. Word Endings—Altered Roots

(Have students open their books to Lesson 16, page 64.)

1. da<u>t</u>ing	4. fla<u>k</u>ing	7. tra<u>d</u>ing
2. pla<u>nn</u>ing	5. sha<u>p</u>ing	8. tra<u>pp</u>ing
3. ha<u>t</u>ing	6. sla<u>pp</u>ing	

1. Find part C in your book.

2. Look at number 1. How many **t**'s? *one*

3. Will you say the name or the sound for the letter **a**? *the name*

4. What is the name? *a*

5. Sound out the word to yourself. What is the word? *dating*

6. Look at number 2. How many **n**'s? *two*

7. Will you say the name or the sound for the letter **a**? *the sound*

8. What is the sound? */aaa/*

9. Sound out the word to yourself. What is the word? *planning*

10. Look at number 3. How many **t**'s? *one*

11. Will you say the name or the sound for the letter **a**? *the name*

12. What is the name? *a*

13. Sound out the word. What is the word? *hating*

14. Look at number 4. How many **k**'s? *one*

15. Will you say the name or the sound for the letter **a**? *the name*

16. What is the name? *a*

17. Sound out the word. What is the word? *flaking*

18. Look at number 5. How many **p**'s? *one*

19. Will you say the name or the sound for the letter **a**? *the name*

20. What is the name? *a*

21. Sound out the word. What is the word? *shaping*

(Repeat steps 18–21 with the remaining words. Adjust step 20 to the specific word—"What is the name?" or "What is the sound?")

22. Let's read these words again. (Call on individual students to read the words.)

D. Challenge Words

Have students open their books to Lesson 16, page 65.)

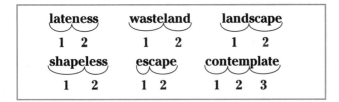

1. Find part D in your book.

2. Touch the first word. Sound out this word to yourself. Put your thumb up when you can say the word. (Wait until thumbs are up.) What is the word? *lateness*

3. Sound out the next word to yourself. Put your thumb up when you can say the word. (Wait until thumbs are up.) What is the word? *wasteland*

(Repeat step 3 with the words **landscape, shapeless, escape,** and **contemplate**.)

4. Let's read these words again. (Call on individual students to read the Challenge Words.)

E. Sight Words

(Have students open their books to Lesson 16, page 65.)

my	by	why	cry	dry
where	some	do	what	work
there	after	all	have	down

1. Find part E in your book.

2. Touch the first word. This word is **my**.
   What is the word? *my*
   Spell and read. *m-y. my*

3. The next word is **by**.
   What is the word? *by*
   Spell and read. *b-y. by*

(Repeat step 3 with the remaining words.)

4. Let's read these words again. (Call on individual students to read the Sight Words.)

F. Sentences and Stories

(Have students open their books to Lesson 16, page 65.)

1. Find part F in your book.

2. Touch the title of the story. Let's read the title together. *Crates to Pack*

3. Read Part 1 to yourself. Read it very carefully. Put your thumb up when you are done. (Wait until thumbs are up.)

4. Let's read Part 1 together. When you are not reading aloud, follow along in your book. (Call on a student to read one or two sentences. Continue until Part 1 has been read.)

5. Look at the three pictures. Put a number 1 under the picture that goes with Part 1.

(Repeat steps 3–5 with Parts 2 and 3.)

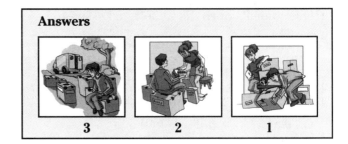

Answers

G. Spelling

(Have students open their books to Lesson 16, page 66.)

1. Find part G in your book.

2. Your first spelling word is **plate**. Write **plate**.

3. (Write the word on the board or display it on-screen.) Check and correct your word. (Monitor.)

(Repeat steps 2 and 3 with the word **plant**.)

4. Your next spelling word is **escape**.
   Say the parts in **escape**. First part. *es*
   Next part. *cape* Write the word.

5. (Write the word on the board or display it on-screen.) Check and correct your word.

(Repeat steps 4 and 5 with the word **contemplate**.)

6. Listen. **Did you see a flake of snow?**
   Write the sentence. (Monitor.)

7. (Write the sentence on the board or display it on-screen.) Check and correct each word. (Monitor.)

Answers
1. plate   3. escape
2. plant   4. contemplate
5. **Did you see a flake of snow?**

H. Practice Activity 1

(Have students open their books to Lesson 16, page 66.)

1. Find part H in your book.

2. Follow along as I read the directions. **Read the story. Answer the questions.**

3. Read the story to yourself. Do number 1. Put your thumb up when you are finished. (Monitor and check.)

4. You will finish part H later.

I. Practice Activity 2

(Have students open their books to Lesson 16, page 67.)

1. Find part I in your book.

2. Follow along as I read the directions. **Read each question. Look back at the story on page 65. Fill in each blank with the best word.**

3. Do number 1. Put your thumb up when you are finished. (Monitor and check.)

4. Now go back and finish parts H and I.

◀)) Work Check for Parts H and I
(Oral Teacher-Directed Activity)

1. Find part H in your book.

2. Let's check your work. If you made a mistake, circle the number. You will fix all mistakes at the end of the lesson. (Call on individual students to read their answers.)

3. Count how many correct answers you have, and write that number in the box at the bottom of the page. (Monitor students.)

(Repeat steps 1–3 with part I.)

4. Now go back and correct any mistakes. (Monitor students.)

Answers for Part H
1. **Skate Shop**
2. **ten**
3. **skates**
4. **skates**

Answers for Part I
1. stuff   5. flakes
2. skate   6. crates
3. case   7. plates
4. shelf   8. shame

◀)) Checking Up
(Oral Teacher-Directed Activity)

Practice reading Part 1 of the story on page 65. I am going to listen to each of you read. Your goal is to make fewer than two errors. Keep practicing Part 1 until you can read it without any errors.

(Ask each student to read Part 1. Record the number of errors in his or her book.

NOTE: If 90 percent of the students make two errors or fewer, you may move on to Lesson 17. If not, repeat Lesson 16.)

LESSON 17

OBJECTIVES

- *to introduce CVCe words with* i
- *to practice words altered by the word ending* -ing

🔊 New Sound

(Have students open their books to Lesson 17, page 68.)

1. Look at the top of page 68 in your book.

2. Touch the word.

3. This word is **five**. Say the word. *five*

4. Touch the letter **i**. When a word ends in **e**, we say the <u>name</u> of this letter. What is the <u>name</u> of this letter? *i*

(Have students close their books. Then do the Sound Drill activity.)

🔊 Sound Drill
(Oral Teacher-Directed Activity)

(Write the following on the board or display it on-screen:)

1. i	ai	oa	ow
2. ow	ea	ay	a
3. o	igh	u	ay
4. ee	e	ai	ea
5. oa	a	ee	igh

1. Let's practice saying the sounds in the words that we will be reading. Look at the letters in line 1. Say the sounds. */iii/, /āāā/, /ōōō/, /ōōō/*

2. Look at the letters in line 2. Say the sounds. */ōōō/, /ēēē/, /āāā/, /aaa/*

(Repeat step 2 with lines 3–5. Then call on individual students to say the sounds in a line.)

(NOTE: As an alternative, review the sounds with flash cards.)

A. New Words

(Have students open their books to Lesson 17, page 68.)

1.	line	ride	nine
2.	dim	dime	time
3.	hide	hid	white
4.	Tim	kite	kit
5.	ripe	rip	fine
6.	fin	smile	five

7. **The last train is at nine tonight.**
8. **Gill will loan you a dime.**
9. **The white shirt turned pink in the wash.**
10. **Pam was upset when her kite got stuck in the tree.**
11. **Do not eat the peach unless it is ripe.**
12. **Glen's smile told me that he had won.**

1. Find part A in your book.

2. Touch the first word in line 1. Does the word end in **e**? *yes*

3. Will you say the name or the sound for the letter **i**? *the name*

4. What is the name? *i*

5. Sound out the word to yourself. Put your thumb up when you can say the whole word. (Wait until thumbs are up.) What is the word? *line*

6. Touch the next word in line 1. Does this word end in **e**? *yes*

7. Will you say the name or the sound for the letter **i**? *the name*

8. What is the name? *i*

9. Sound out the word to yourself. Put your thumb up when you can say the whole word. (Wait until thumbs are up.) What is the word? *ride*

10. Touch the next word. Does this word end in **e**? *yes*

11. Will you say the name or the sound for the letter **i**? *the name*

12. What is the name? *i*

13. Sound out the word to yourself. Put your thumb up when you can say the whole word. (Wait until thumbs are up.) What is the word? *nine*

14. Touch the first word in line 2. Does the word end in **e**? *no*

15. Will you say the name or the sound for the letter **i**? *the sound*

16. What is the sound? */iii/*

17. Sound out the word to yourself. Put your thumb up when you can say the whole word. (Wait until thumbs are up.) What is the word? *dim*

18. Touch the next word. Does this word end in **e**? *yes*

19. Will you say the name or the sound for the letter **i**? *the name*

20. What is the name? *i*

21. Sound out the word to yourself. Put your thumb up when you can say the whole word. (Wait until thumbs are up.) What is the word? *dime*

(Repeat steps 18–21 with the remaining words in lines 2–3. Adjust step 20 to the specific word— "What is the name?" or "What is the sound?")

22. Touch the first word in line 4. Sound out this word to yourself. Say the sounds carefully. Put your thumb up when you can say the whole word. (Wait until thumbs are up.) What is the word? *Tim*

23. Touch the next word. Sound out the word to yourself. Put your thumb up when you can say the whole word. (Wait until thumbs are up.) What is the word? *kite*

(Repeat step 23 with the remaining words in lines 4–6. Then call on a student to read a line.)

24. Read sentence 7 to yourself. Put your thumb up when you are done. (Wait until thumbs are up. Then call on a student to read the sentence.)

(Repeat step 24 with sentences 8–12.)

B. Review Words

(Have students open their books to Lesson 17, page 68.)

1.	train	roam	grow
2.	green	grain	pray
3.	reel	rail	cheek
4.	fail	feel	sneak
5.	tent	fight	toast

1. Find part B in your book.

2. Read the words in line 1 to yourself. When you can read all three words, put your thumb up. (Wait until thumbs are up.)

3. Get ready to read the words in line 1 together. Begin. *train, roam, grow*

(Repeat steps 2 and 3 with lines 2–5. Then call on a student to read the words in a line.)

C. Word Endings—Altered Roots

(Have students open their books to Lesson 17, page 68.)

1.	ri<u>d</u>ing	4.	ti<u>m</u>ing	7.	li<u>n</u>ing
2.	hi<u>d</u>ing	5.	si<u>pp</u>ing	8.	smi<u>l</u>ing
3.	si<u>tt</u>ing	6.	wi<u>nn</u>ing		

1. Find part C in your book.

2. Look at number 1. How many **d**'s? *one*

3. Will you say the name or the sound for the letter **i**? *the name*

4. What is the name? *i*

5. Sound out the word to yourself. What is the word? *riding*

6. Look at number 2. How many **d**'s? *one*

7. Will you say the name or the sound for the letter **i**? *the name*

8. What is the name? *i*

9. Sound out the word to yourself. What is the word? *hiding*

10. Look at number 3. How many **t**'s? *two*

11. Will you say the name or the sound for the letter **i**? *the sound*

12. What is the sound? */iii/*

13. Sound out the word. What is the word? *sitting*

14. Look at number 4. How many **m**'s? *one*

15. Will you say the name or the sound for the letter **i**? *the name*

16. What is the name? *i*

17. Sound out the word. What is the word? *timing*

18. Look at number 5. How many **p**'s? *two*

19. Will you say the name or the sound for the letter **i**? *the sound*

20. What is the sound? */iii/*

21. Sound out the word. What is the word? *sipping*

(Repeat steps 18–21 with the remaining words. Adjust step 20 to the specific word—"What is the name?" or "What is the sound?")

22. Let's read these words again. (Call on individual students to read the words.)

D. Challenge Words

(Have students open their books to Lesson 17, page 69.)

dislike	nineteen	bathrobe	reptile
1 2	1 2	1 2	1 2

sideways	intimidate
1 2	1 2 3 4

1. Find part D in your book.

2. Touch the first word. Sound out this word to yourself. Put your thumb up when you can say the word. (Wait until thumbs are up.) What is the word? *dislike*

3. Sound out the next word to yourself. Put your thumb up when you can say the word. (Wait until thumbs are up.) What is the word? *nineteen*

(Repeat step 3 with the words **bathrobe, reptile, sideways,** and **intimidate**.)

4. Let's read these words again. (Call on individual students to read the Challenge Words.)

E. Sight Words

(Have students open their books to Lesson 17, page 69.)

my	why	try	dry	cry
what	school	after	where	some
do	were	there	of	all

1. Find part E in your book.

2. Touch the first word. This word is **my**. What is the word? *my* Spell and read. *m-y. my*

3. The next word is **why**. What is the word? *why* Spell and read. *w-h-y. why*

(Repeat step 3 with the remaining words.)

4. Let's read these words again. (Call on individual students to read the Sight Words.)

F. Sentences and Stories

(Have students open their books to Lesson 17, page 69.)

1. Find part F in your book.

2. Touch the title of the story. Let's read the title together. *The Plans*

3. Read Part 1 to yourself. Read it very carefully. Put your thumb up when you are done. (Wait until thumbs are up.)

4. Let's read Part 1 together. When you are not reading aloud, follow along in your book. (Call on a student to read one or two sentences. Continue until Part 1 has been read.)

5. Look at the three pictures. Put a number 1 under the picture that goes with Part 1.

(Repeat steps 3–5 with Parts 2 and 3.)

G. Spelling

(Have students open their books to Lesson 17, page 70.)

1. Find part G in your book.

2. Your first spelling word is **smile**. Write **smile**.

3. (Write the word on the board or display it on-screen.) Check and correct your word. (Monitor.)

(Repeat steps 2 and 3 with the word **white**.)

4. Your next spelling word is **nineteen**. Say the parts in **nineteen**. First part. *nine* Next part. *teen* Write the word.

5. (Write the word on the board or display it on-screen.) Check and correct your word.

(Repeat steps 4 and 5 with the word **reptile**.)

6. Listen. **Will you loan me a dime?** Write the sentence. (Monitor.)

7. (Write the sentence on the board or display it on-screen.) Check and correct each word. (Monitor.)

Answers
1. smile   3. nineteen
2. white   4. reptile
5. **Will you loan me a dime?**

H. Practice Activity 1

(Have students open their books to Lesson 17, page 70.)

1. Find part H in your book.

2. Follow along as I read the directions. **Read the story. Answer the questions.**

3. Read the story to yourself. Do number 1. Put your thumb up when you are finished. (Monitor and check.)

4. You will finish part H later.

I. Practice Activity 2

(Have students open their books to Lesson 17, page 71.)

1. Find part I in your book.

2. Follow along as I read the directions. **Read each question. Look back at the story on page 69. Fill in each blank with the best word.**

3. Do number 1. Put your thumb up when you are finished. (Monitor and check.)

4. Now go back and finish parts H and I.

🔊 Work Check for Parts H and I
(Oral Teacher-Directed Activity)

1. Find part H in your book.

2. Let's check your work. If you made a mistake, circle the number. You will fix all mistakes at the end of the lesson. (Call on individual students to read their answers.)

3. Count how many correct answers you have, and write that number in the box at the bottom of the page. (Monitor students.)

(Repeat steps 1–3 with part I.)

4. Now go back and correct any mistakes. (Monitor students.)

Answers for Part H
1. desk
2. five
3. plane
4. help

Answers for Part I

Part 1	Part 2	Part 3
1. peach tree	5. bike	7. club
2. May	6. kite	8. Trish, Meg
3. nine days		
4. peach		

LESSON 18

OBJECTIVES

- *to introduce CVCe words with o*
- *to practice words altered by the word ending -ing*

◀)) New Sound

(Have students open their books to Lesson 18, page 72.)

1. Look at the top of page 72 in your book.

2. Touch the word.

3. This word is **joke**. Say the word. *joke*

4. Touch the letter **o**. When a word ends in **e**, we say the <u>name</u> of this letter. What is the <u>name</u> of this letter? *o*

(Have students close their books. Then do the Sound Drill activity.)

◀)) Sound Drill
(Oral Teacher-Directed Activity)

(Write the following on the board or display it on-screen:)

1.	ay	igh	a	e
2.	ai	ea	oa	ee
3.	ow	o	ee	i
4.	oa	ee	igh	ow
5.	ea	ai	ay	o

1. Let's practice saying the sounds in the words that we will be reading. Look at the letters in line 1. Say the sounds. /$\overline{aaa}$/, /$\overline{iii}$/, /aaa/, /eee/

2. Look at the letters in line 2. Say the sounds. /$\overline{aaa}$/, /$\overline{eee}$/, /$\overline{ooo}$/, /$\overline{eee}$/

(Repeat step 2 with lines 3–5. Then call on individual students to say the sounds in a line.)

(NOTE: As an alternative, review the sounds with flash cards.)

A. New Words

(Have students open their books to Lesson 18, page 72.)

1.	robe	joke	bone
2.	rode	vote	rod
3.	hope	rob	note
4.	rose	not	hole
5.	hop	woke	poke
6.	cone	nose	code

7. **There was nothing left but the bone.**
8. **Do not forget to vote today.**
9. **I admit that I wrote the note.**
10. **The workers dug a hole for the new stoplight.**
11. **Nick insists that he woke up at six.**
12. **The child's cone fell on the sidewalk.**

1. Find part A in your book.

2. Touch the first word in line 1. Does the word end in **e**? *yes*

3. Will you say the name or the sound for the letter **o**? *the name*

4. What is the name? *o*

5. Sound out the word to yourself. Put your thumb up when you can say the whole word. (Wait until thumbs are up.) What is the word? *robe*

6. Touch the next word in line 1. Does this word end in **e**? *yes*

7. Will you say the name or the sound for the letter **o**? *the name*

8. What is the name? *o*

9. Sound out the word to yourself. Put your thumb up when you can say the whole word. (Wait until thumbs are up.) What is the word? *joke*

10. Touch the next word. Does this word end in **e**? *yes*

11. Will you say the name or the sound for the letter **o**? *the name*

12. What is the name? *o*

13. Sound out the word to yourself. Put your thumb up when you can say the whole word. (Wait until thumbs are up.) What is the word? *bone*

14. Touch the first word in line 2. Does the word end in **e**? *yes*

15. Will you say the name or the sound
    for the letter **o**? *the name*

16. What is the name? *o*

17. Sound out the word to yourself. Put your thumb
    up when you can say the whole word. (Wait
    until thumbs are up.) What is the word? *rode*

18. Touch the next word. Does this word
    end in **e**? *yes*

19. Will you say the name or the sound
    for the letter **o**? *the name*

20. What is the name? *o*

21. Sound out the word to yourself. Put your thumb
    up when you can say the whole word. (Wait
    until thumbs are up.) What is the word? *vote*

(Repeat steps 18–21 with the remaining words
in lines 2–3. Adjust step 20 to the specific word—
"What is the name?" or "What is the sound?")

22. Touch the first word in line 4. Sound out this
    word to yourself. Say the sounds carefully.
    Put your thumb up when you can say the
    whole word. (Wait until thumbs are up.)
    What is the word? *rose*

23. Touch the next word. Sound out the word to
    yourself. Put your thumb up when you can say
    the whole word. (Wait until thumbs are up.)
    What is the word? *not*

(Repeat step 23 with the remaining words in lines 4–6.
Then call on a student to read a line.)

24. Read sentence 7 to yourself. Put your thumb up
    when you are done. (Wait until thumbs are up.
    Then call on a student to read the sentence.)

(Repeat step 24 with sentences 8–12.)

B. Review Words

(Have students open their books to Lesson 18,
page 72.)

1. show	greet	spray
2. rain	ship	sleep
3. slip	bow	bee
4. soap	spend	coach
5. beast	seep	beat

1. Find part B in your book.

2. Read the words in line 1 to yourself. When you
   can read all three words, put your thumb up.
   (Wait until thumbs are up.)

3. Get ready to read the words in line 1
   together. Begin. *show, greet, spray*

(Repeat steps 2 and 3 with lines 2–5. Then call
on a student to read the words in a line.)

C. Word Endings—Altered Roots

(Have students open their books to Lesson 18,
page 72.)

1. hoping	4. noting	7. jogging
2. hopping	5. rotting	8. roping
3. joking	6. voting	

1. Find part C in your book.

2. Look at number 1. How many **p**'s? *one*

3. Will you say the name or the sound
   for the letter **o**? *the name*

4. What is the name? *o*

5. Sound out the word to yourself.
   What is the word? *hoping*

6. Look at number 2. How many **p**'s? *two*

7. Will you say the name or the sound
   for the letter **o**? *the sound*

8. What is the sound? */ooo/*

9. Sound out the word to yourself.
   What is the word? *hopping*

10. Look at number 3. How many **k**'s? *one*

11. Will you say the name or the sound
    for the letter **o**? *the name*

12. What is the name? *o*

13. Sound out the word. What is the word? *joking*

14. Look at number 4. How many **t**'s? *one*

15. Will you say the name or the sound
    for the letter **o**? *the name*

16. What is the name? *o*

17. Sound out the word. What is the word? *noting*

18. Look at number 5. How many **t**'s? *two*

19. Will you say the name or the sound for the letter **o**? *the sound*

20. What is the sound? */ooo/*

21. Sound out the word. What is the word? *rotting*

(Repeat steps 18–21 with the remaining words. Adjust step 20 to the specific word— "What is the name?" or "What is the sound?")

22. Let's read these words again. (Call on individual students to read the words.)

D. Challenge Words

(Have students open their books to Lesson 18, page 73.)

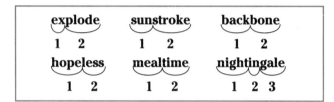

1. Find part D in your book.

2. Touch the first word. Sound out this word to yourself. Put your thumb up when you can say the word. (Wait until thumbs are up.) What is the word? *explode*

3. Sound out the next word to yourself. Put your thumb up when you can say the word. (Wait until thumbs are up.) What is the word? *sunstroke*

(Repeat step 3 with the words **backbone, hopeless, mealtime,** and **nightingale**.)

4. Let's read these words again. (Call on individual students to read the Challenge Words.)

E. Sight Words

(Have students open their books to Lesson 18, page 73.)

by	try	why	dry	cry
where	what	after	were	put
there	of	do	you	all

1. Find part E in your book.

2. Touch the first word. This word is **by**. What is the word? *by* Spell and read. *b-y. by*

3. The next word is **try**. What is the word? *try* Spell and read. *t-r-y. try*

(Repeat step 3 with the remaining words.)

4. Let's read these words again. (Call on individual students to read the Sight Words.)

F. Sentences and Stories

(Have students open their books to Lesson 18, page 73.)

1. Find part F in your book.

2. Touch the title of the story. Let's read the title together. *The Club*

3. Read Part 1 to yourself. Read it very carefully. Put your thumb up when you are done. (Wait until thumbs are up.)

4. Let's read Part 1 together. When you are not reading aloud, follow along in your book. (Call on a student to read one or two sentences. Continue until Part 1 has been read.)

5. Look at the three pictures. Put a number 1 under the picture that goes with Part 1.

(Repeat steps 3–5 with Parts 2 and 3.)

Answers

G. Spelling

(Have students open their books to Lesson 18, page 74.)

1. Find part G in your book.

2. Your first spelling word is **hope**. Write **hope**.

3. (Write the word on the board or display it on-screen.) Check and correct your word. (Monitor.)

(Repeat steps 2 and 3 with the word **cone**.)

4. Your next spelling word is **explode**. Say the parts in **explode**. First part. *ex* Next part. *plode* Write the word.

5. (Write the word on the board or display it on-screen.) Check and correct your word.

(Repeat steps 4 and 5 with the word **sunstroke**.)

6. Listen. **Did you vote today?** Write the sentence. (Monitor.)

7. (Write the sentence on the board or display it on-screen.) Check and correct each word. (Monitor.)

Answers
1. hope   3. explode
2. cone   4. sunstroke
5. Did you vote today?

H. Practice Activity 1

(Have students open their books to Lesson 18, page 74.)

1. Find part H in your book.

2. Follow along as I read the directions. **Read the story. Answer the questions.**

3. Read the story to yourself. Do number 1. Put your thumb up when you are finished. (Monitor and check.)

4. You will finish part H later.

I. Practice Activity 2

(Have students open their books to Lesson 18, page 75.)

1. Find part I in your book.

2. Follow along as I read the directions. **Read each question. Look back at the story on page 73. Fill in each blank with the best word.**

3. Do number 1. Put your thumb up when you are finished. (Monitor and check.)

4. Now go back and finish parts H and I.

🔊 Work Check for Parts H and I
(Oral Teacher-Directed Activity)

1. Find part H in your book.

2. Let's check your work. If you made a mistake, circle the number. You will fix all mistakes at the end of the lesson. (Call on individual students to read their answers.)

3. Count how many correct answers you have, and write that number in the box at the bottom of the page. (Monitor students.)

(Repeat steps 1–3 with part I.)

4. Now go back and correct any mistakes. (Monitor students.)

Answers for Part H
1. dock
2. rod, reel
3. fish
4. three

Answers for Part I

Part 1	Part 2	Part 3
1. grass	4. Slow Pokes	6. code
2. club code	5. STEAM	7. Bike
3. pine tree		8. Kite

LESSON 19

OBJECTIVES

- *to practice CVCe words with* a, i, *and* o
- *to practice words altered by the word ending* -ing

 Sound Drill
(Oral Teacher-Directed Activity)

(Write the following on the board or display it on-screen:)

1.	i	ai	a	oa
2.	ea	igh	ow	ee
3.	ay	oa	igh	o
4.	ow	a	ee	ai
5.	e	igh	ay	ea

1. Let's practice saying the sounds in the words that we will be reading. Look at the letters in line 1. Say the sounds. /iii/, /āāā/, /aaa/, /ōōō/

2. Look at the letters in line 2. Say the sounds. /ēēē/, /ūū/, /ōōō/, /ēēē/

(Repeat step 2 with lines 3–5. Then call on individual students to say the sounds in a line.)

(NOTE: As an alternative, review the sounds with flash cards.)

A. New Words

(Have students open their books to Lesson 19, page 76.)

1.	pave	pill	pile
2.	fine	fin	shade
3.	ram	those	frame
4.	smoke	rope	smock
5.	pine	pin	side
6.	Sid	spoke	drive

7. When are they going to pave the road?
8. It is fine with us if you stay here.
9. Those pancakes smell so good.
10. Tie the rope onto the handrail.
11. The pine tree cast a long shadow.
12. Drive on the highway for six miles.

1. Find part A in your book.

2. Touch the first word in line 1. Does the word end in **e**? *yes*

3. Will you say the name or the sound for the letter **a**? *the name*

4. What is the name? *a*

5. Sound out the word to yourself. Put your thumb up when you can say the whole word. (Wait until thumbs are up.) What is the word? *pave*

6. Touch the next word in line 1. Does this word end in **e**? *no*

7. Will you say the name or the sound for the letter **i**? *the sound*

8. What is the sound? */iii/*

9. Sound out the word to yourself. Put your thumb up when you can say the whole word. (Wait until thumbs are up.) What is the word? *pill*

10. Touch the next word. Does this word end in **e**? *yes*

11. Will you say the name or the sound for the letter **i**? *the name*

12. What is the name? *i*

13. Sound out the word to yourself. Put your thumb up when you can say the whole word. (Wait until thumbs are up.) What is the word? *pile*

14. Touch the first word in line 2. Does the word end in **e**? *yes*

15. Will you say the name or the sound for the letter **i**? *the name*

16. What is the name? *i*

17. Sound out the word to yourself. Put your thumb up when you can say the whole word. (Wait until thumbs are up.) What is the word? *fine*

18. Touch the next word. Does this word end in **e**? *no*

19. Will you say the name or the sound for the letter **i**? *the sound*

20. What is the sound? */iii/*

21. Sound out the word to yourself. Put your thumb up when you can say the whole word. (Wait until thumbs are up.) What is the word? *fin*

(Repeat steps 18–21 with the remaining words in lines 2–3. Adjust step 20 to the specific word— "What is the name?" or "What is the sound?")

22. Touch the first word in line 4. Sound out this word to yourself. Say the sounds carefully. Put your thumb up when you can say the whole word. (Wait until thumbs are up.) What is the word? *smoke*

23. Touch the next word. Sound out the word to yourself. Put your thumb up when you can say the whole word. (Wait until thumbs are up.) What is the word? *rope*

(Repeat step 23 with the remaining words in lines 4–6. Then call on a student to read a line.)

24. Read sentence 7 to yourself. Put your thumb up when you are done. (Wait until thumbs are up. Then call on a student to read the sentence.)

(Repeat step 24 with sentences 8–12.)

B. Review Words

(Have students open their books to Lesson 19, page 76.)

1. treat	road	train
2. dream	grain	groan
3. stay	show	sheep
4. ship	hail	might
5. grow	stream	stem

1. Find part B in your book.

2. Read the words in line 1 to yourself. When you can read all three words, put your thumb up. (Wait until thumbs are up.)

3. Get ready to read the words in line 1 together. Begin. *treat, road, train*

(Repeat steps 2 and 3 with lines 2–5. Then call on a student to read the words in a line.)

C. Word Endings—Altered Roots

(Have students open their books to Lesson 19, page 76.)

1. pa<u>v</u>ing	4. smoking	7. di<u>gg</u>ing
2. di<u>pp</u>ing	5. fi<u>tt</u>ing	8. dri<u>v</u>ing
3. si<u>pp</u>ing	6. pi<u>l</u>ing	

1. Find part C in your book.

2. Look at number 1. How many **v**'s? *one*

3. Will you say the name or the sound for the letter **a**? *the name*

4. What is the name? *a*

5. Sound out the word to yourself. What is the word? *paving*

6. Look at number 2. How many **p**'s? *two*

7. Will you say the name or the sound for the letter **i**? *the sound*

8. What is the sound? */iii/*

9. Sound out the word to yourself. What is the word? *dipping*

10. Look at number 3. How many **p**'s? *two*

11. Will you say the name or the sound for the letter **i**? *the sound*

12. What is the sound? */iii/*

13. Sound out the word. What is the word? *sipping*

14. Look at number 4. How many **k**'s? *one*

15. Will you say the name or the sound for the letter **o**? *the name*

16. What is the name? *o*

17. Sound out the word. What is the word? *smoking*

18. Look at number 5. How many **t**'s? *two*

19. Will you say the name or the sound for the letter **i**? *the sound*

20. What is the sound? */iii/*

21. Sound out the word. What is the word? *fitting*

(Repeat steps 18–21 with the remaining words. Adjust step 20 to the specific word—"What is the name?" or "What is the sound?")

22. Let's read these words again. (Call on individual students to read the words.)

D. Challenge Words

(Have students open their books to Lesson 19, page 77.)

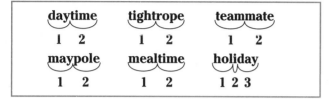

1. Find part D in your book.

2. Touch the first word. Sound out this word to yourself. Put your thumb up when you can say the word. (Wait until thumbs are up.) What is the word? *daytime*

3. Sound out the next word to yourself. Put your thumb up when you can say the word. (Wait until thumbs are up.) What is the word? *tightrope*

(Repeat step 3 with the words **teammate, maypole, mealtime,** and **holiday**.)

4. Let's read these words again. (Call on individual students to read the Challenge Words.)

E. Sight Words

(Have students open their books to Lesson 19, page 77.)

my	dry	why	cry	by
what	school	where	from	are
all	you	saw	do	there

1. Find part E in your book.

2. Touch the first word. This word is **my**.
   What is the word? *my*
   Spell and read. *m-y. my*

3. The next word is **dry**.
   What is the word? *dry*
   Spell and read. *d-r-y. dry*

(Repeat step 3 with the remaining words.)

4. Let's read these words again. (Call on individual students to read the Sight Words.)

F. Sentences and Stories

(Have students open their books to Lesson 19, page 77.)

1. Find part F in your book.

2. Touch the title of the story. Let's read the title together. *The Note*

3. Read Part 1 to yourself. Read it very carefully. Put your thumb up when you are done. (Wait until thumbs are up.)

4. Let's read Part 1 together. When you are not reading aloud, follow along in your book. (Call on a student to read one or two sentences. Continue until Part 1 has been read.)

5. Look at the three pictures. Put a number 1 under the picture that goes with Part 1.

(Repeat steps 3–5 with Parts 2 and 3.)

G. Spelling

(Have students open their books to Lesson 19, page 78.)

1. Find part G in your book.

2. Your first spelling word is **shade**. Write **shade**.

3. (Write the word on the board or display it on-screen.) Check and correct your word. (Monitor.)

(Repeat steps 2 and 3 with the word **those**.)

4. Your next spelling word is **daytime**.
   Say the parts in **daytime**. First part. *day*
   Next part. *time* Write the word.

5. (Write the word on the board or display it on-screen.) Check and correct your word.

(Repeat steps 4 and 5 with the word **holiday**.)

6. Listen. **Are they going to pave the road?**
Write the sentence. (Monitor.)

7. (Write the sentence on the board or display it on-screen.) Check and correct each word. (Monitor.)

```
Answers
1.  shade      3.  daytime
2.  those      4.  holiday
5.  Are they going to pave the road?
```

H. Practice Activity 1

(Have students open their books to Lesson 19, page 78.)

1. Find part H in your book.

2. Follow along as I read the directions. **Fill in each blank with the best word.**

3. Do number 1. Put your thumb up when you are finished. (Monitor and check.)

4. You will finish part H later.

I. Practice Activity 2

(Have students open their books to Lesson 19, page 79.)

1. Find part I in your book.

2. Follow along as I read the directions. **Read each question. Look back at the story on page 77. Fill in each blank with the best word.**

3. Do number 1. Put your thumb up when you are finished. (Monitor and check.)

4. Now go back and finish parts H and I.

Work Check for Parts H and I
(Oral Teacher-Directed Activity)

1. Find part H in your book.

2. Let's check your work. If you made a mistake, circle the number. You will fix all mistakes at the end of the lesson. (Call on individual students to read their answers.)

3. Count how many correct answers you have, and write that number in the box at the bottom of the page. (Monitor students.)

(Repeat steps 1–3 with part I.)

4. Now go back and correct any mistakes. (Monitor students.)

```
Answers for Part H
1.  spoke      4.  smiling
2.  cone       5.  digging
3.  tame
```

```
Answers for Part I
Part 1            Part 2            Part 3
1.  pine tree     4.  code name     6.  five
2.  note          5.  school        7.  code name
3.  Lane Bank                       8.  STREAM
                                        Club
```

LESSON 20

OBJECTIVES

- *to practice CVCe words with* a, i, *and* o
- *to practice words altered by the word ending* -ing

 Sound Drill
(Oral Teacher-Directed Activity)

(Write the following on the board or display it on-screen:)

1.	ea	ay	igh	i
2.	ai	ea	e	oa
3.	ee	a	i	ai
4.	oa	igh	ow	o
5.	ee	ow	a	ay

1. Let's practice saying the sounds in the words that we will be reading. Look at the letters in line 1. Say the sounds. /ēēē/, /āāā/, /īīī/, /iii/

2. Look at the letters in line 2. Say the sounds. /āāā/, /ēēē/, /eee/, /ōōō/

(Repeat step 2 with lines 3–5. Then call on individual students to say the sounds in a line.)

(NOTE: As an alternative, review the sounds with flash cards.)

A. New Words

(Have students open their books to Lesson 20, page 80.)

1.	bike	brat	save
2.	blame	glob	globe
3.	lick	vase	like
4.	mill	mile	shape
5.	cave	whip	wide
6.	slid	broke	slide

7. **Can I save this basket to keep my crayons in?**
8. **Use the globe to show us where you were.**
9. **Jim would like a new jacket.**
10. **Traffic was backed up for a mile.**
11. **We saw a dim light in the cave.**
12. **The eggshell broke when I dropped the egg.**

1. Find part A in your book.

2. Touch the first word in line 1. Does the word end in **e**? *yes*

3. Will you say the name or the sound for the letter **i**? *the name*

4. What is the name? *i*

5. Sound out the word to yourself. Put your thumb up when you can say the whole word. (Wait until thumbs are up.) What is the word? *bike*

6. Touch the next word in line 1. Does this word end in **e**? *no*

7. Will you say the name or the sound for the letter **a**? *the sound*

8. What is the sound? */aaa/*

9. Sound out the word to yourself. Put your thumb up when you can say the whole word. (Wait until thumbs are up.) What is the word? *brat*

10. Touch the next word. Does this word end in **e**? *yes*

11. Will you say the name or the sound for the letter **a**? *the name*

12. What is the name? *a*

13. Sound out the word to yourself. Put your thumb up when you can say the whole word. (Wait until thumbs are up.) What is the word? *save*

14. Touch the first word in line 2. Does the word end in **e**? *yes*

15. Will you say the name or the sound for the letter **a**? *the name*

16. What is the name? *a*

17. Sound out the word to yourself. Put your thumb up when you can say the whole word. (Wait until thumbs are up.) What is the word? *blame*

18. Touch the next word. Does this word end in **e**? *no*

19. Will you say the name or the sound for the letter **o**? *the sound*

20. What is the sound? */ooo/*

21. Sound out the word to yourself. Put your thumb up when you can say the whole word. (Wait until thumbs are up.) What is the word? *glob*

(Repeat steps 18–21 with the remaining words in lines 2–3. Adjust step 20 to the specific word— What is the name?" or "What is the sound?")

22. Touch the first word in line 4. Sound out this word to yourself. Say the sounds carefully. Put your thumb up when you can say the whole word. (Wait until thumbs are up.) What is the word? *mill*

23. Touch the next word. Sound out the word to yourself. Put your thumb up when you can say the whole word. (Wait until thumbs are up.) What is the word? *mile*

(Repeat step 23 with the remaining words in lines 4–6. Then call on a student to read a line.)

24. Read sentence 7 to yourself. Put your thumb up when you are done. (Wait until thumbs are up. Then call on a student to read the sentence.)

(Repeat step 24 with sentences 8–12.)

B. Review Words

(Have students open their books to Lesson 20, page 80.)

1.	flow	stain	stop
2.	steam	soap	coat
3.	cot	blown	clean
4.	clap	nail	right
5.	fight	fit	float

1. Find part B in your book.

2. Read the words in line 1 to yourself. When you can read all three words, put your thumb up. (Wait until thumbs are up.)

3. Get ready to read the words in line 1 together. Begin. *flow, stain, stop*

(Repeat steps 2 and 3 with lines 2–5. Then call on a student to read the words in a line.)

C. Word Endings—Altered Roots

(Have students open their books to Lesson 20, page 80.)

1.	bik<u>ing</u>	4.	hi<u>tt</u>ing	7.	sa<u>v</u>ing
2.	bla<u>m</u>ing	5.	li<u>k</u>ing	8.	sli<u>d</u>ing
3.	ho<u>pp</u>ing	6.	sto<u>pp</u>ing		

1. Find part C in your book.

2. Look at number 1. How many **k**'s? *one*

3. Will you say the name or the sound for the letter **i**? *the name*

4. What is the name? *i*

5. Sound out the word to yourself. What is the word? *biking*

6. Look at number 2. How many **m**'s? *one*

7. Will you say the name or the sound for the letter **a**? *the name*

8. What is the name? *a*

9. Sound out the word to yourself. What is the word? *blaming*

10. Look at number 3. How many **p**'s? *two*

11. Will you say the name or the sound for the letter **o**? *the sound*

12. What is the sound? */ooo/*

13. Sound out the word. What is the word? *hopping*

14. Look at number 4. How many **t**'s? *two*

15. Will you say the name or the sound for the letter **i**? *the sound*

16. What is the sound? */iii/*

17. Sound out the word. What is the word? *hitting*

18. Look at number 5. How many **k**'s? *one*

19. Will you say the name or the sound for the letter **i**? *the name*

20. What is the name? *i*

21. Sound out the word. What is the word? *liking*

(Repeat steps 18–21 with the remaining words. Adjust step 20 to the specific word—"What is the name?" or "What is the sound?")

22. Let's read these words again. (Call on individual students to read the words.)

D. Challenge Words

(Have students open their books to Lesson 20, page 81.)

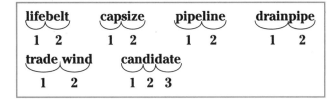

lifebelt	capsize	pipeline	drainpipe
1 2	1 2	1 2	1 2

trade wind	candidate
1 2	1 2 3

1. Find part D in your book.

2. Touch the first word. Sound out this word to yourself. Put your thumb up when you can say the word. (Wait until thumbs are up.) What is the word? *lifebelt*

3. Sound out the next word to yourself. Put your thumb up when you can say the word. (Wait until thumbs are up.) What is the word? *capsize*

(Repeat step 3 with the words **pipeline, drainpipe, trade wind,** and **candidate**.)

4. Let's read these words again. (Call on individual students to read the Challenge Words.)

E. Sight Words

(Have students open their books to Lesson 20, page 81.)

my	by	why	cry	dry
what	after	were	where	you
all	said	there	do	she

1. Find part E in your book.

2. Touch the first word. This word is **my**. What is the word? *my* Spell and read. *m-y. my*

3. The next word is **by**. What is the word? *by* Spell and read *b-y. by*

(Repeat step 3 with the remaining words.)

4. Let's read these words again. (Call on individual students to read the Sight Words.)

F. Sentences and Stories

(Have students open their books to Lesson 20, page 81.)

1. Find part F in your book.

2. Touch the title of the story. Let's read the title together. *Beth's Frog Game*

3. Read Part 1 to yourself. Read it very carefully. Put your thumb up when you are done. (Wait until thumbs are up.)

4. Let's read Part 1 together. When you are not reading aloud, follow along in your book. (Call on a student to read one or two sentences. Continue until Part 1 has been read.)

5. Look at the three pictures. Put a number 1 under the picture that goes with Part 1.

(Repeat step 3–5 with Parts 2 and 3.)

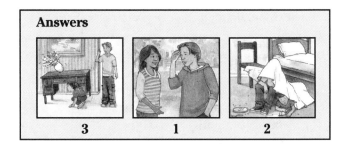

Answers

3	1	2

G. Spelling

(Have students open their books to Lesson 20, page 82.)

1. Find part G in your book.

2. Your first spelling word is **globe**. Write **globe**.

3. (Write the word on the board or display it on-screen.) Check and correct your word. (Monitor.)

(Repeat steps 2 and 3 with the word **shape**.)

4. Your next spelling word is **pipeline**. Say the parts in **pipeline**. First part. *pipe* Next part. *line* Write the word.

5. (Write the word on the board or display it on-screen.) Check and correct your word.

(Repeat steps 4 and 5 with the word **trade wind**.)

6. Listen. **Traffic was backed up for a mile.** Write the sentence. (Monitor.)

7. (Write the sentence on the board or display it on-screen.) Check and correct each word. (Monitor.)

```
Answers
1.  globe      3.  pipeline
2.  shape      4.  trade wind
5.  Traffic was backed up for a mile.
```

H. Practice Activity 1

(Have students open their books to Lesson 20, page 82.)

1. Find part H in your book.

2. Follow along as I read the directions. **Read the story. Fill in each blank with the best word.**

3. Read the story to yourself. Do number 1. Put your thumb up when you are finished. (Monitor and check.)

4. You will finish part H later.

I. Practice Activity 2

(Have students open their books to Lesson 20, page 83.)

1. Find part I in your book.

2. Follow along as I read the directions. **Read each question. Look back at the story on page 81. Fill in each blank with the best word.**

3. Do number 1. Put your thumb up when you are finished. (Monitor and check.)

4. Now go back and finish parts H and I.

Work Check for Parts H and I
(Oral Teacher-Directed Activity)

1. Find part H in your book.

2. Let's check your work. If you made a mistake, circle the number. You will fix all mistakes at the end of the lesson. (Call on individual students to read their answers.)

3. Count how many correct answers you have, and write that number in the box at the bottom of the page. (Monitor students.)

(Repeat steps 1–3 with part I.)

4. Now go back and correct any mistakes. (Monitor students.)

```
Answers for Part H
1.  dry      3.  five
2.  drive    4.  show
```

```
Answers for Part I
Part 1            Part 2           Part 3
1.  show          4.  cave         7.  frog
2.  play          5.  side         8.  desk
3.  stay home     6.  cave
```

Checking Up
(Oral Teacher-Directed Activity)

Practice reading Part 1 of the story on page 81. I am going to listen to each of you read. Your goal is to make fewer than two errors. Keep practicing Part 1 until you can read it without any errors.

(Ask each student to read part 1. Record the number of errors in his or her book.

NOTE: If 90 percent of the students make two errors or fewer, you may move on to Lesson 21. If not, repeat Lesson 20.)

LESSON 21

OBJECTIVES

- *to introduce words with* ar
- *to practice words with the word endings* -ed *and* -ing

🔊 New Sound

(Have students open their books to Lesson 21, page 84.)

1. Look at the top of page 84 in your book.

2. Touch the word.

3. This word is **car**. Say the word. *car*

4. The underlined sound is **/ar/**. Say the sound. */ar/*

5. Say the sound again. */ar/*

(Have students close their books. Then do the Sound Drill activity.)

🔊 Sound Drill
(Oral Teacher-Directed Activity)

(Write the following on the board or display it on-screen:)

1.	ar	igh	ea	ai
2.	ee	ar	ow	oa
3.	o	ea	ar	ay
4.	ai	ar	oa	igh
5.	ar	ow	o	ee

1. Let's practice saying the sounds in the words that we will be reading. Look at the letters in line 1. Say the sounds. */ar/, /īī/, /ēēē/, /āāā/*

2. Look at the letters in line 2. Say the sounds. */ēēē/, /ar/, /ōōō/, /ōōō/*

(Repeat step 2 with lines 3–5. Then call on individual students to say the sounds in a line.)

(NOTE: As an alternative, review the sounds with flash cards.)

A. New Words

(Have students open their books to Lesson 21, page 84.)

1.	car	bark	far
2.	farm	foam	Barb
3.	star	part	stay
4.	park	peek	fight
5.	march	barn	paint
6.	start	steam	smart

7. How far is it to the cabin?
8. Our farm will go up for sale next week.
9. Barb is hoping to get the star role in the play.
10. Don't park your car too close to mine.
11. Soon the barn will be filled with wheat.
12. "Smart people make mistakes too," he said.

1. Find part A in your book.

2. Touch the first word in line 1. Look at the underlined letters. What is the sound? */ar/*

3. Sound out the word to yourself. Put your thumb up when you can say the whole word. (Wait until thumbs are up.) What is the word? *car*

4. Touch the next word. Look at the underlined letters. What is the sound? */ar/* Sound out the word to yourself. Put your thumb up when you can say the whole word. (Wait until thumbs are up.) What is the word? *bark*

(Repeat step 4 with the remaining words in lines 1–3.)

5. Touch the first word in line 4. Sound out this word to yourself. Put your thumb up when you can say the whole word. (Wait until thumbs are up.) What is the word? *park*

6. Touch the next word. Sound out the word to yourself. Put your thumb up when you can say the whole word. (Wait until thumbs are up.) What is the word? *peek*

(Repeat step 6 with the remaining words in lines 4–6. Then call on individual students to read a line.)

7. Read sentence 7 to yourself. Put your thumb up when you are done. (Wait until thumbs are up. Then call on a student to read the sentence.)

(Repeat step 7 with sentences 8–12.)

B. Review Words

(Have students open their books to Lesson 21, page 84.)

1. twin	twine	drape
2. pride	spine	spin
3. stone	grave	blaze
4. robe	rob	while
5. wide	chase	close

1. Find part B in your book.

2. Read the words in line 1 to yourself. When you can read all three words, put your thumb up. (Wait until thumbs are up.)

3. Get ready to read the words in line 1 together. Begin. *twin, twine, drape*

(Repeat steps 2 and 3 with lines 2–5. Then call on a student to read the words in a line.)

C. Word Endings—Altered Roots

(Have students open their books to Lesson 21, page 84.)

1. spi<u>nn</u>ing	6. <u>barked</u> <u>barking</u>	9. <u>parked</u> <u>parking</u>
2. bla<u>z</u>ing		
3. ro<u>bb</u>ed	7. <u>farmed</u> <u>farming</u>	10. <u>painted</u> <u>painting</u>
4. cha<u>s</u>ed		
5. clo<u>s</u>ed	8. <u>started</u> <u>starting</u>	

1. Find part C in your book.

2. Look at number 1. How many **n**'s? *two*

3. Will you say the name or the sound for the letter **i**? *the sound*

4. What is the sound? */iii/*

5. Sound out the word to yourself. What is the word? *spinning*

6. Look at number 2. How many **z**'s? *one*

7. Will you say the name or the sound for the letter **a**? *the name*

8. What is the name? *a*

9. Sound out the word to yourself. What is the word? *blazing*

10. Sound out number 3 to yourself. Put your thumb up when you can read the word. (Wait until thumbs are up.) What is the word? *robbed*

(Repeat step 10 with the words **chased** and **closed**.)

11. Let's read these five words again. (Call on individual students to read the words.)

12. Look at number 6. Sound out the underlined word to yourself. Put your thumb up when you can say the underlined word. (Wait until thumbs are up.) What is the word? *bark*

13. Read **bark** with the endings.
    What is the first word? *barked*
    What is the second word? *barking*

(Repeat steps 12 and 13 with the remaining words.)

14. Let's read these words again. (Call on individual students to read the words.)

D. Challenge Words

(Have students open their books to Lesson 21, page 85.)

artist	carpet	marlin	garden
1 2	1 2	1 2	1 2
harvest	artistic		
1 2	1 2 3		

1. Find part D in your book.

2. Touch the first word. Sound out this word to yourself. Put your thumb up when you can say the word. (Wait until thumbs are up.) What is the word? *artist*

3. Sound out the next word to yourself. Put your thumb up when you can say the word. (Wait until thumbs are up.) What is the word? *carpet*

(Repeat step 3 with the words **marlin, garden, harvest,** and **artistic**.)

4. Let's read these words again. (Call on individual students to read the Challenge Words.)

E. Sight Words

(Have students open their books to Lesson 21, page 85.)

would	should	could	been	what
some	by	where	you	all
do	of	said		

1. Find part E in your book.

2. Touch the first word. This word is **would**.
   What is the word? *would*
   Spell and read. *w-o-u-l-d. would*

3. The next word is **should**.
   What is the word? *should*
   Spell and read. *s-h-o-u-l-d. should*

(Repeat step 3 with the remaining words.)

4. Let's read these words again. (Call on individual students to read the Sight Words.)

F. Sentences and Stories

(Have students open their books to Lesson 21, page 85.)

1. Find part F in your book.

2. Touch the title of the story. Let's read the title together. *Dad Tells the Plan*

3. Read Part 1 to yourself. Read it very carefully. Put your thumb up when you are done.
   (Wait until thumbs are up.)

4. Let's read Part 1 together. When you are not reading aloud, follow along in your book.
   (Call on a student to read one or two sentences. Continue until Part 1 has been read.)

5. Look at the three pictures. Put a number 1 under the picture that goes with Part 1.

(Repeat steps 3–5 with Parts 2 and 3.)

Answers

(pictures numbered 3, 1, 2)

G. Spelling

(Have students open their books to Lesson 21, page 86.)

1. Find part G in your book.

2. Your first spelling word is **farm**. Write **farm**.

3. (Write the word on the board or display it on-screen.) Check and correct your word. (Monitor.)

(Repeat steps 2 and 3 with the word **march**.)

4. Your next spelling word is **carpet**.
   Say the parts in **carpet**. First part. *car*
   Next part. *pet* Write the word.

5. (Write the word on the board or display it on-screen.) Check and correct your word.

(Repeat steps 4 and 5 with the word **artistic**.)

6. Listen. **Barb has a star role in the play.**
   Write the sentence. (Monitor.)

7. (Write the sentence on the board or display it on-screen.) Check and correct each word. (Monitor.)

Answers
1. farm   3. carpet
2. march   4. artistic
5. **Barb has a star role in the play.**

H. Practice Activity 1

(Have students open their books to Lesson 21, page 86.)

1. Find part H in your book.

2. Follow along as I read the directions. **Read the story. Answer the questions.**

3. Read the story to yourself. Do number 1. Put your thumb up when you are finished. (Monitor and check.)

4. You will finish part H later.

I. Practice Activity 2

(Have students open their books to Lesson 21, page 87.)

1. Find part I in your book.

2. Follow along as I read the directions. **Read each question. Look back at the story on page 85. Fill in each blank with the best word.**

3. Do number 1. Put your thumb up when you are finished. (Monitor and check.)

4. Now go back and finish parts H and I.

Work Check for Parts H and I
(Oral Teacher-Directed Activity)

1. Find part H in your book.

2. Let's check your work. If you made a mistake, circle the number. You will fix all mistakes at the end of the lesson. (Call on individual students to read their answers.)

3. Count how many correct answers you have, and write that number in the box at the bottom of the page. (Monitor students.)

(Repeat steps 1–3 with part I.)

4. Now go back and correct any mistakes. (Monitor students.)

Answers for Part H
1. show
2. ten
3. Beach Road
4. steam

Answers for Part I

Part 1	Part 2	Part 3
1. ill	3. beach	6. tonight
2. farm	4. look	7. ten
	5. time	8. three

LESSON 22

OBJECTIVES

- *to practice words with* ar
- *to practice words with the word endings* -ed *and* -ing

🔊 Sound Drill
(Oral Teacher-Directed Activity)

(Write the following on the board or display it on-screen:)

1.	ai	oa	a	ar
2.	ow	ar	ea	ay
3.	i	ee	igh	ar
4.	ar	oa	o	ea
5.	ai	i	a	ar

1. Let's practice saying the sounds in the words that we will be reading. Look at the letters in line 1. Say the sounds. /$\overline{aaa}$/, /$\overline{ooo}$/, /aaa/, /ar/

2. Look at the letters in line 2. Say the sounds. /$\overline{ooo}$/, /ar/, /$\overline{eee}$/, /$\overline{aaa}$/

(Repeat step 2 with lines 3–5. Then call on individual students to say the sounds in a line.)

(NOTE: As an alternative, review the sounds with flash cards.)

A. New Words

(Have students open their books to Lesson 22, page 88.)

1.	jar	arm	hard
2.	scar	Jay	speed
3.	aim	spark	art
4.	eat	mark	card
5.	marsh	meek	might
6.	yard	oats	scarf

7. Fill the glass jar with water.
8. Will there be a scar when the cut heals?
9. Don took the canvas to art class.
10. Mark your mistakes in red pen.
11. This bird makes its nest in the tall marsh.
12. I will plant a garden in part of the yard.

1. Find part A in your book.
2. Touch the first word in line 1. Look at the underlined letters. What is the sound? /ar/
3. Sound out the word. Put your thumb up when you can say the whole word. (Wait until thumbs are up.) What is the word? *jar*
4. Touch the next word. Look at the underlined letters. What is the sound? /ar/ Sound out the word to yourself. Put your thumb up when you can say the whole word. (Wait until thumbs are up.) What is the word? *arm*

(Repeat step 4 with the remaining words in lines 1–3.)

5. Touch the first word in line 4. Sound out this word to yourself. Put your thumb up when you can say the whole word. (Wait until thumbs are up.) What is the word? *eat*
6. Touch the next word. Sound out the word to yourself. Put your thumb up when you can say the whole word. (Wait until thumbs are up.) What is the word? *mark*

(Repeat step 6 with the remaining words in lines 4–6. Then call on a student to read a line.)

7. Read sentence 7 to yourself. Put your thumb up when you are done. (Wait until thumbs are up. Then call on a student to read the sentence.)

(Repeat step 7 with sentences 8–12.)

B. Review Words

(Have students open their books to Lesson 22, page 88.)

1.	mope	mop	home
2.	prize	fill	file
3.	choke	graze	blade
4.	bad	fin	fine
5.	froze	tap	tape

1. Find part B in your book.
2. Read the words in line 1 to yourself. When you can read all three words, put your thumb up. (Wait until thumbs are up.)
3. Get ready to read the words in line 1 together. Begin. *mope, mop, home*

(Repeat steps 2 and 3 with lines 2–5. Then call on a student to read the words in a line.)

C. Word Endings—Altered Roots

(Have students open their books to Lesson 22, page 88.)

1.	fi<u>l</u>ed	6.	<u>aimed</u>	9.	<u>steamed</u>
2.	ta<u>pp</u>ed		<u>aiming</u>		<u>steaming</u>
3.	cho<u>k</u>ed	7.	<u>marked</u>	10.	<u>parted</u>
4.	wi<u>nn</u>ing		<u>marking</u>		<u>parting</u>
5.	ta<u>p</u>ed	8.	<u>stayed</u>		
			<u>staying</u>		

1. Find part C in your book.

2. Look at number 1. How many **l**'s? *one*

3. Will you say the name or the sound for the letter **i**? *the name*

4. What is the name? *i*

5. Sound out the word to yourself. What is the word? *filed*

6. Look at number 2. How many **p**'s? *two*

7. Will you say the name or the sound for the letter **a**? *the sound*

8. What is the sound? */aaa/*

9. Sound out the word to yourself. What is the word? *tapped*

10. Sound out number 3 to yourself. Put your thumb up when you can read the word. (Wait until thumbs are up.) What is the word? *choked*

(Repeat step 10 with the words **winning** and **taped**.)

11. Let's read these five words again. (Call on individual students to read the words.)

12. Look at number 6. Sound out the underlined word to yourself. Put your thumb up when you can say the underlined word. (Wait until thumbs are up.) What is the word? *aim*

13. Read **aim** with the endings. What is the first word? *aimed* What is the second word? *aiming*

(Repeat steps 12 and 13 with the remaining words.)

14. Let's read these words again. (Call on individual students to read the words.)

D. Challenge Words

(Have students open their books to Lesson 22, page 89.)

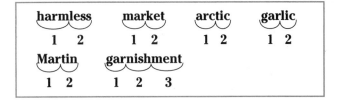

1. Find part D in your book.

2. Touch the first word. Sound out this word to yourself. Put your thumb up when you can say the word. (Wait until thumbs are up.) What is the word? *harmless*

3. Sound out the next word to yourself. Put your thumb up when you can say the word. (Wait until thumbs are up.) What is the word? *market*

(Repeat step 3 with the words **arctic, garlic, Martin,** and **garnishment**.)

4. Let's read these words again. (Call on individual students to read the Challenge Words.)

E. Sight Words

(Have students open their books to Lesson 22, page 89.)

could	should	would	been	there
what	work	where	all	you
of	after	they		

1. Find part E in your book.

2. Touch the first word. This word is **could**. What is the word? *could* Spell and read. *c-o-u-l-d. could*

3. The next word is **should**. What is the word? *should* Spell and read. *s-h-o-u-l-d. should*

(Repeat step 3 with the remaining words.)

4. Let's read these words again. (Call on individual students to read the Sight Words.)

F. Sentences and Stories

(Have students open their books to Lesson 22, page 89.)

1. Find part F in your book.

2. Touch the title of the story. Let's read the title together. *Off to the Farm*

3. Read Part 1 to yourself. Read it very carefully. Put your thumb up when you are done. (Wait until thumbs are up.)

4. Let's read Part 1 together. When you are not reading aloud, follow along in your book. (Call on a student to read one or two sentences. Continue until Part 1 has been read.)

5. Look at the three pictures. Put a number 1 under the picture that goes with Part 1.

(Repeat steps 3–5 with Parts 2 and 3.)

Answers		
1	2	3

G. Spelling

(Have students open their books to Lesson 22, page 90.)

1. Find part G in your book.

2. Your first spelling word is **spark**. Write **spark**.

3. (Write the word on the board or display it on-screen.) Check and correct your word. (Monitor.)

(Repeat steps 2 and 3 with the word **hard**.)

4. Your next spelling word is **market**. Say the parts in **market**. First part. *mar* Next part. *ket* Write the word.

5. (Write the word on the board or display it on-screen.) Check and correct your word.

(Repeat steps 4 and 5 with the word **harmless**.)

6. Listen. **Mark your mistakes in red.** Write the sentence. (Monitor.)

7. (Write the sentence on the board or display it on-screen.) Check and correct each word. (Monitor.)

Answers	
1. spark	3. market
2. hard	4. harmless
5. **Mark your mistakes in red.**	

H. Practice Activity 1

(Have students open their books to Lesson 22, page 90.)

1. Find part H in your book.

2. Follow along as I read the directions. **Draw a line under the sentence that goes with each picture.**

3. Do number 1. Put your thumb up when you are finished. (Monitor and check.)

4. You will finish part H later.

I. Practice Activity 2

(Have students open their books to Lesson 22, page 91.)

1. Find part I in your book.

2. Follow along as I read the directions. **Read each question. Look back at the story on page 89. Fill in each blank with the best word.**

3. Do number 1. Put your thumb up when you are finished. (Monitor and check.)

4. Now go back and finish parts H and I.

 ## Work Check for Parts H and I
(Oral Teacher-Directed Activity)

1. Find part H in your book.

2. Let's check your work. If you made a mistake, circle the number. You will fix all mistakes at the end of the lesson. (Call on individual students to read their answers.)

3. Count how many correct answers you have, and write that number in the box at the bottom of the page. (Monitor students.)

(Repeat steps 1–3 with part I.)

4. Now go back and correct any mistakes. (Monitor students.)

Answers for Part H
1. <u>Jeff has a cut on his arm.</u>
2. <u>Beth sits in the barn.</u>
3. <u>Jan played the harp.</u>
4. <u>Fred sent a card to Kay.</u>
5. <u>His home is far away.</u>

Answers for Part I

Part 1	Part 2	Part 3
1. up	4. seat	7. card
2. gate	5. cards	8. three
3. three	6. barn	

LESSON 23

OBJECTIVES

- *to practice words with* ar
- *to practice words with the word endings* -ed *and* -ing

🔊 Sound Drill
(Oral Teacher-Directed Activity)

(Write the following on the board or display it on-screen:)

1.	ea	ar	ay	oa
2.	ar	a	ai	igh
3.	o	ai	ar	ow
4.	ar	ow	ee	o
5.	e	ar	ow	e

1. Let's practice saying the sounds in the words that we will be reading. Look at the letters in line 1. Say the sounds. /ēēē/, /ar/, /āāā/, /ōōō/

2. Look at the letters in line 2. Say the sounds. /ar/, /aaa/, /āāā/, /īīī/

(Repeat step 2 with lines 3–5. Then call on individual students to say the sounds in a line.)

(NOTE: As an alternative, review the sounds with flash cards.)

A. New Words

(Have students open their books to Lesson 23, page 92.)

1	d**ar**t	y**ar**n	t**ar**
2.	t**ow**	M**ar**s	h**ar**k
3.	b**ar**	b**ow**	ch**ar**m
4.	ch**ea**t	ch**ar**t	h**ar**p
5.	c**ar**t	c**oa**t	d**ay**
6.	sh**ar**p	sh**ee**p	sh**ar**k

7. Don't dart across the street in traffic.
8. Do you think there is life on Mars?
9. My dog will run when he sees this bar of soap.
10. Your chart shows that you are still growing.
11. His shopping cart bumped into the pile of cans.
12. The blades on the skates are sharp.

---

1. Find part A in your book.

2. Touch the first word in line 1. Look at the underlined letters. What is the sound? /ar/

3. Sound out the word to yourself. Put your thumb up when you can say the whole word. (Wait until thumbs are up.) What is the word? *dart*

4. Touch the next word. Look at the underlined letters. What is the sound? /ar/ Sound out the word to yourself. Put your thumb up when you can say the whole word. (Wait until thumbs are up.) What is the word? *yarn*

(Repeat step 4 with the remaining words in lines 1–3.)

5. Touch the first word in line 4. Sound out this word to yourself. Put your thumb up when you can say the whole word. (Wait until thumbs are up.) What is the word? *cheat*

6. Touch the next word. Sound out the word to yourself. Put your thumb up when you can say the whole word. (Wait until thumbs are up.) What is the word? *chart*

(Repeat step 6 with the remaining words in lines 4–6. Then call on a student to read a line.)

7. Read sentence 7 to yourself. Put your thumb up when you are done. (Wait until thumbs are up. Then call on a student to read the sentence.)

(Repeat step 7 with sentences 8–12.)

B. Review Words

(Have students open their books to Lesson 23, page 92.)

1.	cane	can	crane
2.	plane	plan	stove
3.	shine	tribe	trip
4.	drove	stroke	man
5.	stripe	mane	strip

1. Find part B in your book.

2. Read the words in line 1 to yourself. When you can read all three words, put your thumb up. (Wait until thumbs are up.)

3. Get ready to read the words in line 1 together. Begin. *cane, can, crane*

(Repeat steps 2 and 3 with lines 2–5. Then call on a student to read the words in a line.)

C. Word Endings—Altered Roots

(Have students open their books to Lesson 23, page 92.)

1. piled	6. <u>darted</u>	9. <u>charted</u>
2. tripped	<u>darting</u>	<u>charting</u>
3. stripped	7. <u>cheated</u>	10. <u>towed</u>
4. pla<u>nn</u>ed	<u>cheating</u>	<u>towing</u>
5. stri<u>p</u>ed	8. <u>charmed</u>	
	<u>charming</u>	

1. Find part C in your book.

2. Look at number 1. How many **l**'s? *one*

3. Will you say the name or the sound for the letter **i**? *the name*

4. What is the name? *i*

5. Sound out the word to yourself. What is the word? *piled*

6. Look at number 2. How many **p**'s? *two*

7. Will you say the name or the sound for the letter **i**? *the sound*

8. What is the sound? */iii/*

9. Sound out the word to yourself. What is the word? *tripped*

10. Sound out number 3 to yourself. Put your thumb up when you can read the word. (Wait until thumbs are up.) What is the word? *stripped*

(Repeat step 10 with the words **planned** and **striped**.)

11. Let's read these five words again. (Call on individual students to read the words.)

12. Look at number 6. Sound out the underlined word to yourself. Put your thumb up when you can say the underlined word. (Wait until thumbs are up.) What is the word? *dart*

13. Read **dart** with the endings. What is the first word? *darted* What is the second word? *darting*

(Repeat steps 12 and 13 with the remaining words.)

14. Let's read these words again. (Call on individual students to read the words.)

D. Challenge Words

(Have students open their books to Lesson 23, page 93.)

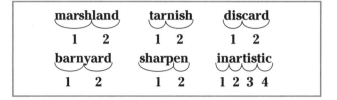

1. Find part D in your book.

2. Touch the first word. Sound out this word to yourself. Put your thumb up when you can say the word. (Wait until thumbs are up.) What is the word? *marshland*

3. Sound out the next word to yourself. Put your thumb up when you can say the word. (Wait until thumbs are up.) What is the word? *tarnish*

(Repeat step 3 with the words **discard, barnyard, sharpen,** and **inartistic**.)

4. Let's read these words again. (Call on individual students to read the Challenge Words.)

E. Sight Words

(Have students open their books to Lesson 23, page 93.)

should	could	would	where	been
after	what	saw	were	from
you	there	water	said	

1. Find part E in your book.

2. Touch the first word. This word is **should**. What is the word? *should* Spell and read. *s-h-o-u-l-d. should*

3. The next word is **could**. What is the word? *could* Spell and read. *c-o-u-l-d. could*

(Repeat step 3 with the remaining words.)

4. Let's read these words again. (Call on individual students to read the Sight Words.)

F. Sentences and Stories

(Have students open their books to Lesson 23, page 93.)

1. Find part F in your book.

2. Touch the title of the story. Let's read the title together. *A Walk in the Park*

3. Read Part 1 to yourself. Read it very carefully. Put your thumb up when you are done. (Wait until thumbs are up.)

4. Let's read Part 1 together. When you are not reading aloud, follow along in your book. (Call on a student to read one or two sentences. Continue until Part 1 has been read.)

5. Look at the three pictures. Put a number 1 under the picture that goes with Part 1.

(Repeat steps 3–5 with Parts 2 and 3.)

Answers

1	3	2

G. Spelling

(Have students open their books to Lesson 23, page 94.)

1. Find part G in your book.

2. Your first spelling word is **charm**. Write **charm**.

3. (Write the word on the board or display it on-screen.) Check and correct your word. (Monitor.)

(Repeat steps 2 and 3 with the word **sharp**.)

4. Your next spelling word is **tarnish**. Say the parts in **tarnish**. First part. *tar* Next part. *nish* Write the word.

5. (Write the word on the board or display it on-screen.) Check and correct your word.

(Repeat steps 4 and 5 with the word **discard**.)

6. Listen. **The man will park his car.** Write the sentence. (Monitor.)

7. (Write the sentence on the board or display it on-screen.) Check and correct each word. (Monitor.)

Answers

1. charm 3. tarnish
2. sharp 4. discard
5. The man will park his car.

H. Practice Activity 1

(Have students open their books to Lesson 23, page 94.)

1. Find part H in your book.

2. Follow along as I read the directions. **Draw a line under the phrase that best completes each sentence.**

3. Do number 1. Put your thumb up when you are finished. (Monitor and check.)

4. You will finish part H later.

I. Practice Activity 2

(Have students open their books to Lesson 23, page 95.)

1. Find part I in your book.

2. Follow along as I read the directions. **Read each question. Look back at the story on page 93. Fill in each blank with the best word.**

3. Do number 1. Put your thumb up when you are finished. (Monitor and check.)

4. Now go back and finish parts H and I.

 ## Work Check for Parts H and I
(Oral Teacher-Directed Activity)

1. Find part H in your book.

2. Let's check your work. If you made a mistake, circle the number. You will fix all mistakes at the end of the lesson. (Call on individual students to read their answers.)

3. Count how many correct answers you have, and write that number in the box at the bottom of the page. (Monitor students.)

(Repeat steps 1–3 with part I.)

4. Now go back and correct any mistakes. (Monitor students.)

Answers for Part H
1. <u>park the car</u>
2. <u>march with the band</u>
3. <u>bark at you</u>
4. <u>carve the roast</u>
5. <u>play with the yarn</u>
6. <u>very sharp</u>
7. <u>a cut on his arm</u>

Answers for Part I

Part 1	Part 2	Part 3
1. park	3. town	6. dog
2. scar	4. vet	7. Sparky
	5. barnyard	

 ## Checking Up
(Oral Teacher-Directed Activity)

Practice reading Part 1 of the story on page 93. I am going to listen to each of you read. Your goal is to make fewer than two errors. Keep practicing Part 1 until you can read it without any errors.

(Ask each student to read Part 1. Record the number of errors in his or her book.

NOTE: If 90 percent of the students make two errors or fewer, you may move on to Lesson 24. If not, repeat Lesson 23.)

LESSON 24

OBJECTIVES

- *to introduce words with* er
- *to practice words with the word endings* -ed *and* -ing
- *to introduce words with the word ending* -er

🔊 New Sound

(Have students open their books to Lesson 24, page 96.)

1. Look at the top of page 96 in your book.

2. Touch the word.

3. This word is **fern**. Say the word. *fern*

4. The underlined sound is /**er**/. Say the sound. */er/*

5. Say the sound again. */er/*

(Have students close their books. Then do the Sound Drill activity.)

🔊 Sound Drill
(Oral Teacher-Directed Activity)

(Write the following on the board or display it on-screen:)

1.	er	ar	oa	igh
2.	ay	er	i	ar
3.	an	a	er	ai
4.	ow	ar	ee	en
5.	er	ea	ar	u

1. Let's practice saying the sounds in the words that we will be reading. Look at the letters in line 1. Say the sounds. */er/, /ar/, /ooo/, /iii/*

2. Look at the letters in line 2. Say the sounds. /$\overline{aaa}$/, /er/, /iii/, /ar/

(Repeat step 2 with lines 3–5. Then call on individual students to say the sounds in a line.)

(NOTE: As an alternative, review the sounds with flash cards.)

A. New Words

(Have students open their books to Lesson 24, page 96.)

1.	her	fern	farm
2.	hay	term	train
3.	verb	herd	hard
4.	own	tart	Herb
5.	clerk	cloak	cheek
6.	germ	smart	perk

7. This kind of fern grows near the swamp.
8. What grade did you get in math last term?
9. We followed the tracks of the herd down to the water.
10. Herb capsized the sailboat in the lake.
11. I asked the clerk if she could cash my paycheck.
12. The robins will perk up at sunrise.

1. Find part A in your book.

2. Touch the first word in line 1. Look at the underlined letters. What is the sound? */er/*

3. Sound out the word to yourself. Put your thumb up when you can say the whole word. (Wait until thumbs are up.) What is the word? *her*

4. Touch the next word. Look at the underlined letters. What is the sound? */er/* Sound out the word to yourself. Put your thumb up when you can say the whole word. (Wait until thumbs are up.) What is the word? *fern*

(Repeat step 4 with the remaining words in lines 1–3.)

5. Touch the first word in line 4. Sound out this word to yourself. Put your thumb up when you can say the whole word. (Wait until thumbs are up.) What is the word? *own*

6. Touch the next word. Sound out the word to yourself. Put your thumb up when you can say the whole word. (Wait until thumbs are up.) What is the word? *tart*

(Repeat step 6 with the remaining words in lines 4–6. Then call on a student to read a line.)

7. Read sentence 7 to yourself. Put your thumb up when you are done. (Wait until thumbs are up. Then call on a student to read the sentence.)

(Repeat step 7 with sentences 8–12.)

B. Review Words

(Have students open their books to Lesson 24, page 96.)

1. rote	rot	throne
2. glide	stack	stake
3. shake	rip	ripe
4. dime	dim	slim
5. plan	plane	slime

1. Find part B in your book.

2. Read the words in line 1 to yourself. When you can read all three words, put your thumb up. (Wait until thumbs are up.)

3. Get ready to read the words in line 1 together. Begin. *rote, rot, throne*

(Repeat steps 2 and 3 with lines 2–5. Then call on a student to read the words in a line.)

C. Word Endings—Altered Roots

(Have students open their books to Lesson 24, page 96.)

1. gli<u>d</u>ing	5. ripped	9. <u>owner</u>
2. pla<u>nn</u>ing	6. <u>farmer</u>	10. <u>starter</u>
3. sha<u>k</u>ing	7. <u>harder</u>	
4. pla<u>nn</u>ed	8. <u>trainer</u>	

1. Find part C in your book.

2. Look at number 1. How many **d**'s? *one*

3. Will you say the name or the sound for the letter **i**? *the name*

4. What is the name? *i*

5. Sound out the word to yourself. What is the word? *gliding*

6. Look at number 2. How many **n**'s? *two*

7. Will you say the name or the sound for the letter **a**? *the sound*

8. What is the sound? */aaa/*

9. Sound out the word to yourself. What is the word? *planning*

10. Sound out number 3 to yourself. Put your thumb up when you can read the word. (Wait until thumbs are up.) What is the word? *shaking*

(Repeat step 10 with the words **planned** and **ripped**.)

11. Let's read these five words again. (Call on individual students to read the words.)

12. Look at number 6. Sound out the underlined word to yourself. Put your thumb up when you can say the underlined word. (Wait until thumbs are up.) What is the word? *farm*

13. Read **farm** with the ending. What is the word? *farmer*

(Repeat steps 12 and 13 with the remaining words.)

14. Let's read these words again. (Call on individual students to read the words.)

D. Challenge Words

(Have students open their books to Lesson 24, page 97.)

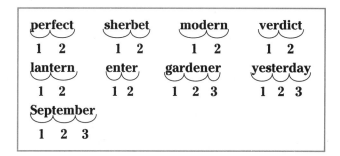

1. Find part D in your book.

2. Touch the first word. Sound out this word to yourself. Put your thumb up when you can say the word. (Wait until thumbs are up.) What is the word? *perfect*

3. Sound out the next word to yourself. Put your thumb up when you can say the word. (Wait until thumbs are up.) What is the word? *sherbet*

(Repeat step 3 with the words **modern, verdict, lantern, enter, gardener, yesterday,** and **September**.)

4. Let's read these words again. (Call on individual students to read the Challenge Words.)

E. Sight Words

(Have students open their books to Lesson 24, page 97.)

my	why	by	cry	dry
come	who	been	where	there
said	were	what	you	school

1. Find part E in your book.

2. Touch the first word. This word is **my**.
   What is the word? *my*
   Spell and read. *m-y. my*

3. The next word is **why**.
   What is the word? *why*
   Spell and read. *w-h-y. why*

(Repeat step 3 with the remaining words.)

4. Let's read these words again. (Call on individual students to read the Sight Words.)

F. Sentences and Stories

(Have students open their books to Lesson 24, page 97.)

1. Find part F in your book.

2. Touch the title of the story. Let's read the title together. *The Last Term*

3. Read Part 1 to yourself. Read it very carefully. Put your thumb up when you are done. (Wait until thumbs are up.)

4. Let's read Part 1 together. When you are not reading aloud, follow along in your book. (Call on a student to read one or two sentences. Continue until Part 1 has been read.)

5. Look at the three pictures. Put a number 1 under the picture that goes with Part 1.

(Repeat steps 3–5 with Parts 2 and 3.)

Answers
2 1 3

G. Spelling

(Have students open their books to Lesson 24, page 98.)

1. Find part G in your book.

2. Your first spelling word is **term**. Write **term**.

3. (Write the word on the board or display it on-screen.) Check and correct your word. (Monitor.)

(Repeat steps 2 and 3 with the word **fern**.)

4. Your next spelling word is **perfect**.
   Say the parts in **perfect**. First part. *per*
   Next part. *fect* Write the word.

5. (Write the word on the board or display it on-screen.) Check and correct your word.

(Repeat steps 4 and 5 with the word **yesterday**.)

6. Listen. **The herd ate hay on the farm.**
   Write the sentence. (Monitor.)

7. (Write the sentence on the board or display it on-screen.) Check and correct each word. (Monitor.)

Answers		
1. term	3.	perfect
2. fern	4.	yesterday
5. **The herd ate hay on the farm.**		

H. Practice Activity 1

(Have students open their books to Lesson 24, page 98.)

1. Find part H in your book.

2. Follow along as I read the directions. **Read the story. Answer the questions.**

3. Read the story to yourself. Do number 1. Put your thumb up when you are finished. (Monitor and check.)

4. You will finish part H later.

I. Practice Activity 2

(Have students open their books to Lesson 24, page 99.)

1. Find part I in your book.

2. Follow along as I read the directions. **Read each question. Look back at the story on page 97. Fill in each blank with the best word.**

3. Do number 1. Put your thumb up when you are finished. (Monitor and check.)

4. Now go back and finish parts H and I.

Work Check for Parts H and I
(Oral Teacher-Directed Activity)

1. Find part H in your book.

2. Let's check your work. If you made a mistake, circle the number. You will fix all mistakes at the end of the lesson. (Call on individual students to read their answers.)

3. Count how many correct answers you have, and write that number in the box at the bottom of the page. (Monitor students.)

(Repeat steps 1–3 with part I.)

4. Now go back and correct any mistakes. (Monitor students.)

Answers for Part H	
1. cloak	3. coat
2. three	4. coat

Answers for Part I		
Part 1	Part 2	Part 3
1. Fern High	4. plans	7. Market
2. Meg	5. Mike	8. Herb Train
3. Jane	6. State U.	

LESSON 25

OBJECTIVES

- *to practice words with* er
- *to practice words with the word endings* -ed, -ing, *and* -er

 Sound Drill
(Oral Teacher-Directed Activity)

(Write the following on the board or display it on-screen:)

1.	er	ee	ar	ai
2.	ar	er	ow	ar
3.	ea	er	ay	o
4.	er	igh	oa	ar
5.	igh	a	er	e

1. Let's practice saying the sounds in the words that we will be reading. Look at the letters in line 1. Say the sounds. /er/, /ēēē/, /ar/, /āāā/

2. Look at the letters in line 2. Say the sounds. /ar/, /er/, /ōōō/, /ar/

(Repeat step 2 with lines 3–5. Then call on individual students to say the sounds in a line.)

(NOTE: As an alternative, review the sounds with flash cards.)

A. New Words

(Have students open their books to Lesson 25, page 100.)

1.	B**er**t	**jer**k	j**ee**p
2.	h**ar**p	t**er**m	H**er**b
3.	B**ar**t	t**ea**m	p**er**ch
4.	s**er**ve	s**igh**t	p**ea**ch
5.	p**ar**t	n**igh**t	n**er**ve
6.	sw**er**ve	y**ar**d	c**ar**d

7. Jerk the strings on the puppet to make it work.
8. Herb hopes to be a carpenter when he grows up.
9. The robin won't sing until it is on its perch.
10. At midday the waitress will serve you a hot meal.
11. My dentist said that with time the nerve will heal.
12. Bert, close the gate and stay in the yard!

1. Find part A in your book.

2. Touch the first word in line 1. Look at the underlined letters. What is the sound? */er/*

3. Sound out the word to yourself. Put your thumb up when you can say the whole word. (Wait until thumbs are up.) What is the word? *Bert*

4. Touch the next word. Look at the underlined letters. What is the sound? */er/* Sound out the word to yourself. Put your thumb up when you can say the whole word. (Wait until thumbs are up.) What is the word? *jerk*

(Repeat step 4 with the remaining words in lines 1–3.)

5. Touch the first word in line 4. Sound out this word to yourself. Put your thumb up when you can say the whole word. (Wait until thumbs are up.) What is the word? *serve*

6. Touch the next word. Sound out the word to yourself. Put your thumb up when you can say the whole word. (Wait until thumbs are up.) What is the word? *sight*

(Repeat step 6 with the remaining words in lines 4–6. Then call on a student to read a line.)

7. Read sentence 7 to yourself. Put your thumb up when you are done. (Wait until thumbs are up. Then call on a student to read the sentence.)

(Repeat step 7 with sentences 8–12.)

B. Review Words

(Have students open their books to Lesson 25, page 100.)

1.	snake	snack	grove
2.	grip	zone	gripe
3.	scope	spine	spin
4.	glad	glade	scrap
5.	fine	scrape	fin

1. Find part B in your book.

2. Read the words in line 1 to yourself. When you can read all three words, put your thumb up. (Wait until thumbs are up.)

3. Get ready to read the words in line 1 together. Begin. *snake, snack, grove*

(Repeat steps 2 and 3 with lines 2–5. Then call on a student to read the words in a line.)

C. Word Endings—Altered Roots

(Have students open their books to Lesson 25, page 100.)

1.	gri**pp**ing	5.	fi<u>n</u>er	9.	<u>team</u>ed
2.	gri**p**ing	6.	jerked	10.	<u>own</u>ed
3.	scra**p**er	7.	perched		
4.	spi<u>nn</u>ing	8.	parted		

1. Find part C in your book.

2. Look at number 1. How many **p**'s? *two*

3. Will you say the name or the sound for the letter **i**? *the sound*

4. What is the sound? */iii/*

5. Sound out the word to yourself. What is the word? *gripping*

6. Look at number 2. How many **p**'s? *one*

7. Will you say the name or the sound for the letter **i**? *the name*

8. What is the name? *i*

9. Sound out the word to yourself. What is the word? *griping*

10. Sound out number 3 to yourself. Put your thumb up when you can read the word. (Wait until thumbs are up.) What is the word? *scraper*

(Repeat step 10 with the words **spinning** and **finer**.)

11. Let's read these five words again. (Call on individual students to read the words.)

12. Look at number 6. Sound out the underlined word to yourself. Put your thumb up when you can say the underlined word. (Wait until thumbs are up.) What is the word? *jerk*

13. Read **jerk** with the ending. What is the word? *jerked*

(Repeat steps 12 and 13 with the remaining words.)

14. Let's read these words again. (Call on individual students to read the words.)

D. Challenge Words

(Have students open their books to Lesson 25, page 101.)

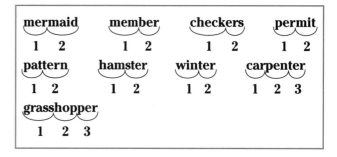

1. Find part D in your book.

2. Touch the first word. Sound out this word to yourself. Put your thumb up when you can say the word. (Wait until thumbs are up.) What is the word? *mermaid*

3. Sound out the next word to yourself. Put your thumb up when you can say the word. (Wait until thumbs are up.) What is the word? *member*

(Repeat step 3 with the words **checkers, permit, pattern, hamster, winter, carpenter,** and **grasshopper**.)

4. Let's read these words again. (Call on individual students to read the Challenge Words.)

E. Sight Words

(Have students open their books to Lesson 25, page 101.)

she	he	me	be	we
come	who	been	would	where
school	what	are	work	after

1. Find part E in your book.

2. Touch the first word. This word is **she**. What is the word? *she* Spell and read. *s-h-e. she*

3. The next word is **he**. What is the word? *he* Spell and read. *h-e. he*

(Repeat step 3 with the remaining words.)

4. Let's read these words again. (Call on individual students to read the Sight Words.)

F. Sentences and Stories

(Have students open their books to Lesson 25, page 101.)

1. Find part F in your book.

2. Touch the title of the story. Let's read the title together. *Job Plans*

3. Read Part 1 to yourself. Read it very carefully. Put your thumb up when you are done. (Wait until thumbs are up.)

4. Let's read Part 1 together. When you are not reading aloud, follow along in your book. (Call on a student to read one or two sentences. Continue until Part 1 has been read.)

5. Look at the three pictures. Put a number 1 under the picture that goes with Part 1.

(Repeat steps 3–5 with Parts 2 and 3.)

Answers

3   2   1

G. Spelling

(Have students open their books to Lesson 25, page 102.)

1. Find part G in your book.

2. Your first spelling word is **jerk**. Write **jerk**.

3. (Write the word on the board or display it on-screen.) Check and correct your word. (Monitor.)

(Repeat steps 2 and 3 with the word **perch**.)

4. Your next spelling word is **member**. Say the parts in **member**. First part. *mem* Next part. *ber* Write the word.

5. (Write the word on the board or display it on-screen.) Check and correct your word.

(Repeat step 4 and 5 with the word **permit**.)

6. Listen. **Bert is a carpenter.** Write the sentence. (Monitor.)

7. (Write the sentence on the board or display it on-screen.) Check and correct each word. (Monitor.)

Answers
1. jerk   3. member
2. perch   4. permit
5. Bert is a carpenter.

H. Practice Activity 1

(Have students open their books to Lesson 25, page 102.)

1. Find part H in your book.

2. Follow along as I read the directions. **Fill in each blank with the best word.**

3. Do number 1. Put your thumb up when you are finished. (Monitor and check.)

4. You will finish part H later.

I. Practice Activity 2

(Have students open their books to Lesson 25, page 103.)

1. Find part I in your book.

2. Follow along as I read the directions. **Read each question. Look back at the story on page 101. Fill in each blank with the best word.**

3. Do number 1. Put your thumb up when you are finished. (Monitor and check.)

4. Now go back and finish parts H and I.

Work Check for Parts H and I
(Oral Teacher-Directed Activity)

1. Find part H in your book.

2. Let's check your work. If you made a mistake, circle the number. You will fix all mistakes at the end of the lesson. (Call on individual students to read their answers.)

3. Count how many correct answers you have, and write that number in the box at the bottom of the page. (Monitor students.)

(Repeat steps 1–3 with part I.)

4. Now go back and correct any mistakes. (Monitor students.)

Answers for Part H

1. harp		5. herd	
2. clerk		6. spark	
3. farm		7. scarf	
4. part		8. verb	

Answers for Part I

Part 1	Part 2	Part 3
1. peach tarts	4. teacher	6. grass
2. trade school	5. market	7. whales
3. carpenter		8. trainers

LESSON 26

OBJECTIVES

- *to practice words with* er
- *to practice words with the word endings* -ed, -ing, *and* -er

 Sound Drill
(Oral Teacher-Directed Activity)

(Write the following on the board or display it on-screen:)

1.	ow	er	ch	ar
2.	th	igh	ee	ck
3.	ar	wh	er	oa
4.	ai	ar	i	ay
5.	er	ea	ar	e

1. Let's practice saying the sounds in the words that we will be reading. Look at the letters in line 1. Say the sounds. /o͞o/, /er/, /ch/, /ar/

2. Look at the letters in line 2. Say the sounds. /th/, /ī/, /ēē/, /k/

(Repeat step 2 with lines 3–5. Then call on individual students to say the sounds in a line.)

(NOTE: As an alternative, review the sounds with flash cards.)

A. New Words

(Have students open their books to Lesson 26, page 104.)

1.	h<u>er</u>	b<u>er</u>g	bright
2.	v<u>er</u>se	b<u>ar</u>k	v<u>er</u>b
3.	clay	p<u>er</u>k	p<u>ar</u>k
4.	cl<u>er</u>k	Cl<u>ar</u>k	h<u>er</u>b
5.	st<u>ar</u>t	st<u>er</u>n	stain
6.	d<u>ar</u>k	s<u>er</u>ve	h<u>ar</u>m

7. **Her yellow dress is on the line.**
8. **The dog might bark at the people in the rowboat.**
9. **Will you demonstrate how you can park the car?**
10. **The clerk at the desk asked us our names.**
11. **The carpenter will start work next week.**
12. **Don't be afraid of the dark.**

1. Find part A in your book.

2. Touch the first word in line 1. Look at the underlined letters. What is the sound? /er/

3. Sound out the word to yourself. Put your thumb up when you can say the whole word. (Wait until thumbs are up.) What is the word? *her*

4. Touch the next word. Look at the underlined letters. What is the sound? /er/ Sound out the word to yourself. Put your thumb up when you can say the whole word. (Wait until thumbs are up.) What is the word? *berg*

(Repeat step 4 with the remaining words in lines 1–3.)

5. Touch the first word in line 4. Sound out this word to yourself. Put your thumb up when you can say the whole word. (Wait until thumbs are up.) What is the word? *clerk*

6. Touch the next word. Sound out the word to yourself. Put your thumb up when you can say the whole word. (Wait until thumbs are up.) What is the word? *Clark*

(Repeat step 6 with the remaining words in lines 4–6. Then call on a student to read a line.)

7. Read sentence 7 to yourself. Put your thumb up when you are done. (Wait until thumbs are up. Then call on a student to read the sentence.)

(Repeat step 7 with sentences 8–12.)

B. Review Words

(Have students open their books to Lesson 26, page 104.)

1.	lake	lack	close
2.	fate	not	note
3.	crave	mine	fat
4.	shake	swipe	whale
5.	swim	slide	shrine

1. Find part B in your book.

2. Read the words in line 1 to yourself. When you can read all three words, put your thumb up. (Wait until thumbs are up.)

3. Get ready to read the words in line 1 together. Begin. *lake, lack, close*

(Repeat steps 2 and 3 with lines 2–5. Then call on a student to read the words in a line.)

C. Word Endings—Altered Roots

(Have students open their books to Lesson 26, page 104.)

1. noting	5. swimmer	9. brighter
2. mining	6. starter	10. sterner
3. fatter	7. barking	
4. shaking	8. stained	

1. Find part C in your book.

2. Look at number 1. How many **t**'s? *one*

3. Will you say the name or the sound for the letter **o**? *the name*

4. What is the name? *o*

5. Sound out the word to yourself. What is the word? *noting*

6. Look at number 2. How many **n**'s? *one*

7. Will you say the name or the sound for the letter **i**? *the name*

8. What is the name? *i*

9. Sound out the word to yourself. What is the word? *mining*

10. Sound out number 3 to yourself. Put your thumb up when you can read the word. (Wait until thumbs are up.) What is the word? *fatter*

(Repeat step 10 with the words **shaking** and **swimmer**.)

11. Let's read these five words again. (Call on individual students to read the words.)

12. Look at number 6. Sound out the underlined word to yourself. Put your thumb up when you can say the underlined word. (Wait until thumbs are up.) What is the word? *start*

13. Read **start** with the ending. What is the word? *starter*

(Repeat steps 12 and 13 with the remaining words.)

14. Let's read these words again. (Call on individual students to read the words.)

D. Challenge Words

(Have students open their books to Lesson 26, page 105.)

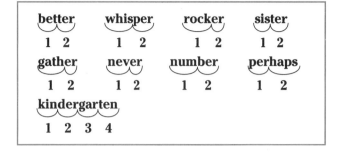

1. Find part D in your book.

2. Touch the first word. Sound out this word to yourself. Put your thumb up when you can say the word. (Wait until thumbs are up.) What is the word? *better*

3. Sound out the next word to yourself. Put your thumb up when you can say the word. (Wait until thumbs are up.) What is the word? *whisper*

(Repeat step 3 with the words **rocker, sister, gather, never, number, perhaps,** and **kindergarten.**)

4. Let's read these words again. (Call on individual students to read the Challenge Words.)

E. Sight Words

(Have students open their books to Lesson 26, page 105.)

could	should	would	come	who
been	where	very	they	you
what	work	said		

1. Find part E in your book.

2. Touch the first word. This word is **could**. What is the word? *could* Spell and read. *c-o-u-l-d. could*

3. The next word is **should**. What is the word? *should* Spell and read. *s-h-o-u-l-d. should*

(Repeat step 3 with the remaining words.)

4. Let's read these words again. (Call on individual students to read the Sight Words.)

F. Sentences and Stories

(Have students open their books to Lesson 26, page 105.)

1. Find part F in your book.

2. Touch the title of the story. Let's read the title together. *Pat and Rex*

3. Read Part 1 to yourself. Read it very carefully. Put your thumb up when you are done. (Wait until thumbs are up.)

4. Let's read Part 1 together. When you are not reading aloud, follow along in your book. (Call on a student to read one or two sentences. Continue until Part 1 has been read.)

5. Look at the three pictures. Put a number 1 under the picture that goes with Part 1.

(Repeat steps 3–5 with Parts 2 and 3.)

Answers

| 1 | 3 | 2 |

G. Spelling

(Have students open their books to Lesson 26, page 106.)

1. Find part G in your book.

2. Your first spelling word is **clerk**. Write **clerk**.

3. (Write the word on the board or display it on-screen.) Check and correct your word. (Monitor.)

(Repeat steps 2 and 3 with the word **serve**.)

4. Your next spelling word is **whisper**. Say the parts in **whisper**. First part. *whis* Next part. *per* Write the word.

5. (Write the word on the board or display it on-screen.) Check and correct your word.

(Repeat steps 4 and 5 with the word **never**.)

6. Listen. **The clerk was very stern.** Write the sentence. (Monitor.)

7. (Write the sentence on the board or display it on-screen.) Check and correct each word. (Monitor.)

Answers
1. clerk   3. whisper
2. serve   4. never
5. The clerk was very stern.

H. Practice Activity 1

(Have students open their books to Lesson 26, page 106.)

1. Find part H in your book.

2. Follow along as I read the directions. **Draw a line under the phrase that best completes each sentence.**

3. Do number 1. Put your thumb up when you are finished. (Monitor and check.)

4. You will finish part H later.

I. Practice Activity 2

(Have students open their books to Lesson 26, page 107.)

1. Find part I in your book.

2. Follow along as I read the directions. **Read each question. Look back at the story on page 105. Fill in each blank with the best word.**

3. Do number 1. Put your thumb up when you are finished. (Monitor and check.)

4. Now go back and finish parts H and I.

 Work Check for Parts H and I
(Oral Teacher-Directed Activity)

1. Find part H in your book.

2. Let's check your work. If you made a mistake, circle the number. You will fix all mistakes at the end of the lesson. (Call on individual students to read their answers.)

3. Count how many correct answers you have, and write that number in the box at the bottom of the page. (Monitor students.)

(Repeat steps 1–3 with part I.)

4. Now go back and correct any mistakes. (Monitor students.)

Answers for Part H
1. a. <u>put on her coat</u>
2. b. <u>with a ball of yarn</u>
3. b. <u>park the car</u>
4. a. <u>very bright</u>
5. b. <u>send a card</u>
6. a. <u>filled with herbs</u>
7. b. <u>say each verse</u>

Answers for Part I

Part 1	Part 2	Part 3
1. Herb	4. sleep	6. Bergs
2. dog	5. work	7. clock
3. week		8. work

 Checking Up
(Oral Teacher-Directed Activity)

Practice reading Part 1 of the story on page 105. I am going to listen to each of you read. Your goal is to make fewer than two errors. Keep practicing Part 1 until you can read it without any errors.

(Ask each student to read Part 1. Record the number of errors in his or her book.

NOTE: If 90 percent of the students make two errors or fewer, you may move on to Lesson 27. If not, repeat Lesson 26.)

LESSON 27

OBJECTIVES

- *to introduce words with* or
- *to practice words with the word endings* -ed, -ing, *and* -er

New Sound

(Have students open their books to Lesson 27, page 108.)

1. Look at the top of page 108 in your book.

2. Touch the word.

3. This word is **corn**. Say the word. *corn*

4. The underlined sound is **/or/**. Say the sound. */or/*

5. Say the sound again. */or/*

(Have students close their books. Then do the Sound Drill activity.)

Sound Drill
(Oral Teacher-Directed Activity)

(Write the following on the board or display it on-screen:)

1.	er	ea	or	ai
2.	ee	oa	ar	e
3.	ow	or	ir	igh
4.	or	ay	ar	ch
5.	ir	i	or	ck

1. Let's practice saying the sounds in the words that we will be reading. Look at the letters in line 1. Say the sounds. */er/, /ēēē/, /or/, /āāā/*

2. Look at the letters in line 2. Say the sounds. */ēēē/, /ōōō/, /ar/, /eee/*

(Repeat step 2 with lines 3–5. Then call on individual students to say the sounds in a line.)

(NOTE: As an alternative, review the sounds with flash cards.)

A. New Words

(Have students open their books to Lesson 27, page 108.)

1.	for	corn	fort
2.	fern	worn	cart
3.	sport	spark	storm
4.	north	speed	star
5.	coach	horse	tore
6.	shore	need	wore

7. The children made a fort out of snow.
8. This is the coat that was worn in the play.
9. The window broke in the storm.
10. Drive north on the freeway until you reach the coast.
11. Lead the horse into the barn at nightfall.
12. The artist likes to go to the shore to paint.

1. Find part A in your book.

2. Touch the first word in line 1. Look at the underlined letters. What is the sound? */or/*

3. Sound out the word to yourself. Put your thumb up when you can say the whole word. (Wait until thumbs are up.) What is the word? *for*

4. Touch the next word. Look at the underlined letters. What is the sound? */or/* Sound out the word to yourself. Put your thumb up when you can say the whole word. (Wait until thumbs are up.) What is the word? *corn*

(Repeat step 4 with the remaining words in lines 1–3.)

5. Touch the first word in line 4. Sound out this word to yourself. Put your thumb up when you can say the whole word. (Wait until thumbs are up.) What is the word? *north*

6. Touch the next word. Sound out the word to yourself. Put your thumb up when you can say the whole word. (Wait until thumbs are up.) What is the word? *speed*

(Repeat step 6 with the remaining words in lines 4–6. Then call on a student to read a line.)

7. Read sentence 7 to yourself. Put your thumb up when you are done. (Wait until thumbs are up. Then call on a student to read the sentence.)

(Repeat step 7 with sentences 8–12.)

B. Review Words

(Have students open their books to Lesson 27, page 108.)

1. shave	strike	stick
2. stock	stroke	shape
3. strain	throat	stain
4. slip	stream	throne
5. screech	strap	slight

1. Find part B in your book.

2. Read the words in line 1 to yourself. When you can read all three words, put your thumb up. (Wait until thumbs are up.)

3. Get ready to read the words in line 1 together. Begin. *shave, strike, stick*

(Repeat steps 2 and 3 with lines 2–5. Then call on a student to read the words in a line.)

C. Word Endings—Altered Roots

(Have students open their books to Lesson 27, page 108.)

1. sha<u>v</u>ing	5. sli<u>pp</u>er	9. <u>stormed</u>
2. sli<u>pp</u>ed	6. <u>sparked</u>	10. <u>speeder</u>
3. stri<u>k</u>ing	7. <u>needed</u>	
4. ska<u>t</u>ed	8. <u>coached</u>	

1. Find part C in your book.

2. Look at number 1. How many **v**'s? *one*

3. Will you say the name or the sound for the letter **a**? *the name*

4. What is the name? *a*

5. Sound out the word to yourself. What is the word? *shaving*

6. Look at number 2. How many **p**'s? *two*

7. Will you say the name or the sound for the letter **i**? *the sound*

8. What is the sound? */iii/*

9. Sound out the word to yourself. What is the word? *slipped*

10. Sound out number 3 to yourself. Put your thumb up when you can read the word. (Wait until thumbs are up.) What is the word? *striking*

(Repeat step 10 with the words **skated** and **slipper**.)

11. Let's read these five words again. (Call on individual students to read the words.)

12. Look at number 6. Sound out the underlined word to yourself. Put your thumb up when you can say the underlined word. (Wait until thumbs are up.) What is the word? *spark*

13. Read **spark** with the ending. What is the word? *sparked*

(Repeat steps 12 and 13 with the remaining words.)

14. Let's read these words again. (Call on individual students to read the words.)

D. Challenge Words

(Have students open their books to Lesson 27, page 109.)

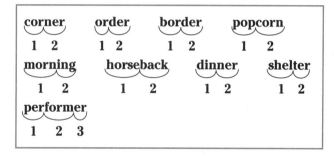

1. Find part D in your book.

2. Touch the first word. Sound out this word to yourself. Put your thumb up when you can say the word. (Wait until thumbs are up.) What is the word? *corner*

3. Sound out the next word to yourself. Put your thumb up when you can say the word. (Wait until thumbs are up.) What is the word? *order*

(Repeat step 3 with the words **border, popcorn, morning, horseback, dinner, shelter,** and **performer.**)

4. Let's read these words again. (Call on individual students to read the Challenge Words.)

E. Sight Words

(Have students open their books to Lesson 27, page 109.)

my	by	cry	dry	why
your	come	down	who	where
little	she	been	what	could

1. Find part E in your book.

2. Touch the first word. This word is **my**.
   What is the word? *my*
   Spell and read. *m-y. my*

3. The next word is **by**.
   What is the word? *by*
   Spell and read. *b-y. by*

(Repeat step 3 with the remaining words.)

4. Let's read these words again. (Call on individual students to read the Sight Words.)

F. Sentences and Stories

(Have students open their books to Lesson 27, page 109.)

1. Find part F in your book.

2. Touch the title of the story. Let's read the title together. *Flight to the Fort*

3. Read Part 1 to yourself. Read it very carefully. Put your thumb up when you are done.
   (Wait until thumbs are up.)

4. Let's read Part 1 together. When you are not reading aloud, follow along in your book.
   (Call on a student to read one or two sentences. Continue until Part 1 has been read.)

5. Look at the three pictures. Put a number 1 under the picture that goes with Part 1.

(Repeat steps 3–5 with Parts 2 and 3.)

Answers

3 2 1

G. Spelling

(Have students open their books to Lesson 27, page 110.)

1. Find part G in your book.

2. Your first spelling word is **corn**. Write **corn**.

3. (Write the word on the board or display it on-screen.) Check and correct your word. (Monitor.)

(Repeat steps 2 and 3 with the word **sport**.)

4. Your next spelling word is **morning**.
   Say the parts in **morning**. First part. *morn*
   Next part. *ing* Write the word.

5. (Write the word on the board or display it on-screen.) Check and correct your word.

(Repeat steps 4 and 5 with the word **performer**.)

6. Listen. **Lead the horse into the barn.**
   Write the sentence. (Monitor.)

7. (Write the sentence on the board or display it on-screen.) Check and correct each word. (Monitor.)

Answers
1. corn   3. morning
2. sport   4. performer
5. Lead the horse into the barn.

H. Practice Activity 1

(Have students open their books to Lesson 27, page 110.)

1. Find part H in your book.

2. Follow along as I read the directions. **Draw a line under the sentence that goes with each picture.**

3. Do number 1. Put your thumb up when you are finished. (Monitor and check.)

4. You will finish part H later.

I. Practice Activity 2

(Have students open their books to Lesson 27, page 111.)

1. Find part I in your book.

2. Follow along as I read the directions. **Read each question. Look back at the story on page 109. Fill in each blank with the best word.**

3. Do number 1. Put your thumb up when you are finished. (Monitor and check.)

4. Now go back and finish parts H and I.

🔊 Work Check for Parts H and I
(Oral Teacher-Directed Activity)

1. Find part H in your book.

2. Let's check your work. If you made a mistake, circle the number. You will fix all mistakes at the end of the lesson. (Call on individual students to read their answers.)

3. Count how many correct answers you have, and write that number in the box at the bottom of the page. (Monitor students.)

(Repeat steps 1–3 with part I.)

4. Now go back and correct any mistakes. (Monitor students.)

Answers for Part H
1. <u>The waitress gave us more water.</u>
2. <u>Nan mended her torn scarf.</u>
3. <u>The horse is in the barn.</u>
4. <u>Tom will sort the mail.</u>
5. <u>Sal plays a horn in the band.</u>

Answers for Part I

Part 1	Part 2	Part 3
1. Jane	5. coat	7. coat
2. winter storms	6. Carl	8. fort
3. fort		
4. tonight		

LESSON 28

OBJECTIVES

- *to practice words with or*
- *to practice words with the word endings -ed, -ing, and -er*

🔊 Sound Drill
(Oral Teacher-Directed Activity)

(Write the following on the board or display it on-screen:)

1.	or	ee	er	igh
2.	ow	or	o	ea
3.	er	ay	or	ar
4.	or	ar	oa	ai
5.	a	er	i	ar

1. Let's practice saying the sounds in the words that we will be reading. Look at the letters in line 1. Say the sounds. /or/, /ēēē/, /er/, /īīī/

2. Look at the letters in line 2. Say the sounds. /ōōō/, /or/, /ooo/, /ēēē/

(Repeat step 2 with lines 3–5. Then call on individual students to say the sounds in a line.)

(NOTE: As an alternative, review the sounds with flash cards.)

A. New Words

(Have students open their books to Lesson 28, page 112.)

1.	nor	born	barn
2.	clerk	more	coat
3.	port	part	cord
4.	fleet	fork	torch
5.	torn	short	lord
6.	team	thorn	term

7. **When were the twins born?**
8. **I can eat six more pancakes.**
9. **The ship will stop at this port in the morning.**
10. **Do not eat the oatmeal with a fork.**
11. **My sister Jill is very short.**
12. **A thorn cut my leg when I was working in the garden.**

1. Find part A in your book.

2. Touch the first word in line 1. Look at the underlined letters. What is the sound? /or/

3. Sound out the word to yourself. Put your thumb up when you can say the whole word. (Wait until thumbs are up.) What is the word? *nor*

4. Touch the next word. Look at the underlined letters. What is the sound? /or/ Sound out the word to yourself. Put your thumb up when you can say the whole word. (Wait until thumbs are up.) What is the word? *born*

(Repeat step 4 with the remaining words in lines 1–3.)

5. Touch the first word in line 4. Sound out this word to yourself. Put your thumb up when you can say the whole word. (Wait until thumbs are up.) What is the word? *fleet*

6. Touch the next word. Sound out the word to yourself. Put your thumb up when you can say the whole word. (Wait until thumbs are up.) What is the word? *fork*

(Repeat step 6 with the remaining words in lines 4–6. Then call on a student to read a line.)

7. Read sentence 7 to yourself. Put your thumb up when you are done. (Wait until thumbs are up. Then call on a student to read the sentence.)

(Repeat step 7 with sentences 8–12.)

B. Review Words

(Have students open their books to Lesson 28, page 112.)

1.	shake	shack	thin
2.	thrive	stove	ship
3.	faith	script	right
4.	screen	scream	risk
5.	fond	toast	task

1. Find part B in your book.

2. Read the words in line 1 to yourself. When you can read all three words, put your thumb up. (Wait until thumbs are up.)

3. Get ready to read the words in line 1 together. Begin. *shake, shack, thin*

(Repeat steps 2 and 3 with lines 2–5. Then call on a student to read the words in a line.)

C. Word Endings—Altered Roots

(Have students open their books to Lesson 28, page 112.)

1.	sha<u>k</u>ing	5.	shi<u>pp</u>ed	9.	parted
2.	thi<u>nn</u>er	6.	<u>short</u>er	10.	parting
3.	shipping	7.	toaster		
4.	thri<u>v</u>ing	8.	teaming		

1. Find part C in your book.

2. Look at number 1. How many **k**'s? *one*

3. Will you say the name or the sound for the letter **a**? *the name*

4. What is the name? *a*

5. Sound out the word to yourself. What is the word? *shaking*

6. Look at number 2. How many **n**'s? *two*

7. Will you say the name or the sound for the letter **i**? *the sound*

8. What is the sound? */iii/*

9. Sound out the word to yourself. What is the word? *thinner*

10. Sound out number 3 to yourself. Put your thumb up when you can read the word. (Wait until thumbs are up.) What is the word? *shipping*

(Repeat step 10 with the words **thriving** and **shipped**.)

11. Let's read these five words again. (Call on individual students to read the words.)

12. Look at number 6. Sound out the underlined word to yourself. Put your thumb up when you can say the underlined word. (Wait until thumbs are up.) What is the word? *short*

13. Read **short** with the ending. What is the word? *shorter*

(Repeat steps 12 and 13 with the remaining words.)

14. Let's read these words again. (Call on individual students to read the words.)

D. Challenge Words

(Have students open their books to Lesson 28, page 113.)

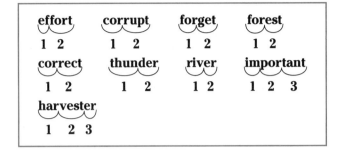

1. Find part D in your book.

2. Touch the first word. Sound out this word to yourself. Put your thumb up when you can say the word. (Wait until thumbs are up.) What is the word? *effort*

3. Sound out the next word to yourself. Put your thumb up when you can say the word. (Wait until thumbs are up.) What is the word? *corrupt*

(Repeat step 3 with the words **forget, forest, correct, thunder, river, important,** and **harvester**.)

4. Let's read these words again. (Call on individual students to read the Challenge Words.)

E. Sight Words

(Have students open their books to Lesson 28, page 113.)

should	would	could	your	who
come	saw	where	been	you
why	what	said		

1. Find part E in your book.

2. Touch the first word. This word is **should**. What is the word? *should* Spell and read. *s-h-o-u-l-d. should*

3. The next word is **would**. What is the word? *would* Spell and read. *w-o-u-l-d. would*

(Repeat step 3 with the remaining words.)

4. Let's read these words again. (Call on individual students to read the Sight Words.)

F. Sentences and Stories

(Have students open their books to Lesson 28, page 113.)

1. Find part F in your book.

2. Touch the title of the story.
   Let's read the title together. *Lord Carl*

3. Read Part 1 to yourself. Read it very carefully.
   Put your thumb up when you are done.
   (Wait until thumbs are up.)

4. Let's read Part 1 together. When you are not
   reading aloud, follow along in your book.
   (Call on a student to read one or two sentences.
   Continue until Part 1 has been read.)

5. Look at the three pictures. Put a number 1
   under the picture that goes with Part 1.

(Repeat steps 3–5 with Parts 2 and 3.)

Answers

| 2 | 3 | 1 |

G. Spelling

(Have students open their books to Lesson 28, page 114.)

1. Find part G in your book.

2. Your first spelling word is **more**. Write **more**.

3. (Write the word on the board or display it
   on-screen.) Check and correct your word.
   (Monitor.)

(Repeat steps 2 and 3 with the word **short**.)

4. Your next spelling word is **forget**.
   Say the parts in **forget**. First part. *for*
   Next part. *get* Write the word.

5. (Write the word on the board or display it
   on-screen.) Check and correct your word.

(Repeat steps 4 and 5 with the word **important**.)

6. Listen. **My sister Jill is very short.**
   Write the sentence. (Monitor.)

7. (Write the sentence on the board or display it
   on-screen.) Check and correct each word.
   (Monitor.)

Answers
1. more   3. forget
2. short   4. important
5. My sister Jill is very short.

H. Practice Activity 1

(Have students open their books to Lesson 28, page 114.)

1. Find part H in your book.

2. Follow along as I read the directions. **Fill in each blank with the best word.**

3. Do number 1. Put your thumb up when you are finished. (Monitor and check.)

4. You will finish part H later.

I. Practice Activity 2

(Have students open their books to Lesson 28, page 115.)

1. Find part I in your book.

2. Follow along as I read the directions. **Read each question. Look back at the story on page 113. Fill in each blank with the best word.**

3. Do number 1. Put your thumb up when you are finished. (Monitor and check.)

4. Now go back and finish parts H and I.

🔊 Work Check for Parts H and I
(Oral Teacher-Directed Activity)

1. Find part H in your book.

2. Let's check your work. If you made a mistake, circle the number. You will fix all mistakes at the end of the lesson. (Call on individual students to read their answers.)

3. Count how many correct answers you have, and write that number in the box at the bottom of the page. (Monitor students.)

(Repeat steps 1–3 with part I.)

4. Now go back and correct any mistakes. (Monitor students.)

Answers for Part H	
1. fork	5. port
2. born	6. horse
3. more	7. thorns
4. torch	8. shorts

Answers for Part I		
Part 1	**Part 2**	**Part 3**
1. fork	4. Lord Norman	7. forest
2. torch	5. north	8. throne
3. Lord Carl	6. storm	

LESSON 29

OBJECTIVES

- *to practice words with* or
- *to practice words with the word endings* -ed, -ing, *and* -er

 Sound Drill
(Oral Teacher-Directed Activity)

(Write the following on the board or display it on-screen:)

1.	or	ck	u	ea
2.	oa	ar	er	ay
3.	ee	e	ar	l
4.	ea	er	ai	igh
5.	or	ow	er	sh

1. Let's practice saying the sounds in the words that we will be reading. Look at the letters in line 1. Say the sounds. /or/, /k/, /uuu/, /eee/

2. Look at the letters in line 2. Say the sounds. /ooo/, /ar/, /er/, /aaa/

(Repeat step 2 with lines 3–5. Then call on individual students to say the sounds in a line.)

(NOTE: As an alternative, review the sounds with flash cards.)

A. New Words

(Have students open their books to Lesson 29, page 116.)

1.	p<u>or</u>k	h<u>or</u>n	s<u>or</u>t
2.	h<u>er</u>d	p<u>ar</u>k	sp<u>or</u>t
3.	st<u>or</u>k	l<u>ar</u>d	str<u>ee</u>t
4.	pr<u>ay</u>	sn<u>or</u>e	st<u>or</u>e
5.	s<u>or</u>e	ch<u>or</u>e	sn<u>ea</u>k
6.	f<u>or</u>m	f<u>er</u>n	c<u>or</u>e

7. **Bob will play his horn in the band.**
8. **Nan was a good sport when we lost the game.**
9. **Some people think that the stork brings good luck.**
10. **Will you explain to me why you snore?**
11. **Cleaning my room is a chore I dislike.**
12. **Write your order on the correct form.**

1. Find part A in your book.

2. Touch the first word in line 1. Look at the underlined letters. What is the sound? */or/*

3. Sound out the word to yourself. Put your thumb up when you can say the whole word. (Wait until thumbs are up.) What is the word? *pork*

4. Touch the next word. Look at the underlined letters. What is the sound? */or/* Sound out the word to yourself. Put your thumb up when you can say the whole word. (Wait until thumbs are up.) What is the word? *horn*

(Repeat step 4 with the remaining words in lines 1–3.)

5. Touch the first word in line 4. Sound out this word to yourself. Put your thumb up when you can say the whole word. (Wait until thumbs are up.) What is the word? *pray*

6. Touch the next word. Sound out the word to yourself. Put your thumb up when you can say the whole word. (Wait until thumbs are up.) What is the word? *snore*

(Repeat step 6 with the remaining words in lines 4–6. Then call on a student to read a line.)

7. Read sentence 7 to yourself. Put your thumb up when you are done. (Wait until thumbs are up. Then call on a student to read the sentence.)

(Repeat step 7 with sentences 8–12.)

B. Review Words

(Have students open their books to Lesson 29, page 116.)

1.	plate	chime	stop
2.	plan	stole	chin
3.	nose	preach	peach
4.	trail	tweed	trade
5.	poach	pond	night

1. Find part B in your book.

2. Read the words in line 1 to yourself. When you can read all three words, put your thumb up. (Wait until thumbs are up.)

3. Get ready to read the words in line 1 together. Begin. *plate, chime, stop*

(Repeat steps 2 and 3 with lines 2–5. Then call on a student to read the words in a line.)

C. Word Endings—Altered Roots

(Have students open their books to Lesson 29, page 116.)

1.	chim<u>i</u>ng	5.	tra<u>d</u>er	9.	<u>parked</u>
2.	tra<u>d</u>ed	6.	<u>sorti</u>ng	10.	<u>sort</u>er
3.	plan<u>n</u>ing	7.	<u>sneak</u>ing		
4.	stop<u>p</u>ing	8.	<u>pray</u>ed		

1. Find part C in your book.

2. Look at number 1. How many **m**'s? *one*

3. Will you say the name or the sound for the letter **i**? *the name*

4. What is the name? *i*

5. Sound out the word to yourself. What is the word? *chiming*

6. Look at number 2. How many **d**'s? *one*

7. Will you say the name or the sound for the letter **a**? *the name*

8. What is the name? *a*

9. Sound out the word to yourself. What is the word? *traded*

10. Sound out number 3 to yourself. Put your thumb up when you can read the word. (Wait until thumbs are up.) What is the word? *planning*

(Repeat step 10 with the words **stopping** and **trader**.)

11. Let's read these five words again. (Call on individual students to read the words.)

12. Look at number 6. Sound out the underlined word to yourself. Put your thumb up when you can say the underlined word. (Wait until thumbs are up.) What is the word? *sort*

13. Read **sort** with the ending. What is the word? *sorting*

(Repeat steps 12 and 13 with the remaining words.)

14. Let's read these words again. (Call on individual students to read the words.)

D. Challenge Words

(Have students open their books to Lesson 29, page 117.)

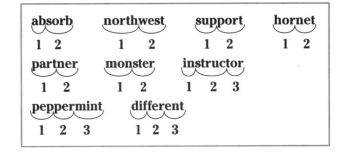

1. Find part D in your book.

2. Touch the first word. Sound out this word to yourself. Put your thumb up when you can say the word. (Wait until thumbs are up.) What is the word? *absorb*

3. Sound out the next word to yourself. Put your thumb up when you can say the word. (Wait until thumbs are up.) What is the word? *northwest*

(Repeat step 3 with the words **support, hornet, partner, monster, instructor, peppermint,** and **different**.)

4. Let's read these words again. (Call on individual students to read the Challenge Words.)

E. Sight Words

(Have students open their books to Lesson 29, page 117.)

she	**he**	**be**	**me**	**we**
your	**where**	**who**	**been**	**come**
should	**what**	**could**	**school**	**have**

1. Find part E in your book.

2. Touch the first word. This word is **she**. What is the word? *she* Spell and read. *s-h-e. she*

3. The next word is **he**. What is the word? *he* Spell and read. *h-e. he*

(Repeat step 3 with the remaining words.)

4. Let's read these words again. (Call on individual students to read the Sight Words.)

F. Sentences and Stories

(Have students open their books to Lesson 29, page 117.)

1. Find part F in your book.

2. Touch the title of the story. Let's read the title together. *Mark's Sore Throat*

3. Read Part 1 to yourself. Read it very carefully. Put your thumb up when you are done. (Wait until thumbs are up.)

4. Let's read Part 1 together. When you are not reading aloud, follow along in your book. (Call on a student to read one or two sentences. Continue until Part 1 has been read.)

5. Look at the three pictures. Put a number 1 under the picture that goes with Part 1.

(Repeat steps 3–5 with Parts 2 and 3.)

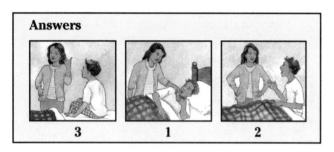

Answers

3   1   2

G. Spelling

(Have students open their books to Lesson 29, page 118.)

1. Find part G in your book.

2. Your first spelling word is **store**. Write **store**.

3. (Write the word on the board or display it on-screen.) Check and correct your word. (Monitor.)

(Repeat steps 2 and 3 with the word **sort**.)

4. Your next spelling word is **northwest**. Say the parts in **northwest**. First part. *north* Next part. *west* Write the word.

5. (Write the word on the board or display it on-screen.) Check and correct your word.

(Repeat steps 4 and 5 with the word **instructor**.)

6. Listen. **Nan was a good sport when we lost.** Write the sentence. (Monitor.)

7. (Write the sentence on the board or display it on-screen.) Check and correct each word. (Monitor.)

Answers
1. store   3. northwest
2. sort   4. instructor
5. **Nan was a good sport when we lost.**

H. Practice Activity 1

(Have students open their books to Lesson 29, page 118.)

1. Find part H in your book.

2. Follow along as I read the directions. **Read the story. Answer the questions.**

3. Read the story to yourself. Do number 1. Put your thumb up when you are finished. (Monitor and check.)

4. You will finish part H later.

I. Practice Activity 2

(Have students open their books to Lesson 29, page 119.)

1. Find part I in your book.

2. Follow along as I read the directions. **Read each question. Look back at the story on page 117. Fill in each blank with the best word.**

3. Do number 1. Put your thumb up when you are finished. (Monitor and check.)

4. Now go back and finish parts H and I.

 ## Work Check for Parts H and I
(Oral Teacher-Directed Activity)

1. Find part H in your book.

2. Let's check your work. If you made a mistake, circle the number. You will fix all mistakes at the end of the lesson. (Call on individual students to read their answers.)

3. Count how many correct answers you have, and write that number in the box at the bottom of the page. (Monitor students.)

(Repeat steps 1–3 with part I.)

4. Now go back and correct any mistakes. (Monitor students.)

Answers for Part H
1. home
2. backyard
3. arm
4. thorn

Answers for Part I		
Part 1	Part 2	Part 3
1. Mark	4. snore	5. art
2. sore		6. today
3. cheek		7. week
		8. Jeff

 ## Checking Up
(Oral Teacher-Directed Activity)

Practice reading Part 1 of the story on page 117. I am going to listen to each of you read. Your goal is to make fewer than two errors. Keep practicing Part 1 until you can read it without any errors.

(Ask each student to read Part 1. Record the number of errors in his or her book.

NOTE: If 90 percent of the students make two errors or fewer, you may move on to Lesson 30. If not, repeat Lesson 29.)

LESSON 30

OBJECTIVES

- *to introduce words with ir and ur*
- *to practice words with the word endings -ed, -ing, and -er*

🔊 New Sound

(Have students open their books to Lesson 30, page 120.)

1. Look at the top of page 120 in your book.

2. Touch the first word.

3. This word is **bird**. Say the word. *bird*

4. The underlined sound is **/ir/**. Say the sound. */ir/*

5. Say the sound again. */ir/*

6. Touch the next word.

7. This word is **turn**. Say the word. *turn*

8. The underlined sound is **/ur/**. Say the sound. */ur/*

9. Say the sound again. */ur/*

(Have students close their books. Then do the Sound Drill activity.)

🔊 Sound Drill
(Oral Teacher-Directed Activity)

(Write the following on the board or display it on-screen:)

1.	ur	ar	a	ir
2.	ow	igh	ur	er
3.	ea	ir	ur	or
4.	ir	oa	er	ee
5.	ar	i	ir	ai

1. Let's practice saying the sounds in the words that we will be reading. Look at the letters in line 1. Say the sounds. */ur/, /ar/, /aaa/, /ir/*

2. Look at the letters in line 2. Say the sounds. $/\overline{ooo}/, /\overline{ii}/, /ur/, /er/$

(Repeat step 2 with lines 3–5. Then call on individual students to say the sounds in a line.)

(NOTE: As an alternative, review the sounds with flash cards.)

A. New Words

(Have students open their books to Lesson 30, page 120.)

1.	f<u>ir</u>	t<u>ur</u>n	t<u>er</u>m
2.	b<u>ur</u>n	f<u>ur</u>	f<u>or</u>
3.	d<u>ir</u>t	d<u>ar</u>t	g<u>ir</u>l
4.	h<u>ur</u>t	st<u>ir</u>	st<u>ar</u>
5.	th<u>u</u>d	f<u>ir</u>st	sp<u>ur</u>t
6.	sp<u>or</u>t	f<u>or</u>t	ch<u>ur</u>n

7. Many fir trees grow in this forest.
8. The fox we saw had gray fur and a long tail.
9. That girl works as a waitress at night.
10. Don't forget to stir the oatmeal.
11. Why do you have to be first in line?
12. A speedboat will churn the water more than a sailboat.

1. Find part A in your book.

2. Touch the first word in line 1. Look at the underlined letters. What is the sound? */ir/*

3. Sound out the word to yourself. Put your thumb up when you can say the whole word. (Wait until thumbs are up.) What is the word? *fir*

4. Touch the next word. Look at the underlined letters. What is the sound? */ur/* Sound out the word to yourself. Put your thumb up when you can say the whole word. (Wait until thumbs are up.) What is the word? *turn*

(Repeat step 4 with the remaining words in lines 1–3.)

5. Touch the first word in line 4. Sound out this word to yourself. Put your thumb up when you can say the whole word. (Wait until thumbs are up.) What is the word? *hurt*

6. Touch the next word. Sound out the word to yourself. Put your thumb up when you can say the whole word. (Wait until thumbs are up.) What is the word? *stir*

(Repeat step 6 with the remaining words in lines 4–6. Then call on a student to read a line.)

7. Read sentence 7 to yourself. Put your thumb up when you are done. (Wait until thumbs are up. Then call on a student to read the sentence.)

(Repeat step 7 with sentences 8–12.)

B. Review Words

(Have students open their books to Lesson 30, page 120.)

1. drive	drip	blade
2. glad	slope	slop
3. bleach	creek	steal
4. stale	might	math
5. snail	bleed	coach

1. Find part B in your book.

2. Read the words in line 1 to yourself. When you can read all three words, put your thumb up. (Wait until thumbs are up.)

3. Get ready to read the words in line 1 together. Begin. *drive, drip, blade*

(Repeat steps 2 and 3 with lines 2–5. Then call on a student to read the words in a line.)

C. Word Endings—Altered Roots

(Have students open their books to Lesson 30, page 120.)

1. dri<u>pp</u>ing	5. dri<u>pp</u>ed	9. <u>turn</u>ing
2. dri<u>v</u>er	6. <u>turn</u>ed	10. <u>stir</u>ring
3. slo<u>pp</u>ed	7. <u>dart</u>ing	
4. slo<u>p</u>ing	8. <u>burn</u>ed	

1. Find part C in your book.

2. Look at number 1. How many **p**'s? *two*

3. Will you say the name or the sound for the letter **i**? *the sound*

4. What is the sound? */iii/*

5. Sound out the word to yourself. What is the word? *dripping*

6. Look at number 2. How many **v**'s? *one*

7. Will you say the name or the sound for the letter **i**? *the name*

8. What is the name? *i*

9. Sound out the word to yourself. What is the word? *driver*

10. Sound out number 3 to yourself. Put your thumb up when you can read the word. (Wait until thumbs are up.) What is the word? *slopped*

(Repeat step 10 with the words **sloping** and **dripped**.)

11. Let's read these five words again. (Call on individual students to read the words.)

12. Look at number 6. Sound out the underlined word to yourself. Put your thumb up when you can say the underlined word. (Wait until thumbs are up.) What is the word? *turn*

13. Read **turn** with the ending. What is the word? *turned*

(Repeat steps 12 and 13 with the remaining words.)

14. Let's read these words again. (Call on individual students to read the words.)

D. Challenge Words

(Have students open their books to Lesson 30, page 121.)

doctor	further	birthday	surprise
1 2	1 2	1 2	1 2
thirteen	occur	confirm	hamburger
1 2	1 2	1 2	1 2 3
frankfurter			
1 2 3			

1. Find part D in your book.

2. Touch the first word. Sound out this word to yourself. Put your thumb up when you can say the word. (Wait until thumbs are up.) What is the word? *doctor*

3. Sound out the next word to yourself. Put your thumb up when you can say the word. (Wait until thumbs are up.) What is the word? *further*

(Repeat step 3 with the words **birthday, surprise, thirteen, occur, confirm, hamburger,** and **frankfurter**.)

4. Let's read these words again. (Call on individual students to read the Challenge Words.)

E. Sight Words

(Have students open their books to Lesson 30, page 121.)

use	your	could	come	have
little	said	been	there	you

1. Find part E in your book.

2. Touch the first word. This word is **use**.
   What is the word? *use*
   Spell and read. *u-s-e. use*

3. The next word is **your**.
   What is the word? *your*
   Spell and read. *y-o-u-r. your*

(Repeat step 3 with the remaining words.)

4. Let's read these words again. (Call on individual students to read the Sight Words.)

F. Sentences and Stories

(Have students open their books to Lesson 30, page 121.)

1. Find part F in your book.

2. Touch the title of the story. Let's read the title together. *A Time to Wait*

3. Read Part 1 to yourself. Read it very carefully. Put your thumb up when you are done. (Wait until thumbs are up.)

4. Let's read Part 1 together. When you are not reading aloud, follow along in your book. (Call on a student to read one or two sentences. Continue until Part 1 has been read.)

5. Look at the three pictures. Put a number 1 under the picture that goes with Part 1.

(Repeat steps 3–5 with Parts 2 and 3.)

Answers

1   3   2

G. Spelling

(Have students open their books to Lesson 30, page 122.)

1. Find part G in your book.

2. Your first spelling word is **turn**. Write **turn**.

3. (Write the word on the board or display it on-screen.) Check and correct your word. (Monitor.)

(Repeat steps 2 and 3 with the word **hurt**.)

4. Your next spelling word is **birthday**.
   Say the parts in **birthday**. First part. *birth*
   Next part. *day* Write the word.

5. (Write the word on the board or display it on-screen.) Check and correct your word.

(Repeat steps 4 and 5 with the word **hamburger**.)

6. Listen. **Fir trees grow in the forest.**
   Write the sentence. (Monitor.)

7. (Write the sentence on the board or display it on-screen.) Check and correct each word. (Monitor.)

Answers
1. turn   3. birthday
2. hurt   4. hamburger
5. **Fir trees grow in the forest.**

H. Practice Activity 1

(Have students open their books to Lesson 30, page 122.)

1. Find part H in your book.

2. Follow along as I read the directions. **Fill in each blank with the best word.**

3. Do number 1. Put your thumb up when you are finished. (Monitor and check.)

4. You will finish part H later.

I. Practice Activity 2

(Have students open their books to Lesson 30, page 123.)

1. Find part I in your book.

2. Follow along as I read the directions. **Read each question. Look back at the story on page 121. Fill in each blank with the best word.**

3. Do number 1. Put your thumb up when you are finished. (Monitor and check.)

4. Now go back and finish parts H and I.

Work Check for Parts H and I
(Oral Teacher-Directed Activity)

1. Find part H in your book.

2. Let's check your work. If you made a mistake, circle the number. You will fix all mistakes at the end of the lesson. (Call on individual students to read their answers.)

3. Count how many correct answers you have, and write that number in the box at the bottom of the page. (Monitor students.)

(Repeat steps 1–3 with part I.)

4. Now go back and correct any mistakes. (Monitor students.)

Answers for Part H	
1. hurt	5. firm
2. fur	6. dirt
3. girl	7. burn
4. bird	8. turn

Answers for Part I		
Part 1	Part 2	Part 3
1. six	4. tests	7. street
2. main	5. bleeding	8. sports car
3. Liz	6. Barb	

LESSON 31

OBJECTIVES

- *to practice words with ir and ur*
- *to practice words with the word endings -ed, -ing, and -er*

 Sound Drill
(Oral Teacher-Directed Activity)

(Write the following on the board or display it on-screen:)

1.	ar	ur	ir	ck
2.	or	u	ar	er
3.	ai	ir	or	e
4.	ur	ch	th	ar
5.	er	a	ir	or

1. Let's practice saying the sounds in the words that we will be reading. Look at the letters in line 1. Say the sounds. */ar/, /ur/, /ir/, /k/*

2. Look at the letters in line 2. Say the sounds. */or/, /uuu/, /ar/, /er/*

(Repeat step 2 with lines 3–5. Then call on individual students to say the sounds in a line.)

(NOTE: As an alternative, review the sounds with flash cards.)

A. New Words

(Have students open their books to Lesson 31, page 124.)

1.	s<u>ir</u>	b<u>ir</u>d	b<u>ea</u>d
2.	sh<u>ir</u>t	c<u>ur</u>b	sh<u>ee</u>t
3.	th<u>ir</u>st	sk<u>ir</u>t	sh<u>ar</u>p
4.	p<u>ur</u>r	ch<u>ai</u>n	ch<u>ur</u>n
5.	st<u>ar</u>t	bl<u>ur</u>	p<u>ur</u>se
6.	h<u>ur</u>l	ch<u>ea</u>p	ch<u>ir</u>p

7. **Sir, you need a permit to park in this lot.**
8. **Do not step off the curb until the stoplight is green.**
9. **The waistband on this skirt is too big.**
10. **Will the cat purr when I pat his fur?**
11. **Mom lost her purse on the subway.**
12. **The instructor will demonstrate how to hurl the ball.**

1. Find part A in your book.

2. Touch the first word in line 1. Look at the underlined letters. What is the sound? */ir/*

3. Sound out the word to yourself. Put your thumb up when you can say the whole word. (Wait until thumbs are up.) What is the word? *sir*

4. Touch the next word. Look at the underlined letters. What is the sound? */ir/* Sound out the word to yourself. Put your thumb up when you can say the whole word. (Wait until thumbs are up.) What is the word? *bird*

(Repeat step 4 with the remaining words in lines 1–3.)

5. Touch the first word in line 4. Sound out this word to yourself. Put your thumb up when you can say the whole word. (Wait until thumbs are up.) What is the word? *purr*

6. Touch the next word. Sound out the word to yourself. Put your thumb up when you can say the whole word. (Wait until thumbs are up.) What is the word? *chain*

(Repeat step 6 with the remaining words in lines 4–6. Then call on a student to read a line.)

7. Read sentence 7 to yourself. Put your thumb up when you are done. (Wait until thumbs are up. Then call on a student to read the sentence.)

(Repeat step 7 with sentences 8–12.)

B. Review Words

(Have students open their books to Lesson 31, page 124.)

1.	globe	glob	prize
2.	chase	clap	plan
3.	bright	swift	boats
4.	frail	braid	yeast
5.	fail	sweet	boast

1. Find part B in your book.

2. Read the words in line 1 to yourself. When you can read all three words, put your thumb up. (Wait until thumbs are up.)

3. Get ready to read the words in line 1 together. Begin. *globe, glob, prize*

(Repeat steps 2 and 3 with lines 2–5. Then call on a student to read the words in a line.)

C. Word Endings—Altered Roots

(Have students open their books to Lesson 31, page 124.)

1.	cha<u>s</u>ing	5.	si<u>z</u>ed	9.	<u>starting</u>
2.	pla<u>nn</u>ed	6.	sharper	10.	<u>churn</u>ed
3.	cha<u>s</u>ed	7.	cheaper		
4.	cla<u>pp</u>ed	8.	chirping		

1. Find part C in your book.

2. Look at number 1. How many **s**'s? *one*

3. Will you say the name or the sound for the letter **a**? *the name*

4. What is the name? *a*

5. Sound out the word to yourself. What is the word? *chasing*

6. Look at number 2. How many **n**'s? *two*

7. Will you say the name or the sound for the letter **a**? *the sound*

8. What is the sound? */aaa/*

9. Sound out the word to yourself. What is the word? *planned*

10. Sound out number 3 to yourself. Put your thumb up when you can read the word. (Wait until thumbs are up.) What is the word? *chased*

(Repeat step 10 with the words **clapped** and **sized**.)

11. Let's read these five words again. (Call on individual students to read the words.)

12. Look at number 6. Sound out the underlined word to yourself. Put your thumb up when you can say the underlined word. (Wait until thumbs are up.) What is the word? *sharp*

13. Read **sharp** with the ending. What is the word? *sharper*

(Repeat steps 12 and 13 with the remaining words.)

14. Let's read these words again. (Call on individual students to read the words.)

D. Challenge Words

(Have students open their books to Lesson 31, page 125.)

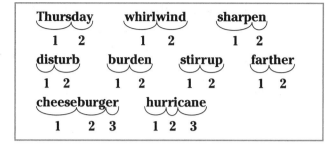

1. Find part D in your book.

2. Touch the first word. Sound out this word to yourself. Put your thumb up when you can say the word. (Wait until thumbs are up.) What is the word? *Thursday*

3. Sound out the next word to yourself. Put your thumb up when you can say the word. (Wait until thumbs are up.) What is the word? *whirlwind*

(Repeat step 3 with the words **sharpen, disturb, burden, stirrup, farther, cheeseburger,** and **hurricane**.)

4. Let's read these words again. (Call on individual students to read the Challenge Words.)

E. Sight Words

(Have students open their books to Lesson 31, page 125.)

would	use	after	your	who
been	come	you	they	what

1. Find part E in your book.

2. Touch the first word. This word is **would**. What is the word? *would* Spell and read. *w-o-u-l-d. would*

3. The next word is *use*. What is the word? *use* Spell and read. *u-s-e. use*

(Repeat step 3 with the remaining words.)

4. Let's read these words again. (Call on individual students to read the Sight Words.)

F. Sentences and Stories

(Have students open their books to Lesson 31, page 125.)

1. Find part F in your book.

2. Touch the title of the story. Let's read the title together. *A Wish for Barb*

3. Read Part 1 to yourself. Read it very carefully. Put your thumb up when you are done. (Wait until thumbs are up.)

4. Let's read Part 1 together. When you are not reading aloud, follow along in your book. (Call on a student to read one or two sentences. Continue until Part 1 has been read.)

5. Look at the three pictures. Put a number 1 under the picture that goes with Part 1.

(Repeat steps 3–5 with Parts 2 and 3.)

G. Spelling

(Have students open their books to Lesson 31, page 126.)

1. Find part G in your book.

2. Your first spelling word is **skirt**. Write **skirt**.

3. (Write the word on the board or display it on-screen.) Check and correct your word. (Monitor.)

(Repeat steps 2 and 3 with the word **sharp**.)

4. Your next spelling word is **Thursday**. Say the parts in **Thursday**. First part. *Thurs* Next part. *day* Write the word.

5. (Write the word on the board or display it on-screen.) Check and correct your word.

(Repeat steps 4 and 5 with the word **cheeseburger**.)

6. Listen. **The nurse wore a white skirt.** Write the sentence. (Monitor.)

7. (Write the sentence on the board or display it on-screen.) Check and correct each word. (Monitor.)

```
Answers
1. skirt      3. Thursday
2. sharp      4. cheeseburger
5. The nurse wore a white skirt.
```

H. Practice Activity 1

(Have students open their books to Lesson 31, page 126.)

1. Find part H in your book.

2. Follow along as I read the directions. **Draw a line under the sentence that goes with each picture.**

3. Do number 1. Put your thumb up when you are finished. (Monitor and check.)

4. You will finish part H later.

I. Practice Activity 2

(Have students open their books to Lesson 31, page 127.)

1. Find part I in your book.

2. Follow along as I read the directions. **Read each question. Look back at the story on page 125. Fill in each blank with the best word.**

3. Do number 1. Put your thumb up when you are finished. (Monitor and check.)

4. Now go back and finish parts H and I.

◄)) Work Check for Parts H and I
(Oral Teacher-Directed Activity)

1. Find part H in your book.

2. Let's check your work. If you made a mistake, circle the number. You will fix all mistakes at the end of the lesson. (Call on individual students to read their answers.)

3. Count how many correct answers you have, and write that number in the box at the bottom of the page. (Monitor students.)

(Repeat steps 1–3 with part I.)

4. Now go back and correct any mistakes. (Monitor students.)

Answers for Part H
1. <u>Carl thirsts for a drink</u>.
2. <u>Rose looked at the shirts</u>.
3. <u>The cat sat on the curb</u>.
4. <u>We saw a nest in the birch tree</u>.
5. <u>The hornet has a sharp stinger</u>.

Answers for Part I

Part 1	Part 2	Part 3
1. nine	4. Clark	7. Barb
2. snack shop	5. star	8. week
3. Barb	6. Barb	

LESSON 32

OBJECTIVES

• *to practice words with* ir *and* ur
• *to practice words with the word endings* -ed, -ing, *and* -er

 Sound Drill
(Oral Teacher-Directed Activity)

(Write the following on the board or display it on-screen:)

1. or	wh	ir	a
2. th	i	igh	ch
3. ur	ck	oa	e
4. ow	or	u	ee
5. ar	o	er	ea

1. Let's practice saying the sounds in the words that we will be reading. Look at the letters in line 1. Say the sounds. */or/, /wh/, /ir/, /aaa/*

2. Look at the letters in line 2. Say the sounds. */th/, /iii/, /ī/, /ch/*

(Repeat step 2 with lines 3–5. Then call on individual students to say the sounds in a line.)

(NOTE: As an alternative, review the sounds with flash cards.)

A. New Words

(Have students open their books to Lesson 32, page 128.)

1.	f<u>ir</u>m	b<u>ur</u>p	farm
2.	c<u>ur</u>l	Barb	Carl
3.	c<u>ur</u>e	bl<u>ur</u>t	bl<u>ee</u>d
4.	n<u>ur</u>se	b<u>ir</u>th	n<u>er</u>ve
5.	b<u>ir</u>ch	K<u>ir</u>k	wh<u>ir</u>l
6.	c<u>ur</u>ve	tw<u>ir</u>l	c<u>ar</u>ve

7. **You must be firm when you are training your dog.**
8. **On a damp day my hair will curl.**
9. **If you have the winning ticket, do not blurt it out.**
10. **The nurse will not disturb you at night.**
11. **Some birch trees have white bark.**
12. **Turn right after the curve in the road.**

1. Find part A in your book.

2. Touch the first word in line 1. Look at the underlined letters. What is the sound? */ir/*

3. Sound out the word to yourself. Put your thumb up when you can say the whole word. (Wait until thumbs are up.) What is the word? *firm*

4. Touch the next word. Look at the underlined letters. What is the sound? */ur/* Sound out the word to yourself. Put your thumb up when you can say the whole word. (Wait until thumbs are up.) What is the word? *burp*

(Repeat step 4 with the remaining words in lines 1–3.)

5. Touch the first word in line 4. Sound out this word to yourself. Put your thumb up when you can say the whole word. (Wait until thumbs are up.) What is the word? *nurse*

6. Touch the next word. Sound out the word to yourself. Put your thumb up when you can say the whole word. (Wait until thumbs are up.) What is the word? *birth*

(Repeat step 6 with the remaining words in lines 4–6. Then call on a student to read a line.)

7. Read sentence 7 to yourself. Put your thumb up when you are done. (Wait until thumbs are up. Then call on a student to read the sentence.)

(Repeat step 7 with sentences 8–12.)

B. Review Words

(Have students open their books to Lesson 32, page 128.)

1.	spine	spin	flame
2.	flap	blond	broke
3.	groan	beast	float
4.	best	flight	grime
5.	steal	grin	braid

1. Find part B in your book.

2. Read the words in line 1 to yourself. When you can read all three words, put your thumb up. (Wait until thumbs are up.)

3. Get ready to read the words in line 1 together. Begin. *spine, spin, flame*

(Repeat steps 2 and 3 with lines 2–5. Then call on a student to read the words in a line.)

C. Word Endings—Altered Roots

(Have students open their books to Lesson 32, page 128.)

1.	spin<u>n</u>ing	5.	bro<u>k</u>er	9.	<u>whirling</u>
2.	flaming	6.	<u>farm</u>er	10.	<u>twirl</u>ed
3.	grin<u>n</u>ing	7.	<u>firm</u>er		
4.	spin<u>n</u>er	8.	<u>bleed</u>ing		

1. Find part C in your book.

2. Look at number 1. How many **n**'s? *two*

3. Will you say the name or the sound for the letter **i**? *the sound*

4. What is the sound? */iii/*

5. Sound out the word to yourself. What is the word? *spinning*

6. Look at number 2. How many **m**'s? *one*

7. Will you say the name or the sound for the letter **a**? *the name*

8. What is the name? *a*

9. Sound out the word to yourself. What is the word? *flaming*

10. Sound out number 3 to yourself. Put your thumb up when you can read the word. (Wait until thumbs are up.) What is the word? *grinning*

(Repeat step 10 with the words **spinner** and **broker**.)

11. Let's read these five words again. (Call on individual students to read the words.)

12. Look at number 6. Sound out the underlined word to yourself. Put your thumb up when you can say the underlined word. (Wait until thumbs are up.) What is the word? *farm*

13. Read **farm** with the ending. What is the word? *farmer*

(Repeat steps 12 and 13 with the remaining words.)

14. Let's read these words again. (Call on individual students to read the words.)

D. Challenge Words

(Have students open their books to Lesson 32, page 129.)

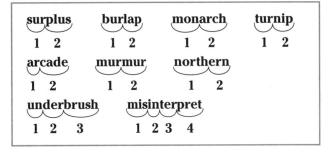

1. Find part D in your book.

2. Touch the first word. Sound out this word to yourself. Put your thumb up when you can say the word. (Wait until thumbs are up.) What is the word? *surplus*

3. Sound out the next word to yourself. Put your thumb up when you can say the word. (Wait until thumbs are up.) What is the word? *burlap*

(Repeat step 3 with the words **monarch, turnip, arcade, murmur, northern, underbrush,** and **misinterpret**.)

4. Let's read these words again. (Call on individual students to read the Challenge Words.)

E. Sight Words

(Have students open their books to Lesson 32, page 129.)

use	**they**	**your**	**should**	**were**
who	**work**	**come**	**are**	**been**

1. Find part E in your book.

2. Touch the first word. This word is **use**. What is the word? *use* Spell and read. *u-s-e. use*

3. The next word is **they**. What is the word? *they* Spell and read. *t-h-e-y. they*

(Repeat step 3 with the remaining words.)

4. Let's read these words again. (Call on individual students to read the Sight Words.)

F. Sentences and Stories

(Have students open their books to Lesson 32, page 129.)

1. Find part F in your book.

2. Touch the title of the story. Let's read the title together. *Kirk Turns Three*

3. Read Part 1 to yourself. Read it very carefully. Put your thumb up when you are done. (Wait until thumbs are up.)

4. Let's read Part 1 together. When you are not reading aloud, follow along in your book. (Call on a student to read one or two sentences. Continue until Part 1 has been read.)

5. Look at the three pictures. Put a number 1 under the picture that goes with Part 1.

(Repeat steps 3–5 with Parts 2 and 3.)

Answers

| 2 | 1 | 3 |

G. Spelling

(Have students open their books to Lesson 32, page 130.)

1. Find part G in your book.

2. Your first spelling word is **nurse**. Write **nurse**.

3. (Write the word on the board or display it on-screen.) Check and correct your word. (Monitor.)

(Repeat steps 2 and 3 with the word **curve**.)

4. Your next spelling word is **surplus**. Say the parts in **surplus**. First part. *sur* Next part. *plus* Write the word.

5. (Write the word on the board or display it on-screen.) Check and correct your word.

(Repeat steps 4 and 5 with the word **misinterpret**.)

6. Listen. **Turn right after the curve in the road.** Write the sentence. (Monitor.)

7. (Write the sentence on the board or display it on-screen.) Check and correct each word. (Monitor.)

Answers
1. nurse   3. surplus
2. curve   4. misinterpret
5. **Turn right after the curve in the road.**

H. Practice Activity 1

(Have students open their books to Lesson 32, page 130.)

1. Find part H in your book.

2. Follow along as I read the directions. **Read the story. Answer the questions.**

3. Read the story to yourself. Do number 1. Put your thumb up when you are finished. (Monitor and check.)

4. You will finish part H later.

I. Practice Activity 2

(Have students open their books to Lesson 32, page 131.)

1. Find part I in your book.

2. Follow along as I read the directions. **Read each question. Look back at the story on page 129. Fill in each blank with the best word.**

3. Do number 1. Put your thumb up when you are finished. (Monitor and check.)

4. Now go back and finish parts H and I.

 ## Work Check for Parts H and I
(Oral Teacher-Directed Activity)

1. Find part H in your book.

2. Let's check your work. If you made a mistake, circle the number. You will fix all mistakes at the end of the lesson. (Call on individual students to read their answers.)

3. Count how many correct answers you have, and write that number in the box at the bottom of the page. (Monitor students.)

(Repeat steps 1–3 with part I.)

4. Now go back and correct any mistakes. (Monitor students.)

Answers for Part H
1. curve
2. leg
3. vet
4. ten

Answers for Part I		
Part 1	Part 2	Part 3
1. birth	4. den	6. Carla
2. His dad	5. play farm	7. fork
3. three		8. game

Checking Up
(Oral Teacher-Directed Activity)

Practice reading Part 1 of the story on page 129. I am going to listen to each of you read. Your goal is to make fewer than two errors. Keep practicing Part 1 until you can read it without any errors.

(Ask each student to read Part 1. Record the number of errors in his or her book.

NOTE: If a number of your students make more than two errors, repeat Lesson 32.)

Answer Key

LESSON 1

F. Sentences and Stories

    1   3   2

G. Spelling

1. stay   3. raindrop   5. The dog has a
2. wait   4. payday   black tail.

H. Practice Activity 1

1. a. a mop in the pail
2. a. have a sail
3. a. wait in the truck
4. b. fail a test
5. b. pay the bill
6. b. sit in the hay
7. a. rain on this day

I. Practice Activity 2

1. The dog has a black tail.
2. The cats play in the box.
3. The rain will fill the pail.
4. Rob put the nail in the box.
5. Chuck will wait until the bus stops.
6. Will Beth fail the test?
7. The maid will dust the lamp.
8. The man will pay with cash.

LESSON 2

F. Sentences and Stories

    3   2   1

G. Spelling

1. play   3. paintbrush   5. The crayon is
2. trail   4. maintain   in the box.

H. Practice Activity 1

1. no   6. yes
2. yes   7. yes
3. no   8. yes
4. yes   9. no
5. no   10. yes

I. Practice Activity 2

1. Rob and Chuck play with the train.
2. Pam's muffin is on the tray.
3. A train runs on a rail.
4. The paintbrush is in the pail.
5. Mom got the mail.
6. Beth has a braid.
7. The hen stands in the hay.
8. Jay painted the shed.

LESSON 3

F. Sentences and Stories

2   1   3

G. Spelling

1. grain   3. explain   5. The mail is in
2. pray   4. paycheck   the mailbox.

H. Practice Activity 1

1. bay   6. mail
2. rain   7. stay
3. tray   8. paint
4. bait   9. braid
5. grain   10. drain

I. Practice Activity 2

1. The men will stay in the cabin.
2. Paint is in the can.
3. Bess will play in the rain.
4. Ray has bait in a pail.
5. The hat has red dots.
6. The dog will run up the trail.
7. Nick and Gail play with clay.
8. The mail is in the mailbox.

LESSON 4

F. Sentences and Stories

3   2   1

G. Spelling

1. week   3. peanut   5. Fish swim in
2. beach   4. seashell   the deep sea.

H. Practice Activity 1

1. bee   5. tea
2. see   6. sea
3. feed   7. each
4. week   8. eat

I. Practice Activity 2

1. The van will need gas.
2. Rob leans on the mailbox.
3. The seaweed is on the beach.
4. He will feed the dog each day.
5. Fish swim in the deep sea.
6. Nan will cut each beet.
7. Beth saw a bee on the seat.
8. Rain fell on the leaf.

LESSON 5

F. Sentences and Stories

2   1   3

G. Spelling

1. deep
2. clean
3. freedom
4. freeway
5. I need to clean my hands.

H. Practice Activity 1

1. Bess and Pat fill the pail with sand.
2. The seal will play on the rocks.
3. The swim team will get a treat.
4. Jay will clean the paintbrush.
5. Dad will hail a cab.
6. Mom will peel the skin off the peach.
7. We got free tickets to the train.

I. Practice Activity 2

1. Ted peeled the egg.
2. Jill reads each day.
3. The seal swims in the water.
4. Nan feels sad.
5. Chuck will meet you at the bus stop.
6. She put weeds in the pail.
7. Dad keeps nails in a box.
8. I need to clean my hands.

LESSON 6

F. Sentences and Stories

1   3   2

G. Spelling

1. green
2. speak
3. teapot
4. sleepless
5. The leaf fell off the tree.

H. Practice Activity 1

1. That shop will fix my mom's heel.
2. Jay speaks to the men on the beach.
3. Jan sprayed the wheels green.
4. The jeep is next to three trees.
5. Bill can reach the gray tray.
6. Sam dreams in his sleep.
7. Clean teeth feel slick.

I. Practice Activity 2

1. Pam speaks to Tom.
2. Stan cleaned his teeth.
3. The pot was filled with steam.
4. Sheep eat green grass.
5. The teen can reach the tray.
6. He can fix the heel.
7. Snow fell on the trees.
8. Bess played at the beach.

LESSON 7

F. Sentences and Stories

    3   1   2

G. Spelling

1. soap
2. grow
3. window
4. oatmeal
5. There is soap in the bowl.

H. Practice Activity 1

1. The boat has a yellow sail.
2. The leaf fell off the tree.
3. Fran will soak her socks.
4. Matt and Jill will row the boat.
5. The van cannot go past the low tree.

I. Practice Activity 2

Story 1
1. coat
2. snow
3. road
4. own

Story 2
1. bowl
2. soap
3. load
4. soak

LESSON 8

F. Sentences and Stories

    1   3   2

G. Spelling

1. throw
2. roast
3. pillow
4. roadway
5. Pam got a loan at the bank.

H. Practice Activity 1

1. Jeff will toss a pass to his coach.
2. The goat eats weeds.
3. Lee saw a crack in the teapot.
4. The tugboat tows the big ship.
5. The coast has lots of rocks.

I. Practice Activity 2

Story 1
1. ill
2. toast
3. beef
4. moaned

Story 2
1. boat
2. tow
3. coats
4. lead

LESSON 9

F. Sentences and Stories

2   1   3

G. Spelling

1. shown   3. seacoast   5. The sailboat is
2. boast   4. sailboat   very slow.

H. Practice Activity 1

1. The little tree will grow.
2. The gulls have flown to the rocks.
3. Ed soaks his feet in the tub.
4. Lim has shown his train set to Nat.
5. I saw my shadow.

I. Practice Activity 2

Story 1	Story 2
1. fleet	1. cleaned
2. flown	2. soak
3. pack	3. green
4. fresh	4. goal

LESSON 10

F. Sentences and Stories

1   3   2

G. Spelling

1. night   3. highway   5. The highway
2. bright   4. insight   went to the
                                   right.

H. Practice Activity 1

1. The wind blows the hay.
2. Her coat is tight.
3. The dog might frighten the cat.
4. The truck went on the highway.
5. The gulls are in flight.

I. Practice Activity 2

Story 1	Story 2
1. gray	1. paint
2. blown	2. bleach
3. high	3. bright
4. sight	4. right

LESSON 11

F. Sentences and Stories

3   1   2

G. Spelling

1. flight
2. high
3. stoplight
4. trainload
5. Jack lifts his right hand.

H. Practice Activity 1

1. Jack lifts his right hand.
2. The sheet is on the bed.
3. Pam put the light on at night.
4. The tree is in the road.
5. The train is fast.

I. Practice Activity 2

Story 1	Story 2
1. road	1. trail
2. light	2. show
3. sheet	3. thigh
4. night	4. right

LESSON 12

F. Sentences and Stories

3   2   1

G. Spelling

1. right
2. sight
3. brightness
4. frighten
5. Nell might see the sights.

H. Practice Activity 1

1. Beth has a braid.
2. Don sweeps the rug.
3. There was bright sun at midday.
4. A duck floats on the pond.
5. The gulls are in flight.

I. Practice Activity 2

Story 1	Story 2
1. ten	1. plant shop
2. snack shop	2. three
3. ham, bun	3. three plants
4. milk	4. tree

LESSON 13

F. Sentences and Stories

    2   3   1

G. Spelling

1. came   3. pancake   5. Nan can bake
2. lake   4. handmade   bran muffins.

H. Practice Activity 1

1. Tom wakes up at six.
2. Nan can bake bran muffins.
3. Fran put tape on the box.
4. The duck floated in the lake.
5. Chet will put cash in the safe.

I. Practice Activity 2

Story 1	Story 2
1. three	1. lunch
2. cape	2. lake
3. desk	3. cake
4. play	4. cake pan

LESSON 14

F. Sentences and Stories

    2   1   3

G. Spelling

1. name   3. classmate   5. Tom will rake
2. late   4. mistake   the grass.

H. Practice Activity 1

1. Tom can rake the grass.
2. Liz chats with her classmate.
3. That man has a cane.
4. Tom is waking up.
5. Beth and Kit have the same dress.

I. Practice Activity 2

Story 1	Story 2
1. six	1. ten
2. grill	2. jeep
3. beef	3. snack
4. grill	4. lake

LESSON 15

F. Sentences and Stories

3   1   2

G. Spelling

1. plane   3. statement   5. You may miss
2. whale   4. demonstrate   your plane.

H. Practice Activity 1

1. flame   6. ate
2. game   7. whale
3. grape   8. rake
4. plane   9. tape
5. snake   10. state

I. Practice Activity 2

Story 1   **Story 2**
1. three   1. last night
2. gate   2. bake shop
3. black   3. muffins
4. snack   4. take

LESSON 16

F. Sentences and Stories

3   2   1

G. Spelling

1. plate   3. escape   5. Did you see a
2. plant   4. contemplate   flake of snow?

H. Practice Activity 1

1. Skate Shop
2. ten
3. skates
4. skates

I. Practice Activity 2

Part 1	Part 2	Part 3
1. stuff	4. shelf	6. crates
2. skate	5. flakes	7. plates
3. case		8. shame

LESSON 17

F. Sentences and Stories

    1   2   3

G. Spelling

1. smile   3. nineteen   5. Will you loan
2. white   4. reptile   me a dime?

H. Practice Activity 1

1. desk
2. five
3. plane
4. help

I. Practice Activity 2

Part 1	Part 2	Part 3
1. peach tree	5. bike	7. club
2. May	6. kite	8. Trish, Meg
3. nine days		
4. peach		

LESSON 18

F. Sentences and Stories

    3   2   1

G. Spelling

1. hope   3. explode   5. Did you vote
2. cone   4. sunstroke   today?

H. Practice Activity 1

1. dock
2. rod, reel
3. fish
4. three

I. Practice Activity 2

Part 1	Part 2	Part 3
1. grass	4. Slow Pokes	6. code
2. club code	5. STEAM	7. Bike
3. pine tree		8. Kite

LESSON 19

F. Sentences and Stories

     3   2   1

G. Spelling

1. shade   3. daytime   5. Are they going
2. those   4. holiday   to pave the road?

H. Practice Activity 1

1. spoke
2. cone
3. tame
4. smiling
5. digging

I. Practice Activity 2

Part 1	Part 2	Part 3
1. pine tree	4. code name	6. five
2. note	5. school	7. code name
3. Lane Bank		8. STREAM Club

LESSON 20

F. Sentences and Stories

     3   1   2

G. Spelling

1. globe   3. pipeline   5. Traffic was
2. shape   4. trade wind   backed up for
                                      a mile.

H. Practice Activity 1

1. dry
2. drive
3. five
4. show

I. Practice Activity 2

Part 1	Part 2	Part 3
1. show	4. cave	7. frog
2. play	5. side	8. desk
3. stay home	6. cave	

LESSON 21

F. Sentences and Stories

    3   1   2

G. Spelling

1. farm
2. march
3. carpet
4. artistic
5. Barb has a star role in the play.

H. Practice Activity 1

1. show
2. ten
3. Beach Road
4. steam

I. Practice Activity 2

Part 1	Part 2	Part 3
1. ill	3. beach	6. tonight
2. farm	4. look	7. ten
	5. time	8. three

LESSON 22

F. Sentences and Stories

    1   2   3

G. Spelling

1. spark
2. hard
3. market
4. harmless
5. Mark your mistakes in red.

H. Practice Activity 1

1. Jeff has a cut on his arm.
2. Beth sits in the barn.
3. Jan played the harp.
4. Fred sent a card to Kay.
5. His home is far away.

I. Practice Activity 2

Part 1	Part 2	Part 3
1. up	4. seat	7. card
2. gate	5. cards	8. three
3. three	6. bam	

LESSON 23

F. Sentences and Stories

1   3   2

G. Spelling

1. charm   3. tarnish   5. The man will
2. sharp   4. discard   park his car.

H. Practice Activity 1

1. park the car
2. march with the band
3. bark at you
4. carve the roast
5. play with the yarn
6. very sharp
7. a cut on his arm

I. Practice Activity 2

Part 1	Part 2	Part 3
1. park	3. town	6. dog
2. scar	4. vet	7. Sparky
	5. barnyard	

LESSON 24

F. Sentences and Stories

2   1   3

G. Spelling

1. term   3. perfect   5. The herd ate
2. fern   4. yesterday   hay on the farm.

H. Practice Activity 1

1. cloak
2. three
3. coat
4. coat

I. Practice Activity 2

Part 1	Part 2	Part 3
1. Fern High	4. plans	7. Market
2. Meg	5. Mike	8. Herb Train
3. Jane	6. State U.	

LESSON 25

F. Sentences and Stories

      3   2   1

G. Spelling

1. jerk
2. perch
3. member
4. permit
5. Bert is a carpenter.

H. Practice Activity 1

1. harp
2. clerk
3. farm
4. part
5. herd
6. spark
7. scarf
8. verb

I. Practice Activity 2

Part 1	Part 2	Part 3
1. peach tarts	4. teacher	6. grass
2. trade school	5. market	7. whales
3. carpenter		8. trainers

LESSON 26

F. Sentences and Stories

      1   3   2

G. Spelling

1. clerk
2. serve
3. whisper
4. never
5. The clerk was very stern.

H. Practice Activity 1

1. a. <u>put on her coat</u>
2. b. <u>with a ball of yarn</u>
3. b. <u>park the car</u>
4. a. <u>very bright</u>
5. b. <u>send a card</u>
6. a. <u>filled with herbs</u>
7. b. <u>say each verse</u>

I. Practice Activity 2

Part 1	Part 2	Part 3
1. Herb	4. sleep	6. Bergs
2. dog	5. work	7. clock
3. week		8. work

LESSON 27

F. Sentences and Stories

     3   2   1

G. Spelling

1. corn   3. morning   5. Lead the horse
2. sport   4. performer   into the barn.

H. Practice Activity 1

1. <u>The waitress gave us more water</u>.
2. <u>Nan mended her torn scarf</u>.
3. <u>The horse is in the barn</u>.
4. <u>Tom will sort the mail</u>.
5. <u>Sal plays a horn in the band</u>.

I. Practice Activity 2

Part 1	Part 2	Part 3
1. Jane	5. coat	7. coat
2. winter storms	6. Carl	8. fort
3. fort		
4. tonight		

LESSON 28

F. Sentences and Stories

     2   3   1

G. Spelling

1. more   3. forget   5. My sister Jill is
2. short   4. important   very short.

H. Practice Activity 1

1. fork   5. port
2. born   6. horse
3. more   7. thorns
4. torch   8. shorts

I. Practice Activity 2

Part 1	Part 2	Part 3
1. fork	4. Lord Norman	7. forest
2. torch	5. north	8. throne
3. Lord Carl	6. storm	

LESSON 29

F. Sentences and Stories

 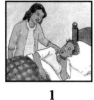

    3   1   2

G. Spelling

1. store 3. northwest 5. Nan was a
2. sort 4. instructor   good sport
                              when we lost.

H. Practice Activity 1

1. home
2. backyard
3. arm
4. thorn

I. Practice Activity 2

Part 1	Part 2	Part 3
1. Mark	4. snore	5. art
2. sore		6. today
3. cheek		7. week
		8. Jeff

LESSON 30

F. Sentences and Stories

    1   3   2

G. Spelling

1. turn 3. birthday 5. Fir trees grow
2. hurt 4. hamburger   in the forest.

H. Practice Activity 1

1. hurt   5. firm
2. fur   6. dirt
3. girl   7. burn
4. bird   8. turn

I. Practice Activity 2

Part 1	Part 2	Part 3
1. six	4. tests	7. street
2. main	5. bleeding	8. sports car
3. Liz	6. Barb	

LESSON 31

F. Sentences and Stories

3   1   2

G. Spelling

1. skirt
2. sharp
3. Thursday
4. cheeseburger
5. The nurse wore a white skirt.

H. Practice Activity 1

1. <u>Carl thirsts for a drink</u>.
2. <u>Rose looked at the shirts</u>.
3. <u>The cat sat on the curb</u>.
4. <u>We saw a nest in the birch tree</u>.
5. <u>The hornet has a sharp stinger</u>.

I. Practice Activity 2

Part 1	Part 2	Part 3
1. nine	4. Clark	7. Barb
2. snack shop	5. star	8. week
3. Barb	6. Barb	

LESSON 32

F. Sentences and Stories

2   1   3

G. Spelling

1. nurse
2. curve
3. surplus
4. misinterpret
5. Turn right after the curve in the road.

H. Practice Activity 1

1. curve
2. leg
3. vet
4. ten

I. Practice Activity 2

Part 1	Part 2	Part 3
1. birth	4. den	6. Carla
2. His dad	5. play farm	7. fork
3. three		8. game

Word Lists

LESSON 1	LESSON 2	LESSON 3	LESSON 4	LESSON 5	LESSON 6
New Words	**New Words**	**New Words**	**New Words**	**New Words**	**New Words**
fail	ray	bay	beef	deep	reach
day	mail	main	eat	keep	three
may	gain	man	sea	team	sheep
wait	Jay	Gail	say	fail	tree
wit	paint	bat	week	feel	tray
tail	pant	bait	tea	read	leak
way	trail	bit	meat	raid	heel
say	rail	pray	beach	jeep	hail
sail	train	pay	need	weed	wheel
maid	brain	stay	see	peel	sleep
mad	play	plan	lead	pail	green
stay	lay	plain	feed	seal	grain
pain	tray	drain	each	clean	speak
pail	braid	grain	deep	meet	steal
play	gray	raid	trail	treat	teeth
hay	clay	Ray	beat	trait	dream
jail	faint	spray	bait	hail	scream
aid	fin	raise	beets	cream	spray
Challenge Words	**Challenge Words**	**Challenge Words**	**Challenge Words**	**Challenge Words**	**Challenge Words**
raindrop	paintbrush	explain	seashell	freeway	teapot
mailbox	waitress	paycheck	peanut	indeed	steamship
midday	pigtail	mainland	seaweed	seasick	sleepless
railway	crayon	subway	payment	reason	treetop
payday	maintain	waistband	sunbeam	freedom	speedway
Sight Words	**Sight Words**	**Sight Words**	**Sight Words**	**Sight Words**	**Sight Words**
were	were	they	there	there	said
you	said	were	were	things	were
of	you	said	things	they	there
said	to	you	have	were	saw
have	of	after	some	some	down
after	are	my	people	water	have
from	look	have	you	into	you
my	was	put	little	you	was
to	my	saw	of	from	to
they	have	of	water	people	little

LESSON 7	LESSON 8	LESSON 9	LESSON 10	LESSON 11	LESSON 12
New Words	**New Words**	**New Words**	**New Words**	**New Words**	**New Words**
own	tow	coal	high	light	light
float	goat	slow	night	slight	bright
toad	loan	flown	fight	high	sigh
road	lean	may	flown	trail	least
read	glow	mow	sight	right	show
flow	rail	goal	saint	screen	might
bail	roast	throw	blown	snail	steal
bowl	bay	Gail	bright	sight	fright
grow	bow	foam	teeth	street	faint
soap	blown	groan	cheat	throat	night
leaf	mean	shown	coast	sheet	braid
loaf	float	green	right	thigh	sight
bait	tea	growth	sigh	flight	sweep
boat	toast	soak	see	tray	flight
show	coach	gray	say	spray	float
soak	coast	cloak	hay	bright	shown
low	fleet	boast	bleach	speech	roast
moan	throw	beast	blow	might	right
Challenge Words	**Challenge Words**	**Challenge Words**	**Challenge Words**	**Challenge Words**	**Challenge Words**
window	pillow	snowdrift	highway	sightless	brightness
roadbed	boatload	shadow	gaslight	stoplight	frighten
elbow	snowman	sailboat	upright	nightfall	soapsuds
oatmeal	rainbow	follow	insight	handrail	ingrown
yellow	fellow	coatrack	railroad	daydream	tailcoat
rowboat	roadway	seacoast	speedboat	trainload	weakness
Sight Words	**Sight Words**	**Sight Words**	**Sight Words**	**Sight Words**	**Sight Words**
all	all	there	do	do	do
there	they	to	after	what	where
water	there	work	all	all	all
they	water	all	saw	where	what
work	are	after	of	said	people
you	were	was	were	there	there
said	said	you	water	have	saw
were	little	little	you	were	were
from	you	said	was	they	work
put	saw	were	there	you	you

LESSON 13	LESSON 14	LESSON 15	LESSON 16	LESSON 17	LESSON 18
New Words	**New Words**	**New Words**	**New Words**	**New Words**	**New Words**
bake	name	state	case	line	robe
came	safe	ate	flat	ride	joke
makc	take	brave	shame	nine	bone
made	same	fate	ham	dim	rode
mad	Sam	at	rate	dime	vote
hate	pane	plane	trade	time	rod
gave	mate	brake	flake	hide	hope
tape	pan	fat	date	hid	rob
sale	rack	plan	lack	white	note
lake	rake	glad	plate	Tim	rose
tap	mat	whale	van	kite	not
cape	flame	shape	slave	kit	hole
mane	gate	clap	sale	ripe	hop
man	cane	lame	plant	rip	woke
wake	can	grape	vane	fine	poke
fad	rat	snake	fame	fin	cone
fade	late	slap	skate	smile	nose
late	rate	wave	crate	five	code
Challenge Words	**Challenge Words**	**Challenge Words**	**Challenge Words**	**Challenge Words**	**Challenge Words**
tailgate	gateway	shipmate	lateness	dislike	explode
keepsake	classmate	statement	wasteland	nineteen	sunstroke
pancake	estate	upgrade	landscape	bathrobe	backbone
handmade	mistake	exhale	shapeless	reptile	hopeless
cupcake	dictate	whaleboat	escape	sideways	mealtime
inhale	estimate	demonstrate	contemplate	intimidate	nightingale
Sight Words	**Sight Words**	**Sight Words**	**Sight Words**	**Sight Words**	**Sight Words**
be	me	he	my	my	by
we	she	me	by	why	try
she	he	she	why	try	why
me	be	we	cry	dry	dry
they	we	be	dry	cry	cry
do	were	where	where	what	where
what	do	they	some	school	what
work	what	do	do	after	after
where	people	what	what	where	were
all	where	water	work	some	put
you	they	there	there	do	there
there	there	down	after	were	of
said	you	look	all	there	do
have	all	all	have	of	you
	of	were	down	all	all

LESSON 19	LESSON 20	LESSON 21	LESSON 22	LESSON 23	LESSON 24
New Words	**New Words**	**New Words**	**New Words**	**New Words**	**New Words**
pave	bike	car	jar	dart	her
pill	brat	bark	arm	yarn	fern
pile	save	far	hard	tar	farm
fine	blame	farm	scar	tow	hay
fin	glob	foam	Jay	Mars	term
shade	globe	Barb	speed	hark	train
ram	lick	star	aim	bar	verb
those	vase	part	spark	bow	herd
frame	like	stay	art	charm	hard
smoke	mill	park	eat	cheat	own
rope	mile	peek	mark	chart	tart
smock	shape	fight	card	harp	Herb
pine	cave	march	marsh	cart	clerk
pin	whip	barn	meek	coat	cloak
side	wide	paint	might	day	cheek
Sid	slid	start	yard	sharp	stern
spoke	broke	steam	oats	sheep	smart
drive	slide	smart	scarf	shark	perk
Challenge Words	**Challenge Words**	**Challenge Words**	**Challenge Words**	**Challenge Words**	**Challenge Words**
daytime	lifebelt	artist	harmless	marshland	perfect
tightrope	capsize	carpet	market	tarnish	sherbet
teammate	pipeline	marlin	arctic	discard	modern
maypole	drainpipe	garden	garlic	barnyard	verdict
mealtime	trade wind	harvest	Martin	sharpen	lantern
holiday	candidate	artistic	garnishment	inartistic	enter
					gardener
					yesterday
					September
Sight Words	**Sight Words**	**Sight Words**	**Sight Words**	**Sight Words**	**Sight Words**
my	my	would	could	should	my
dry	by	should	should	could	why
why	why	could	would	would	by
cry	cry	been	been	where	cry
by	dry	what	there	been	dry
what	what	some	what	after	come
school	after	by	work	what	who
where	were	where	where	saw	been
from	where	you	all	were	where
are	you	all	you	from	there
all	all	do	of	you	said
you	said	of	after	there	were
saw	there	said	they	water	what
do	do			said	you
there	she				school

171

LESSON 25	LESSON 26	LESSON 27	LESSON 28	LESSON 29	LESSON 30
New Words	**New Words**	**New Words**	**New Words**	**New Words**	**New Words**
Bert	her	for	nor	pork	fir
jerk	berg	corn	born	horn	turn
jeep	bright	fort	barn	sort	term
harp	verse	fern	clerk	herd	burn
term	bark	worn	more	park	fur
Herb	verb	cart	coat	sport	for
Bart	clay	sport	port	stork	dirt
team	perk	spark	part	lard	dart
perch	park	storm	cord	street	girl
serve	clerk	north	fleet	pray	hurt
sight	Clark	speed	fork	snore	stir
peach	herb	star	torch	store	star
part	start	coach	torn	sore	thud
night	stern	horse	short	chore	first
nerve	stain	tore	lord	sneak	spurt
swerve	dark	shore	team	form	sport
yard	serve	need	thorn	fern	fort
card	harm	wore	term	core	churn
Challenge Words	**Challenge Words**	**Challenge Words**	**Challenge Words**	**Challenge Words**	**Challenge Words**
mermaid	better	corner	effort	absorb	doctor
member	whisper	order	corrupt	northwest	further
checkers	rocker	border	forget	support	birthday
permit	sister	popcorn	forest	hornet	surprise
pattern	gather	morning	correct	partner	thirteen
hamster	never	horseback	thunder	monster	occur
winter	number	dinner	river	instructor	confirm
carpenter	perhaps	shelter	important	peppermint	hamburger
grasshopper	kindergarten	performer	harvester	different	frankfurter
Sight Words	**Sight Words**	**Sight Words**	**Sight Words**	**Sight Words**	**Sight Words**
she	could	my	should	she	use
he	should	by	would	he	your
me	would	cry	could	be	could
be	come	dry	your	me	come
we	who	why	who	we	have
come	been	your	come	your	little
who	where	come	saw	where	said
been	very	down	where	who	been
would	they	who	been	been	there
where	you	where	you	come	you
school	what	little	why	should	
what	work	she	what	what	
are	said	been	said	could	
work		what		school	
after		could		have	

172

LESSON 31	LESSON 32
New Words	**New Words**
sir	firm
bird	burp
bead	farm
shirt	curl
curb	Barb
sheet	Carl
thirst	cure
skirt	blurt
sharp	bleed
purr	nurse
chain	birth
churn	nerve
start	birch
blur	Kirk
purse	whirl
hurl	curve
cheap	twirl
chirp	carve
Challenge Words	**Challenge Words**
Thursday	surplus
whirlwind	burlap
sharpen	monarch
disturb	turnip
burden	arcade
stirrup	murmur
farther	northern
cheeseburger	underbrush
hurricane	misinterpret
Sight Words	**Sight Words**
would	use
use	they
after	your
your	should
who	were
been	who
come	work
you	come
they	are
what	been

INDIVIDUAL EDUCATION PLAN (IEP)

Name of Student _____ Student's Age _____

Teacher _____ Student's Grade _____

Date Begun _____ Date Completed _____

Long-Term Goal: _____ will be able to read the phonetically regular and irregular words presented in **Phonics for Reading, Second Level,** when those words are presented in lists or within passages.

SHORT-TERM OBJECTIVES   Lessons

One-Syllable Words

1. Given a list of words with *ai* and *ay,* _____   1–3
   will be able to read the words with _____ accuracy.
   (Examples: *rain, play, pail, may*)

2. Given a list of words with *ee* and *ea,* _____   4–6
   will be able to read the words with _____ accuracy.
   (Examples: *beach, lead, beef, sheep*)

3. Given a list of words with *oa* and *ow,* _____   7–9
   will be able to read the words with _____ accuracy.
   (Examples: *coach, toast, flow, show*)

4. Given a list of words with *igh,* _____   10–12
   will be able to read the words with _____ accuracy.
   (Examples: *night, flight*)

5. Given a list of CVCe words with *a,* _____   13–16
   will be able to read the words with _____ accuracy.
   (Examples: *bake, came*)

6. Given a list of CVCe words with *i,* _____   17
   will be able to read the words with _____ accuracy.
   (Examples: *white, time*)

7. Given a list of CVCe words with *o,* _____   18–20
   will be able to read the words with _____ accuracy.
   (Examples: *robe, joke*)

          Phonics for Reading, Second Level

8. Given a list of words with *ar,* _____   21–23
will be able to read the words with _____ accuracy.
(Examples: *smart, farm*)

9. Given a list of words with *er,* _____   24–26
will be able to read the words with _____ accuracy.
(Examples: *herd, serve*)

10. Given a list of words with *or,* _____   27–29
will be able to read the words with _____ accuracy.
(Examples: *sport, horse*)

11. Given a list of words with *ir* and *ur,* _____   30–32
will be able to read the words with _____ accuracy.
(Examples: *girl, turn*)

Multisyllable Words

12. Given a list of multisyllable words with *ai* and *ay,*   1–3
_____ will be able to read the words with
_____ accuracy. (Examples: *railway, raindrop, payday, crayon*)

13. Given a list of multisyllable words with *ee* and *ea,*   4–6
_____ will be able to read the words with
_____ accuracy. (Examples: *freeway, indeed, sunbeam, peanut*)

14. Given a list of multisyllable words with *oa* and *ow,*   7–9
_____ will be able to read the words with
_____ accuracy. (Examples: *window, elbow, oatmeal, rowboat*)

15. Given a list of multisyllable words with *igh,*   10–12
_____ will be able to read the words with
_____ accuracy. (Examples: *highway, brightness*)

16. Given a list of multisyllable words with CVCe syllables with *a,*   13–16
_____ will be able to read the words with
_____ accuracy. (Examples: *landscape, inhale*)

17. Given a list of multisyllable words with CVCe syllables with *i,*   17
_____ will be able to read the words with
_____ accuracy. (Examples: *dislike, reptile*)

18. Given a list of multisyllable words with CVCe syllables with *o*, _____ will be able to read the words with _____ accuracy. (Examples: *sunstroke, hopeless*)

19. Given a list of multisyllable words with *ar*, _____ will be able to read the words with _____ accuracy. (Example: *artist*)

20. Given a list of multisyllable words with er, _____ will be able to read the words with _____ accuracy. (Example: *perfect*)

21. Given a list of multisyllable words with *or*, _____ will be able to read the words with _____ accuracy. (Example: *morning*)

22. Given a list of multisyllable words with *ir* and *ur*, _____ will be able to read the words with _____ accuracy. (Examples: *birthday, confirm, burden, Thursday*)

Words with Word Endings

23. Given a list of words with the word ending *-ed*, _____ will be able to read these words with _____ accuracy. (Examples: *sailed, painted*)

24. Given a list of words with both word endings *-ed* and *-ing*, _____ will be able to read these words with _____ accuracy. (Examples: *camped, camping; lifted, lifting*)

25. Given a list of words with roots that are altered when *-ing* is added (the final *e* is dropped or the final consonant is doubled), _____ will be able to read these words with _____ accuracy. (Examples: *riding, baking, batting, shopping*)

26. Given a list of words ending with -*ed* and -*ing*, some
    of which have altered roots,

    _____ will be able to read

    these words with _____ accuracy.
    (Examples: *closed, spinning, barked, barking*)

27. Given a list of words with the word endings -*er*, -*ed*,
    and -*ing*, some of which have altered roots,

    _____ will be able to read

    these words with _____ accuracy.
    (Examples: *farmer, twirled, flaming*)

Irregular Words or High-Frequency Words

28. Given the following high-frequency words, _____
    will be able to read these words with _____ accuracy.

    people, school, to, my, water, after, of, from, they, very, some, saw,
    where, down, work, said, put, were, you, have, are, look, was, there,
    things, little, into, all, do, what, be, he, we, she, me, by, why, cry, dry,
    would, should, could, been, come, who, your, use, try

Passage Reading

29. Given a passage in ***Phonics for Reading, Second Level,***

    _____ will be able to read the passage

    with _____ accuracy.

PHONICS FOR READING – Letter of Progress

To: _____

From: _____

Re: Progress of _____

I am pleased to inform you that _____ has successfully
completed the first twelve lessons in the Second Level of **Phonics for Reading**. In these lessons,
students learned to read one-syllable words with the vowel combinations *ay, ai, ee, ea, oa,
ow,* and *igh*. The students also learned how to read multisyllable words with the same sounds.
The following words are examples of those taught in the first twelve lessons:

One-Syllable Words		Multisyllable Words	
say	soap	railway	rowboat
feed	right	seaweed	brightness

The students also learned to read words ending with *-ed* and *-ing*. The following words are examples
of those introduced in the program:

waited	stayed	showed	planted
missed	needed	showing	planting

In addition, the students learned to read the following high-frequency words:

were	my	saw	into
you	to	there	down
of	they	things	all
said	are	some	work
have	look	people	do
after	was	little	what
from	put	water	where

I am very pleased with _____'s efforts. Please listen as your child reads the words
listed in this letter.

PHONICS FOR READING – Letter of Progress

Distribute after Lesson 20

To: _____

From: _____

Re: Progress of _____

I am pleased to inform you that _____ has successfully completed the first twenty lessons in the Second Level of *Phonics for Reading*. In Lessons 13 through 20, students learned to read long-vowel words with consonant-vowel-consonant-*e* (CVCe) configurations. The students also learned how to read multisyllable words with the same patterns. The following words are examples of those taught in Lessons 13 through 20:

One-Syllable Words		Multisyllable Words	
bake	shade	tailgate	dislike
kite	save	reptile	backbone
note	mile	inhale	sunstroke
fine	cave		
rope	globe		

The students also learned to read words with roots that are altered when *-ing* is added (the final *-e* is dropped or the final consonant is doubled).

baking	trading	clapping
riding	winning	shipping

In addition, the students learned to read the following high-frequency words:

be	me	dry
he	by	try
we	why	school
she	cry	

I am very pleased with _____'s efforts. Please listen as your child reads the words listed in this letter.

PHONICS FOR READING – Letter of Progress

Distribute after Lesson 32

To: _____

From: _____

Re: Progress of _____

I am pleased to inform you that _____ has successfully
completed the thirty-two lessons in the Second Level of ***Phonics for Reading***. In Lessons 21
through 32, students learned to read words with the *r*-controlled vowel sounds. The students
also learned how to read multisyllable words with the same sounds. The following words
are examples of those taught in Lessons 21 through 32:

One-Syllable Words					Multisyllable Words	
car	clay	shore	burn	cure	garden	performer
herd	verb	fern	curb	carve	enter	yesterday
park	tore	corn	sir	shirt	order	hamburger
nerve	barn	stir	firm	for	confirm	misinterpret

In addition, the students learned to read the following high-frequency words:

would	should	could	been	come	who	very	your	use

I am very pleased with _____'s efforts. Please listen as your child reads the words
listed in this letter and the following paragraphs from Lesson 32.

"Come look at this snapshot, Carla," Mom said. "Kirk was a blond at birth. See the nurse
showing me his blond curls? He still has curls today, but they are dark. He looks a lot like his
dad, I think. Look at the curve of his smile," she said, grinning. "That is just the way his dad
smiles. Kirk should wake up from his nap by three. Then the fun will start!"

"Come look at your birthday gifts, Kirk," Mom said when Kirk woke up. "They are on
the desk in the den." Kirk ran into the den. "Which will you start with?" asked Mom.

"Let me see the big red box," Kirk said with glee. Kirk peeked in the big red box. It had
a play farm in it. The rest of the gifts were a bat, a game, a shirt, and a can of clay.

"Let's cut the cake," Mom said, "and then you may play."

"This cake is a work of art," Carla said. "I hate to carve it up, but I will. Hand me your
plate, Kirk." Carla cut the cake and they started to eat.

"It may be your birthday, Kirk, but you must still use your fork," Mom said.

"After we eat, I will play your game with you," said Carla.

PLACEMENT TEST – Instructions

Purpose: This test can be used for placement of students into the First Level, Second Level, or Third Level of *Phonics for Reading*. It can also be used to measure students' progress in decoding after instruction.

Determining Student Placement

Preparation: Make one copy of the Student Form of the Placement Test for each student to read (pages 182–184). Also, make a copy of the Recording Form to collect test data for each student (pages 185–187).

Starting Place: Start with Subtest A. However, if you anticipate that the student could be placed in a more advanced level, begin with a higher subtest.

Procedure:
1. Ask the student to read aloud the words in each line of the subtest.
2. If the student makes four consecutive errors, terminate the subtest and have the student read a lower subtest.
3. If the student takes more than five seconds to read a word, direct the student to read the next word.
4. If the student correctly reads the criterion number of word parts for the subtest (80% correct), have the student read the words on the next subtest.
5. Terminate the test at the point at which the student does not meet the 80% criterion. Note that multisyllable words are given one point for each decodable word part (e.g., *provide* = 2; *adjustable* = 3).
6. Based on the results of the subtests, you may choose to place a student at the beginning of a level or at an intermediate point within the level.
7. The data collected for each student can be recorded on a copy of the Individual Student Record (page 188).
8. All student data can be summarized on a copy of the Group Record (page 189) for the purpose of forming instructional groups.

Measuring Student Progress

The Placement Test can be used not only as a pretest but also as a post test. When the student completes a level or a portion of a level, the appropriate subtest can be administered again to gauge student growth.

PLACEMENT TEST – Student Form

Phonics for Reading—First Level (1)

Subtest A

mix	pad	hit	cab	dot
hut	jet	hum	cod	yet
habit	muffin	rustic	summit	

Subtest B

less	dill	moss	rack	bath
wish	lock	mesh	rust	desk
shed	thud	whip	chat	ship
crib	clam	grin	plum	trim
potluck	dentist	contest	unpack	

PLACEMENT TEST – Student Form

Phonics for Reading—Second Level (2)

Subtest C

braid	beach	trait	clean	soap
shown	boast	flight	spray	speech
speedway	daydream		brightness	shadow

Subtest D

brave	slap	smoke	wide	plate
drive	spoke	smock	flake	flat
drainpipe	hopeless	sunstroke		trade wind

Subtest E

clerk	smart	birch	torch	nurse
sport	Carl	verse	marsh	twirl
arcade	monarch	northern	border	

PLACEMENT TEST – Student Form

Phonics for Reading—Third Level (3)

Subtest F

smooth	point	grew	cause	Troy
shampoo	turmoil		oyster	exhaust
unload	distrust		expand	return
teachable	extinction		preventable	

Subtest G

blouse	knight	phase	sketch	quote
southwest	dolphin		hopscotch	banquet
contain	handle		provide	smallest
completely	connection		glamorous	

Subtest H

cinch	choice	strange	spool	spread
margin	sagebrush		marshmallow	
understood	gingerbread		homestead	
impressive	adjustable		informally	

©Curriculum Associates, LLC   *Phonics for Reading, Second Level*

PLACEMENT TEST – Recording Form

Name _____ Date _____

Phonics for Reading—First Level (1)

Lessons 1–13   **Subtest A**

mix	pad	hit	cab	dot
hut	jet	hum	cod	yet
habit 2	muffin 2	rustic 2	summit 2	

If the student correctly reads 14 parts, continue with Subtest B.   _____/18 _____%

Lessons 14–30   **Subtest B**

less	dill	moss	rack	bath
wish	lock	mesh	rust	desk
shed	thud	whip	chat	ship
crib	clam	grin	plum	trim
potluck 2	dentist 2	contest 2	unpack 2	

If the student correctly reads 22 parts, continue with Subtest C.   _____/28 _____%

PLACEMENT TEST – Recording Form

Name _____ Date _____

Phonics for Reading—Second Level (2)

Lessons 1–12   **Subtest C**

braid	**beach**	**trait**	**clean**	**soap**
shown	**boast**	**flight**	**spray**	**speech**
speedway 2	**daydream** 2		**brightness** 2	**shadow** 2

If the student correctly reads 14 parts, continue with Subtest D.   _____/18 _____%

Lessons 13–20   **Subtest D**

brave	**slap**	**smoke**	**wide**	**plate**
drive	**spoke**	**smock**	**flake**	**flat**
drainpipe 2	**hopeless** 2		**sunstroke** 2	**trade wind** 2

If the student correctly reads 14 parts, continue with Subtest E.   _____/18 _____%

Lessons 21–32   **Subtest E**

clerk	**smart**	**birch**	**torch**	**nurse**
sport	**Carl**	**verse**	**marsh**	**twirl**
arcade 2	**monarch** 2		**northern** 2	**border** 2

If the student correctly reads 14 parts, continue with Subtest F.   _____/18 _____%

PLACEMENT TEST – Recording Form

Name _____ Date _____

Phonics for Reading—Third Level (3)

Lessons 1–12   **Subtest F**

smooth	point	grew	cause	Troy
shampoo ₂	turmoil ₂	oyster ₂	exhaust ₂
unload ₂	distrust ₂	expand ₂	return ₂
teachable ₂	extinction ₃	preventable ₃	

If the student correctly reads 23 parts, continue with Subtest G.   _____ /29 _____ %

Lessons 13–21   **Subtest G**

blouse	knight	phase	sketch	quote
southwest ₂	dolphin ₂	hopscotch ₂	banquet ₂
contain ₂	handle ₂	provide ₂	smallest ₂
completely ₃	connection ₃	glamorous ₃	

If the student correctly reads 24 parts, continue with Subtest H.   _____ /30 _____ %

Lessons 22–36   **Subtest H**

cinch	choice	strange	spool	spread
margin ₂	sagebrush ₂	marshmallow ₃	
understood ₃	gingerbread ₃	homestead ₂	
impressive ₃	adjustable ₃	informally ₄	

If the student correctly reads 24 parts, the student can be placed
in materials more difficult than *Phonics for Reading*.   _____ /30 _____ %

©Curriculum Associates, LLC   *Phonics for Reading, Second Level*   187

PLACEMENT TEST – Individual Student Record

Name of Student _____

Teacher _____

LEVEL	SUBTEST	PRETEST DATE: _____	POST TEST DATE: _____
1	A	_____/18 correct parts* _____/% correct parts	_____/18 correct parts _____/% correct parts
1	B	_____/28 correct parts _____/% correct parts	_____/28 correct parts _____/% correct parts
2	C	_____/18 correct parts _____/% correct parts	_____/18 correct parts _____/% correct parts
2	D	_____/18 correct parts _____/% correct parts	_____/18 correct parts _____/% correct parts
2	E	_____/18 correct parts _____/% correct parts	_____/18 correct parts _____/% correct parts
3	F	_____/29 correct parts _____/% correct parts	_____/29 correct parts _____/% correct parts
3	G	_____/30 correct parts _____/% correct parts	_____/30 correct parts _____/% correct parts
3	H	_____/30 correct parts _____/% correct parts	_____/30 correct parts _____/% correct parts

*Parts refer to decodable chunks within the word and do not equate directly with syllables.
For example, the word *adjustable* has three parts because the word *able* is taught as a single
word part or decodable chunk.

©Curriculum Associates, LLC   *Phonics for Reading, Second Level*

PLACEMENT TEST – Group Record

Determine the placement level for each student. The placement level will be the lowest level at which the student did not meet the 80% criterion. Begin the list with the name of the student who had the lowest performance and end with the name of the student who had the highest performance. Use this data for grouping students.

NAME OF STUDENT	PLACEMENT LEVEL
	Level _____ Subtest _____
	Level _____ Subtest _____
	Level _____ Subtest _____
	Level _____ Subtest _____
	Level _____ Subtest _____
	Level _____ Subtest _____
	Level _____ Subtest _____
	Level _____ Subtest _____
	Level _____ Subtest _____
	Level _____ Subtest _____
	Level _____ Subtest _____
	Level _____ Subtest _____
	Level _____ Subtest _____
	Level _____ Subtest _____
	Level _____ Subtest _____
	Level _____ Subtest _____
	Level _____ Subtest _____
	Level _____ Subtest _____
	Level _____ Subtest _____
	Level _____ Subtest _____
	Level _____ Subtest _____
	Level _____ Subtest _____

Reading Fluency Graph (correct words per minute)

Name _____

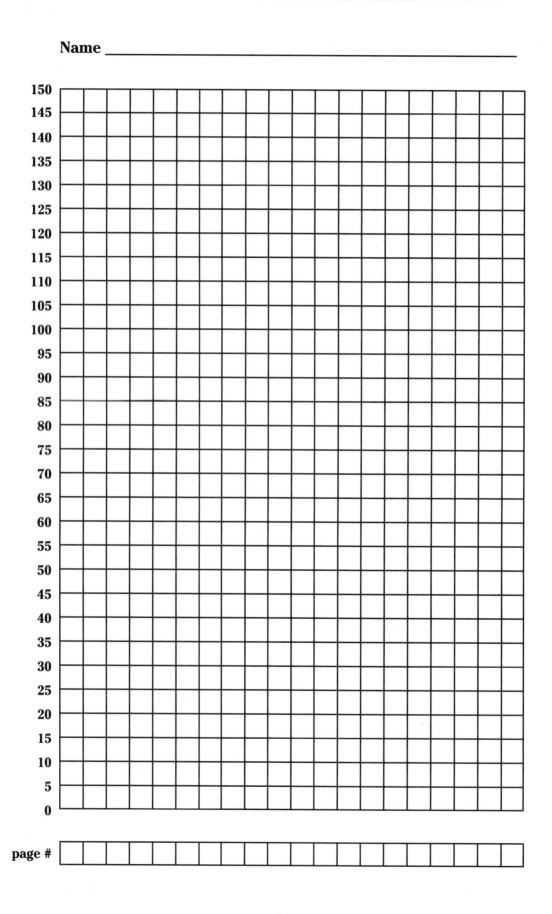

page #

Scope and Sequence Chart – Second Level

The following Scope and Sequence Chart indicates the lessons in which each skill is taught.

Introduction of Letter-Sound Associations				One-Syllable Words		Multisyllable Words		Words with Word Endings		Irregular and/or High-Frequency Words
Lesson	Letter(s)	Sound	Key Word(s)	Word Type	Examples	Syllable Type	Examples	Word Type	Examples	
1–3	ai ay	/āāā/ /āāā/	rain play	Words with ai and ay	fail pain play hay	ai and ay	raindrop railway maintain	Words with -ed ending	failed painted played	were, you, of, said, have, after, from, my, to, they, are, look, was, put, saw
4–6	ee ea	/ēēē/ /ēēē/	feed leaf	Words with ee and ea	beet sheep beach lead	ee and ea	sunbeam freeway indeed	Words with -ed ending	needed peeled cleaned	there, things, some, people, little, water, into, down
7–9	oa ow	/ōōō/ /ōōō/	coat snow	Words with oa and ow	coach toast flow show	oa and ow	window oatmeal rowboat	Words with both -ed and -ing endings	floated floating snowed snowing	all, work
10–12	igh	/ī/	light	Words with igh	night fright	igh	highway nightfall brightness	Words with both -ed and -ing endings	sprayed spraying printed printing	do, what, where
13–16	a	/āāā/	rake	CVCe words with a	bake grape	CVCe with a	handmade inhale	Words with 1 or 2 medial consonants	trading mapping	be, he, we, she, me, by, why, cry, dry
17	i	/ī/	five	CVCe words with i	white time	CVCe with i	dislike reptile	Words with 1 or 2 medial consonants	riding sitting	try, school
18–20	o	/ōōō/	joke	CVCe words with o	vote nose	CVCe with o	sunstroke backbone	Words with 1 or 2 medial consonants	hoping jogging	Review of irregular and/or high-frequency words introduced in previous lessons
21–23	ar	/ar/	car	Words with ar	smart farm	ar	artist harmless market	Review of words with -ed and -ing endings		would, should, could, been
24–26	er	/er/	fern	Words with er	term herd	er	perfect yesterday	Words with -er ending Review of words with -ed and -ing endings		come, who, very
27–29	or	/or/	corn	Words with or	sport horse	or	popcorn corrupt forget	Review of words with -ed, -ing, and -er endings		your
30–32	ir ur	/ir/ /ur/	bird turn	Words with ir and ur	first girl church turn	ir and ur	birthday frankfurter stirrup hamburger	Review of words with -ed, -ing, and -er endings		use